Exporting Perilous Pauline

WOMEN AND FILM HISTORY INTERNATIONAL

Series Editors
Kay Armatage, Jane M. Gaines, and Christine Gledhill

A new generation of motion picture historians is rediscovering the vital and diverse contributions of women to world film history, whether as producers, actors, or spectators. Taking advantage of new print material and moving picture archival discoveries as well as the benefits of digital access and storage, this series investigates the significance of gender in the cinema.

A list of books in the series appears at the end of this book.

Exporting Perilous Pauline

Pearl White and the Serial Film Craze

Edited by

MARINA DAHLQUIST

UNIVERSITY OF ILLINOIS PRESS

Urbana, Chicago, and Springfield

Manufactured in the United States of America
1 2 3 4 5 C P 5 4 3 2 1
∞ This book is printed on acid-free paper.

Library of Congress Control Number: 2013937624

Contents

Acknowledgments

This volume would not have been published without the enthusiasm and supporting midwifery from the series editors of Women and Film History International. Jane Gaines invited me to edit this collection and has indefatigably offered constructive criticism every step of the way. Many thanks also to Christine Gledhill for inspiring suggestions and spirited discussions.

Jennifer M. Bean proposed the idea to examine the impact of one of the most famous American female film stars on an international scale by inviting scholars with expertise on local receptions and film practices around the world. Due to other commitments she was not able to finish the project, and the baton was handed over to me. Jennifer has, however, generously shared her blueprint and notes for the project.

University of Illinois Press offered unfailing support from start to finish. I'm indebted to Daniel M. Nasset, Joan Catapano, and Vijay Shah for astute editorial guidance; to the production and art team, especially Kelly Gray, who designed the book cover; and, not least, to the sharp eyes of Michael L. Levine, whose elegant copyediting took the collection across the finishing line.

I have received generous financial support from the Department of Cinema Studies at Stockholm University for conducting archival research in the United States in order to finalize the manuscript. Bart van der Gaag has provided cheerful technical support at critical junctures of the project. I have benefited immensely from the scholarship of Jan Olsson, whose insights across the field of silent cinema have been a pleasurable and many-pronged reservoir of inspiration for this venture and projects at large.

Finally, I have been fortunate in having a superb cast of contributors, whose commitment to the project and patience over the years has been astonishing. I would like to salute their scholarly imagination and research dexterity.

Stockholm, December 2012

Exporting Perilous Pauline

Introduction

Why Pearl?

MARINA DAHLQUIST

In 1913 four young men enjoyed what turned out to be an ostensibly historic luncheon. William deMille, who was not at the table, in hindsight encapsulates Arthur Friend's attempt between courses to convince Cecil B. DeMille, Samuel Goldfish, and Jesse Lasky that "there was a future in motion pictures":

> He told them about Pearl White, then at the height of her popularity in "The Perils of Pauline"; he described the eagerness with which the country's youth awaited each new peril as it appeared in serial form; he explained that the fair Miss White was, at the moment, the best-known woman in the world, Pauline's perils having proved enthralling to every nation which boasted a cinema, including India and Arabia, and her face having become as familiar in China and Japan as in Norway and Sweden.[1]

This charming tale of a lunch that took place half a year or so before Pauline actually hit the screen is a pregnant memory slip on William deMille's part. Chronology apart, the faux anecdote does, however, attest to Pearl White's impact on the cinema for a chronicler looking back at the blurred pioneering days from the perspective of the late 1930s. And Pearl White was again in the headlines around the time William deMille finished his book manuscript, as she passed away in 1938.

In the late 1910s, a vast mythology surrounded Pearl White. With her soaring stardom, Pearl White was constantly in the news. Numerous articles explored and exploited her private as well as professional life, her background, career, home life, fame, and not least her daring feats on the screen. This Pearl discourse, to which she contributed herself, is filled with gaps, contradictions, and perhaps a few tall tales. During a time when press agents were emerging at the studios, it was anyone's guess regarding which information was reliable and which was only promotion-seeking copy. The hype around Pearl White and the serials in which she acted was of enormous proportions. Was she really "the best-known woman in the world" in the 1910s, as the above quote says, or was this line merely something lifted from wishful ads? White was a studio product to be marketed, just like Charlie Chaplin and comparable first-generation screen luminaries. And efficient machinery was in place for generating copy around the time *The Perils of Pauline* (1914), her first successful film, opened. Capitalizing on her stardom and the boundless interest in the personal lives of stars, an autobiography was published in 1919, when White was only thirty years old. The text, a comprehensive work, sums up the marketing of a star performer emerging in the widely popular serial film format and synthesizes her remarkable career during a time when film culture was reconfigured in a multitude of ways, not least by the promotional machinery fanning the star system. More than anything, the autobiography confirms and underpins the blurred boundaries between her star persona, private life, and film characters.[2]

White's claim to stardom remains current and is reasserted in contemporary scholarship. According to Jane Gaines, for example, "Today, no scholar or silent-era cinephile would challenge the assertion that Pearl White was the first international American star celebrity."[3] Still, the research devoted to White does not match the extent of her many-sided influence both on and off screen. To partly remedy the scant amount of scholarship devoted to female prowess on the screen, this volume addresses the complexities of Pearl White's performance and the overall cultural power of serial queens in many markets at a critical historical juncture in the medium's history. Albeit preceded by others, White's breakthrough as Pauline defined the serial format as a fixture on screens worldwide parallel to the success of full-length features. The serial film was part of a rethinking of production strategies, distribution and advertising patterns, and fan culture. When exported, the format was "glocalized" and emerged in slightly different forms of screen and marketing constellations, depending on the modi operandi of national film cultures. This collection offers clear evidence that a staple of film culture and marketing in one country—say, the tie-ins for the serials in the United States—simply did not exist in, for example, the Swedish market. The essays take off from White's emblematic role for the serial phenomenon and the upsurge for female action heroes on the screen, but they extend the perspective in discussing reception and marketing—of both White's serials and the genre overall—from numerous vantage points within a number of national exhibition contexts. Pivoted around Pearl White, the commissioned texts reframe the discussion of the serial phenomenon by offering cross-cultural perspectives on the reception of the genre and White's stardom parallel to Hollywood's global success at large.

Few film genres have been historically significant on a par with the spectacular American action serials of the 1910s featuring powerful female heroines. The serial queens represented a new and independent female type of protagonist within sensational, action-packed story lines. Irrespective of the composition of actual audiences, which is impossible to accurately determine a century later, the genre offered young women a novel template for negotiating gender stereotypes. This new type of woman, configured in tandem with discourses on the meanings of femininity overall, seeped into the cultural lexicon of the era and thereby took on cultural significance outside as well as within the film theaters. The versatility and bravado of Pauline and her serial "sisters" in performing tasks traditionally associated with masculine brawn—battling in fistfights, handling pistols, and demonstrating agility in stunts—were the genre's most striking, and gender-bending, negotiations.

In a recent article, Hilary A. Hallett demonstrated how early writing about Hollywood, especially that of Louella Parsons, promoted the liberating possibilities in the New West for women. Journalism and moving pictures offered intertwined strands for rethinking identities and gender stereotypes in relation to novel professions open for young women. The strategy of using female writers to appeal to other women was a tactic to attract more women into the theaters during the 1910s but is only one aspect of this discourse. The writings about Los Angeles and California seemingly opened up glorious opportunities and new avenues for the working girl within the new industry. The New Western Woman, as presented in newspaper columns, was described as an expert navigator of the city. As a key grounding of modern feminism, this discourse in fact drew female audiences, especially single working girls, to find professional opportunities in California. Irrespective of whether Pearl White set foot in California or not, her and other serial queens' celebrity rested on the tale of the West, with Los Angeles as its metropolitan frontier, while simultaneously the action serials promoted a fantasy of female power.[4]

The Perils of Pauline, directed by Louis J. Gasnier and Donald MacKenzie, is still the emblematic production of the American serial craze; hence the focus here on Pearl White. The enthusiasm for serials propelled Pearl White's full-fledged stardom, making her one of the most popular film actresses, as deMille's anecdote vividly illustrates.

Promotional portrait of Pearl White for *The Lightning Raider* (1919). Courtesy Monica Dall'Asta. Private collection.

Starting out in 1910 as a rather anonymous actress with the Powers, Lubin, and Crystal studios, it was with Pathé Frères's American branch in Jersey City that she achieved her breakthrough. The actress's popularity boom as Pauline made her a focus of attention in women's magazines, the daily press, and trade journals. In *Motion Picture Magazine*'s popularity contest in 1916, Pearl White was voted the most popular female movie star. Two years later, in December 1918, she was ranked third on *Motion Picture Magazine*'s list, trailing only Mary Pickford and Marguerite Clark. In 1920 Pearl White still came out third in the same contest.[5]

Pearl White was not only a superstar within the United States but one of the first globally recognized American film stars. Second to few screen celebrities—perhaps only Max Linder and Charlie Chaplin—she soon emerged as Pathé Frères's most glimmering star of the 1910s. Her international fame was evidenced by heaps of fan letters pouring in from all over the world. As she put it herself, "Although I don't have time to read them all, I should be heart broken if they ceased. . . . It is really marvelous to get letters from all the different countries generally asking for a photograph or autograph to be sent to them in every corner of the globe—even from far away places like Iceland, Siam, Finland, Guatemala, the Colonies of South Africa, etc. I receive as many as ten thousand letters a month."[6] In 1913, when Pearl White was about to leave London to return to New York after her first European trip, she came across an image of herself in a morning paper with the following headline: "Pearl White, a Rising Young Cinema Star of America, Who Is Visiting London to Get Ideas for Her Forthcoming Photoplays." This was, she claims, her first newspaper headline prior to her serial fame.[7]

Marketing Strategies

The Perils of Pauline's initial success in the United States in 1914 was fueled by the immense publicity resulting from the collaboration between Pathé and the newspaper tycoon William R. Hearst. Realizing the potential of moving pictures, Hearst had started up a newsreel with Selig in 1914 and at the same time entered into a partnership with Pathé to publish novelizations of its films in the Sunday papers.[8] This cooperation was advertised in a two-page spread in the *Moving Picture World* in February 1914 under the headline, "Pathé Pictures and the Hearst Newspapers," as well as in the newspapers.[9] This joint venture took on novel form and scope with Pathé's *The Perils of Pauline*, its first serial.[10] The day before each episode premiered in theaters, the Hearst papers—together with the Hearst syndicated newspapers—carried an illustrated story of that episode in their Sunday issue. Once an episode was in the can, a staff writer for the Hearst newspapers would have it screened so that he or she could write the story, a so-called tie-in, for the Sunday supplement.[11] The campaign was launched by a coalition of leading metropolitan newspapers on a "you-scratch-my-back-and-I'll-scratch-yours" basis, where the papers boosted the film story and the films brought readers to the newspapers in advance of every new episode. As David Nasaw has pointed out, Hearst's nationwide network of publications reached more Americans than any other advertising medium at this time. There were perhaps not the twenty million readers that the Pathé advertising claimed,[12] but certainly millions. This was especially true for the widely circulated Sunday editions, which were often read by all family members.[13] Alan Dale, Hearst's leading drama critic, gave additional attention to the serial as his reviews appeared in all the syndicate's papers. The reviews often found their way into the trade journals, either reprinted in their entirety or quoted in the commentary section. *Motography* wrote in April 1914,

> The newspapers don't usually get excited about anything. But the day after the first showing of the "Perils of Pauline" the criticism reproduced here appeared in one of the biggest morning papers in New York. Alan Dale is known all over the United States as one of the foremost dramatic critics of the present day. His field is particularly the drama and opera, but for the first time in history he broke all precedent to put the review of the "Perils of Pauline" on the dramatic page. Now how about yourself? Have you protected your theater and your patrons by booking "The Perils of Pauline"?[14]

Prize money in the amount of $25,000 was offered in plot-writing contests as a further incentive for readers to engage with the serial. A critical factor for the popularity of Pathé's serials might have been the controversial status attached to Hearst's name in American public life.

The rave reviews and the enormous advertising volume in the syndicate's papers afforded a domestic base for Pathé, a company whose alien Frenchness, both when it came to ownership, as well as the orientation of its movies, for years had drawn heavy criticism, especially in *Moving Picture World* and the *New York Dramatic Mirror*.[15] By producing serials showcasing American heroines in American settings, often New York City, Pathé was no longer subject to criticism from the trade press for not living up to American standards and for not catering to the "American taste." And Pearl White, the most popular serial star, was an all-American, even an icon of the U.S. Marine Corps in 1917. In at least one group of marines, she was the only woman chosen by the men to send them a message of Christmas cheer at a time of war. One marine tellingly declared, "We like Pearl White and we all voted for her because she can do stunts that would stump the best of us, and she comes up smiling after them."[16]

According to Ben Singer, regarded as a scholarly pioneer on serials as a consequence of his essay in *Camera Obscura* in 1990 (following Kalton C. Lahue's more popular efforts), the serials were by far the most widely advertised U.S. film genre during the 1910s, which greatly contributed to the format's success.[17] Producers and exhibitors invested heavily in advertising the serials by resorting to tie-ins in newspapers and magazines, probably the most important and innovative publicity model up to that time, in addition to placing ads in trade journals, marketing on billboards and streetcars, publishing sheet music and postcards, and launching prize contests. The tie-ins in the Sunday editions, Singer claims, primarily targeted a female audience base as the promotional material most commonly was published on the "women's pages,"[18] an observation calling for more research. As Hallett argues, by 1914 the majority of readers of moving picture news consisted of women and girls. And by 1920 *Photoplay*, the largest fan magazine in the United States, was estimating that 75 percent of movie fans were women.[19] The trade promotion for *The Perils of Pauline* argued that the widely circulated advertisements for the serials, especially in newspapers, were perhaps the most important reason why film exhibitors should order this new serial: "Think of it—a story so thrilling, so full of action and interest that the largest single chain of newspapers in the world is featuring it in their Sunday edition."[20] As Shelley Stamp reminds us, the promotions of the serials coincided with a general change in film marketing and advertising in the mid-1910s, which is further underpinned by Richard Abel's scholarship.[21] National publicity ventures supplanted local initiatives as the film industry overall cultivated a female fan base featuring athletic heroines as a modern version of empowered femininity.[22]

The serials received massive exposure from the inception of the format in 1912, when Thomas Edison teamed up with *Ladies' World* for *What Happened to Mary*. In 1914 Selig expanded the formula with *The Adventures of Kathlyn* in collaboration with the *Chicago Tribune*, and somewhat later Pathé's *The Perils of Pauline* serial hooked up with the Hearst organization, which owned the *Chicago American*, a *Tribune* rival. Later, Universal connected with the *Chicago Herald* for *Lucille Love, Girl of Mystery*. As Singer claims, all American serials before 1917 were backed by tie-ins running parallel to the screenings during twelve to fifteen weeks. In spite of its successful launching, the tie-in model was short-lived. The staggering promotional costs and the dubious wisdom of giving the story away before the screenings contributed to its demise, and by 1918 tie-ins had virtually disappeared. Pathé's collaboration with Hearst was one of the longest-lived and ran well into mid-1918.[23]

Seriality

In January 1914 the unprecedented advertising campaign orchestrated around *The Adventures of Kathlyn*, starring Kathlyn Williams, was received with wonder. In commenting on the campaign, a journalist in *Motography* elected to once again brandish criticism of Pathé in terms of foreignness. The company's French origin placed it on the fringe of American culture without a deep-rooted grounding in local manners and customs: "Other organizations may have reason to lie awake nights. Charles Pathé, himself, may discover in this instance one of the reasons why film conditions in this country differ from film conditions in other countries."[24] If Charles Pathé lost sleep over Kathlyn, we do not know, but the publicity campaign around *The Adventures of Kathlyn* most certainly did not pass him by unnoticed.

Selig released *The Adventures of Kathlyn* with twelve prints in Chicago alone against an average of about three;[25] still, exhibitors had problems in meeting the demand from patrons.[26] The next serial, Pathé's *The Perils of Pauline*, was also released with many more prints than customary to ensure that the screenings would be reasonably close to the publishing date of the newspaper tie-ins. According to *Motion Picture News*, 30 prints of each episode were released in New York City alone. The enormous demand was evidently not fully met as 200 theater owners in Chicago and more than 250 in New York ordered the serial in the first release days.[27]

The success of the Kathlyn serial prompted nearly all production companies of importance to begin filming action serials featuring young women. The dominating serial companies during the 1910s were Pathé's American branch, Universal, Mutual, Thanhouser, and Vitagraph. Pathé emerged as the "House of Serials," and according to Lahue, it, together with Vitagraph "showed the greatest taste and restraint in its product," and therefore their serials were seldom cut or mentioned in discussions on censorship in the United States.[28] The Pearl White serials, most of them directed and written by George B. Seitz, became a backbone and money machine for the company. Just like Universal, Pathé for years had two serials running in tandem, one featuring Pearl White (1914–1919) and another showcasing Pathé's other serial queens, such as Ruth Roland, Grace Darmond, or Mollie King. According to Singer, Universal's serial production generated more revenue for the company than any other genre or production branch.[29] Other Pearl White serials produced by Pathé include *The Iron Claw* (1916), *Pearl of the Army* (1916), *The Fatal Ring* (1917), *The House of Hate* (1918), *The Lightning Raider* (1919), *The Black Secret* (1919–1920), and *Plunder* (1923).

The serials' entangled storylines get in the way of clear-cut continuity and obfuscate narrative clarity. Such a chaotic structure with at times unfathomable narratives characterizes many forms of melodrama. Melodramatic series films, with stand-alone episodes featuring recurrent characters and settings, appeared in France even before the 1910s. Éclair was the first French studio to release various detective series, which turned into its specialty and trademark, starting with *Nick Carter* in 1908. This series, telling the adventures of a detective hero, was drawn from American dime novels. Until 1914 the early series tended to build on a complete story in each episode within an overarching framework across episodes. As Singer points out, *The Perils of Pauline* can be considered a transitional serial by sporting both that model and the other, which told a story in segmented parts. Later serials, with the cliffhanger ending as indicative of the genre, used the latter model.[30]

As Stamp has noted, seriality and tie-in publishing had their vicissitudes.[31] *The Perils of Pauline* was to appear on Sundays in the Hearst newspapers, with the films being released the following day, every Monday. The tie-in model's glitches were soon noticed. Audiences not only had to wait a week or two for the next episode, but also had to attend theaters during a narrow window of screening or else miss that episode and thereby key information; upcoming episodes would then be difficult to follow. Another drawback noted in *Motography* was the fact that viewers could not select the time to view any part of the serials but were only offered one episode at a time: "So the serial motion picture is handicapped; for many people cannot or will not 'tie themselves up' to a series of definite dates, missing any one of which would kill the value of those preceding and succeeding it."[32] Several attempts were made by exhibitors to circumvent these difficulties by, for example, showing episodes on a daily basis instead of weekly or biweekly installments after the serial had completed its first run. Exhibitors thereby offered audiences another chance to catch each episode and a different way to experience the serial.[33] The writer in *Motography* argues for series rather than serials where each installment formed a complete story on its own, and so not "forcing" spectators to return for closure.[34]

The Adventures of Kathlyn was released in thirteen biweekly installments in the Chicago area in December 1913 and early 1914 while the story was published weekly in the Sunday editions of the *Chicago Tribune*. Depending on where in Chicago patrons lived, episodes could be seen either before or after reading the installment.[35] *The Perils of Pauline* was also released biweekly, while Pearl White's next serial, *The Exploits of Elaine* (1914), was released on a weekly basis to correspond with the story's publication in the Hearst newspapers—no Elaine episode was released until the story had appeared in the newspapers. Even though an attempt was made to coordinate the releases of films with published tie-ins to allow audiences to read the installments prior to seeing the films, there was, according to Stamp, a considerable variety in terms of exhibition practices. Her research shows that in the San Francisco area, the Elaine episodes were initially screened in downtown San Francisco the following day but would not reach the small neighboring cities until two or three weeks after the tie-ins were published.[36]

Perils and Thrills

According to an unsigned article in *Motography* commenting on the thirteenth episode, massive promotion was the reason for *The Perils of Pauline*'s widespread and lasting popularity in the United States. In addition, "each episode is crowded with thrills, excitement, and adventures; things that are bound to take with any audience."[37] In the mid-1910s, tricks and spectacles were integrated into several narrative genres.[38] In the French and American film serials, striking effects and unhinged continuity launched strings of clashes between heroines and villains. The writer in *Motography* noted a change within the Pauline serial: "The thrills are now carefully worked into the story and come as a natural sequence to the circumstances, instead of being stumbled upon without warning, as was the case in a few of the earlier episodes." The upcoming episode—the thirteenth—"teems with excitement" through thrills not "overstepping the bounds of probability."[39]

Pearl White was most commonly promoted as Pathé's "Peerless fearless Girl" or the "Heroine of a Thousand Stunts" in line with the new marketing methods of the mid-1910s showcasing stars rather than studios or directors as the most important promotional tag for a film.[40] As Stamp has pointed out, the serials were particularly "well-suited" to the growing celebrity culture. The episodic format proved a fitting vehicle for promoting recurring players.[41] Pearl White's undaunted and adventurous persona became emblematic for a career pivoted around action serials during a productive decade, 1914–1924. But as Jennifer Bean has argued, "White's fame may have been unique in scope, but it was certainly not in type."[42] At least some twenty female stars were praised for their outstanding athletic accomplishments. Grace Cunard, Helen Holmes, Ruth Roland, Marie Walcamp, and Kathlyn Williams were all associated with thrilling films set in modern surroundings or with adventure films featuring wild animals—preferably large felines. The serials' female heroines displayed qualities traditionally associated with men—endurance, strength, and authority in a style awash with film tricks, stunts, and spectacular effects set off against the fabric of modern technology.[43] Trains, automobiles, and subways offered powerful settings by which "tricks" were made "realistic" and heroic deeds both possible and plausible. Contemporary metropolitan settings associated with a new brand of liberated female prowess represented an early cinematic negotiation of female emancipation in a modern world. Female independence and mastery were placed at the center of the narrative.

As Bean has argued, the realistic dimension of Pearl White's and other female action stars' spectacular feats in the serials were heavily underlined in trade articles and advertising material.[44] That the dangers she was exposed to in the films were real—she allegedly insisted on performing all the stunts herself—offered one of the most recurrent strands of promotion. It was apparently of critical importance to convince audiences that the courage on screen was genuine and truly hers.[45] Savvy audiences no doubt understood that even if it looked real on the screen, some thrilling actions, like high falls from cliffs, were too dangerous to act out.[46] White's fearless image was, however, somewhat tarnished when a stunt man was killed while doubling for her.[47] Pearl White, or rather Pathé, perpetuated a set of myths mixing her private self with the film character Pauline that added to White's action persona by describing the serials as "'the always in danger' type of pictures."[48] This is also highlighted in her account of the contractual negotiations with Louis Gasnier, the head of production at American Pathé, leading up to her starring in *The Perils of Pauline*:[49] "The farther into the contract I got the worse things looked for me, and when I got to the clause 'the party of the second part, being of age, takes her part in this motion picture play at her own risk, and in case of accident or loss of life she or relations have no claim for damages against the party of the first part . . .'"[50] The script presented to her outlined a number of skills she had not mastered. On the eve of the first episode, she accordingly would have to learn how to play tennis, swim, drive a motorcar, and survive a smashup. She wrote, "And so it has been ever since, even up to the present time. I'm always learning to do something new for each picture. I've even learned to fly an aeroplane, a feat that took me many months. If I have to jump off a moving train, automobile, etceteras, I always take myself out and try it several times until I get to be pretty sure of myself before they take the picture."[51] In contrast to the magicians of the trick films impacting their surroundings with astonishing ease, using fingertips or a magic wand, the female heroines faced almost insurmountable obstacles and challenges. Interestingly, *The Master Mystery* (B. A. Rolfe Productions, 1919), the only serial starring Harry Houdini, was no success. As Lahue has argued, the serial probably failed due to the suspenseless ease with which the master magician solved problems.[52] As Bean emphasizes, suffering, trials, and tribulations, both on and off the screen, were essential for the female star discourse. Their heroic status and the characters' exceptional abilities—marketed as the actresses' very own prowess—were bolstered by the realistic simulation of feats performed in blood and sweat, but without tears.[53] Consequently, publicity material for the serials repeatedly stressed the injuries risked by the stars during shooting. According to producers, stunts were rarely faked by way of film tricks or by the use of doubles. No wonder Pearl White, in *Lectures pour Tous* in 1920, was called: "La femme la plus assassinée du monde" (The most assassinated woman in the world).[54]

In *Melodrama and Modernity*, Singer discusses the victimization of the serial queens. Dangerous events and onslaughts recurrently put the heroines in defenseless and exposed situations. Thereby, female power is linked with its obverse—victimization.[55] The serials put on display a new mobility of woman within public space, but the heroines' abilities are at times on the verge of being eclipsed as the freedom this new mobility supposedly gave them simultaneously put them in life-threatening situations. In this respect, the serial screen melodrama appropriated the sensational stage melodrama by focusing on violent action and stunts. The film serial and its subgenres were, with few exceptions, stamped in the mold of sensational melodramas based on violence and intense action in conflicts between heroine and villains and predicated on riveting chases, entrapments, and last-minute rescues.[56]

Many serial heroines gave their own name to the protagonist, additionally conflating serial characters and actresses. In this process of conflation, the abilities of the heroines were grafted onto the personalities of the stars, which underscores that the breathtaking feats on the screens were daring physical acts unaided by tricks. According to Pearl White, serial work was a tough branch of acting: "The picture business is certainly not one of ease and comfort, and I think I can modestly say that my lot is just a little harder than most of the others in the profession, because I'm always doing some new stunt and nursing a lot of cuts, bruises or sprains in consequence."[57] But these circumstances did not deter the star: "I have actually gotten to like fear, and like the sensation of taking some very dangerous chances that frighten me."[58] The perils White faced seemed to spill over into her private life; in an interview she thus enthusiastically shows off her bruises after an accident while riding a cab in Central Park on a Sunday afternoon. "I take risks, big risks, every day of my life, being the perilous Pauline. But the minute I'm out of danger and attempt to do so gentle a thing as take myself a ride in a hansom-cab, I hurt my bones and shed real blood."[59] Not only accidents made her private life perilous; so, too, did what she said was her penchant for adventure. When relating her European trip in 1913, she tells her readers how she crossed the border into France with a revolver, a dagger, and a couple of decks of playing cards. After trying to run for the train, she was forcibly held by custom officers and gendarmes.[60]

Ad for *Plunder* (George B. Seitz, 1923). Courtesy Monica Dall'Asta. Private collection.

To further highlight the correlation between screen persona and private life and the very real dangers to which she was subjected and which she simultaneously relished, she even performed an off-screen stunt in April 1916 when she painted her initials in large letters on the Gregory Building in New York, hanging from the roof.[61] The event was highly publicized by the New York press. The dovetailing between life and screen made White's characters and her private life emblematic for the modern and independent women of her time—the New Woman. The serial genre can hence be seen as a destabilization of traditional gender norms, placing the heroines far from the confines of Victorian domestic femininity and familial obligations and the meek modesty expected from women. This shift of gender norms was a way to attract a modern female audience to the theaters. But the serial film did not present an absolute break with traditional gender norms. As Singer notices, the promotion of the serials, as well as the episodes themselves, put an emphasis on luxury and extravagant fashion. The combination of athletic performance and fashionable appearance—characteristics almost universally considered as absolute opposites—was unfailingly emphasized.[62] "Amazed" reporters discovered a blond, petite, and gentle person instead of the mannish woman they seemed to have expected. White's femininity is persistently underlined in descriptions of her appearance, and her dress style constantly attracted considerable attention. The heroines put up two sides, the "masculine" and adventurous self when they wore an austere outfit and a more "feminine" one when they were rescued by male chivalry and when they sported luxury fashion to put feminine glamour on display.[63] Fashion was probably another way to get the attention of a female audience.

Despite her extraordinary abilities, constantly advertised, the persona on display was not that of an inimitable divinity but one of an unassuming, ordinary individual. Hard work for success and modest upbringing were central components for the characterization. In the trade press, Pearl White often put up a homely and plain image of herself. In a note at the end of her autobiography with the telling title *Just Me*, she implores, "To you, kind readers, I ask only that you will please look upon me as just 'A regular human being.'"[64] This attitude is also emphasized earlier on in her book: "I am of 'The People,' and it is to 'The People' that I owe most of my good fortune."[65]

Despite, or perhaps due to, her unassuming attitude, the Pearl White serials were highly successful in the United States. The Elaine serials' enormous following inspired Pathé to throw a banquet in July 1915 to celebrate the million dollar profit mark.[66]

Internationalization

In her seminal work on American film export, Kristin Thompson explores the American film industry's expansion on the international market and the business strategies deployed for that purpose in the early 1910s. The profitable serial format, she claims, was an important aspect of the film companies' new zest for expansion during the 1910s and 1920s. World War I facilitated Hollywood's foray into the global market.[67] Film shipping seems to have worked rather smoothly despite the war, and very few celluloid losses at sea were reported in the trade press.[68] One production firm that early on used internationalization as a main strategy for attaining access to, a foothold in, and control of the worldwide market was the French company Pathé Frère—and Pearl White was one of the most important assets of Pathé's American branch in its attempt to produce American films for an American market. But the serials were also exported to scores of other countries, for example, France, Sweden, Italy, India, Russia, and China, where they were integrated into a wide spectrum of cultural contexts and constellations.

Pathé Frère's market design was two-sided. On the one hand, Pathé tailored its products to local markets by opening offices in a number of countries, starting in 1904 with Moscow, New York, and Brussels.[69] It gradually produced films catering to local taste and featuring local talents.[70] One of many examples is the opening of the American studio in Jersey City in 1910, where most of the scenes in *The Perils of Pauline* would be shot.[71] Also in 1910, Pathé opened its Swedish branch in Stockholm, headed by Siegmund Popert, who in 1904 had become Pathé's first general manager in the United States.[72] The decentralization of the motion picture business became a model, with Pathé Frères as the pioneers. On the other hand, the company's international importance and global organization were promoted, perhaps most directly, in the marketing of its newsreels, under the title of *Pathé's Weekly*, which were advertised to "cover the whole world."[73] Positioned virtually everywhere, the studio was able to report all important events worldwide, a fact put forward in an advertisement in the *New York Dramatic Mirror*: "A nation gone, boundaries wiped out, a fertile land made a desert, a king in exile, and the Pathé News cameramen are there."[74] Pathé's promotional campaigns during the early 1910s mostly championed newsreels and serials.

From 1907 to 1910, French film production was losing ground in the U.S. market due to a combination of trust regulations and anti-French agitation; the American film companies by and large took over the market in the United States. Not only the domestic avenue of exhibition was at stake, as the international market shortly became a target for American producers; the exportation of American films soon emerged as a key strategy. During the years before 1910, the western film had gained immense popularity within the United States as well as abroad, a trend Pathé immediately exploited when it began production in New Jersey. However, it was problematic for Pathé—a company still considered French, at least in the United States—to tap into the red-blooded western genre.[75] Despite obstacles, however, Pathé blended in and joined in the growth of American film production and its bid for new markets. In August 1911 the following comments appeared in *Motography*: "It does not seem as if too many of these Indian and cowboy films could be fed to the moving picture goers of the rest of the world. From Liverpool to Moscow and from Stockholm to Melbourne the patrons eagerly watch the unfolding of every one of the highly colored dramas of the prairies and the mountains. . . . This is the America that they have long imagined and heard about."[76] This "profitable trade" of pictures had not come about by chance. Audiences everywhere had been studied in order to map their preferences. Charting the tastes and preferences of different audiences was seen as a prerequisite for global success.[77] In an interview in 1914, Charles Pathé described Pathé's structural decentralization and its presence on many markets as a "considerable evolution." This change of strategy was not only valid for foreign production companies in the U.S.; American studios also had to navigate a

Cover of American promotion booklet for *Pearl of the Army* (1916). Patrimoine Pathé. Paris.

spectrum of cultural tastes and predilections in order to succeed. Pathé said that "each and every country is striving to produce at home subjects which are better adapted to the special mentality and taste of their motion picture patrons. For this reason European manufacturers attain only a relative success with the film they ship to America, and for the same reason the American production, which for the last few years has been in high favor in Europe, is now losing considerable ground in that market."[78] He declared that to attain international success, he had almost completely ceased to produce moving pictures. He compared himself to a publisher who handles books on a royalty basis, a system he considered very satisfying.[79] Pathé was affiliated with studios producing films in a number of countries: France, Germany, Italy, Sweden, Russia, and the United States. Adding to their own production, they also bought films from independent studios. In August 1914 *Motography* declared that Pathé's entire stock company at Jersey City, with the exception of Pearl White, Crane Wilbur, and Paul Panzer, had been released. From now on the company would only hire actors for special engagements.[80] The goal was to become a full-fledged distribution firm, only releasing films produced by other companies. *The Perils of Pauline* was an exception. Pathé's immediate success in producing serials was, according to Lahue, due to the fact that it was a French firm, headed by Gasnier, who had brought with him insights and expertise from French melodrama production.[81] Another important factor was of course its international network and its well-established sales and marketing force.

Adapting to local taste could lead to Pathé's model of hooking up with studios scattered across many markets. Alternatively, companies could, and most soon did, subscribe to the model of film production outlined in *Motography*: namely, finding formulas with international leverage. Motography commented that "motion pictures have one distinct advantage over the regular drama—it is quite easily possible to see what class of films 'go' the best, and then stick to that."[82]

The Serial Craze's International Impact

In the last few years, the serial craze during the 1910s and 1920s has garnered increasing scholarly attention, adding new perspectives to Lahue's documentation in *Bound and Gagged* (1968). Seminal texts have explored the new series/serial format and its impact on exhibition practices, marketing, and the rising fan culture as well as its role as a launching pad for propelling the New Woman. Almost exclusively, however, these texts have riveted their attention to the U.S. market. Among articles and essays about the fearless and athletic female stars is Jennifer Bean's award-winning text, "Technologies of Early Stardom and the Extraordinary Body," in which she explores issues bearing on women performers and female stardom in relation to early film historiography.

This volume brings together seven original essays that cover the genre and its historiographic importance, narrative patterns, marketing, and cultural reception which will challenge the received scholarship by a wider contextualization of the serial phenomenon and its fearless female stars. What made Pearl White and her serial sisters important in an international sense? Why did she became such a popular star worldwide, or did she not?

When exported, the American serial format encountered various types of exhibition contexts, and the films would hence appear in modified forms in step with local practices. The serials illustrate both globalization and an accompanying hegemonic practice of Hollywood cinema and the vicissitudes of glocalization, including both purposeful regional campaigns by the studio and local reappropriations. These cultural shifts illustrate glocalized editorial and production procedures seen from the side, or the "periphery." Roland Robertson's concept of glocalization alongside and Miriam Hansen's analysis of vernacular modernism highlight processes of transactions and patterns of cultural flow between the global and the local.[83] White's serials, made in the United States with an American star by Pathé, originally a French production company, and later localized again for the French market are themselves examples of an inflected glocalization loop. Rudmer Canjels has written a compelling study about the cultural transformations of American serials in France, the Netherlands, and Germany[84] and contributes to this volume with an essay on Pearl White's serials in France and the transformations made in tailoring them to the local French setting during a time of war.

Marina Dahlquist's essay explores the fate of Pearl White's serials on the Swedish market. Here censorship problems, together with traditional forms of marketing without tie-ins, eclipsed the format and reshuffled the chronology for the episodes, which undercut the popularity of the serial queen in a market already geared to features.

Monica Dall'Asta makes a cluster of inquiries, with an emphasis on the Pearl White phenomenon on the French market. She focuses on the French influence on Pathé's American serials and the obvious resemblance between the Pauline character and the amazing French athlete, mountaineer, and aviator Marie Marvingt. Dall'Asta further explores Pearl White's forerunners as well as emulators in the French serial productions from Musidora to Protéa.

By examining the evocation of Pearl White's star persona by avant-garde theorists and filmmakers as varied as Sergei Eisenstein and surrealist George Hugnet, Christina Petersen's contribution uncovers Pearl White's legacy aside from international stardom as an influence upon the avant-garde with revolutionary potential for challenging the status quo.

World War I cut short film production and distribution in a number of countries. In Czechoslovakia and throughout the entire Austro-Hungarian Empire, there was a general ban on American films during World War I. As a consequence, Czech audiences did not become acquainted with Pearl White and other American serial stars until after 1918. Drawing on a series of articles in Czech periodicals from the late 1910s to the 1930s, Kevin Johnson discusses the postponed but still strong and lasting impression Pearl White left on Czech critics, viewers, and the avant-garde.

Pearl White and the American serials present a multitude of intricate issues regarding the international market, the need to come to terms with Hollywood's global reach, and the impact of glocalized Americana for local production. The studies of Rosie Thomas and Weihong Bao analyze the influence White's serials exerted on local production and local genres in India and China. "Fearless Nadia," alias Mary Evans, was one of the biggest female stars on the Indian screen of the 1930s and 1940s. The blonde, blue-eyed, and white-skinned former circus artist became an Indian icon and box-office queen. Billed as the "Indian Pearl White," she seems to have been the personification of the "Heroine of a Thousand Stunts" but without her gentler qualities. Rosie Thomas explores how Nadia's whiteness was negotiated, adjusted, and weakened by the producers to conflate two traditions: the American stunt queen and the legendary Indian warrior woman. In fact, despite her whiteness, Fearless Nadia became part of the nationalist movement during the late colonial period in films that many considered anti-British.

Weihong Bao's contribution discusses the origin of Chinese martial arts films as a mediated encounter between American serial queen adventures and a subgenre of Chinese martial arts films, *nüxiapian*. By highlighting the presence of American serial queen films in the Chinese entertainment world of the 1920s and 1930s, Bao questions the cultural essentialist definition of the martial arts films as a purely Chinese genre largely identified with long-standing domestic tradition and local culture.

In the 1910s the American serials were released on a global film market, which offered novel opportunities for promotional campaigns and a growing market share for American cinema. The globalization of American cinema was to a large extent fueled by the intrepid serial queens' worldwide success. Glocalized tactics in negotiations with screen Americana, in order to reach local markets, are still with us. This book is a contribution to a century-long debate.

NOTES

1. William deMille, *Hollywood Saga* (New York: E. P. Dutton, 1939), 37.

2. Pearl White, *Just Me* (New York: George H. Doran Company, 1919). Charlie Chaplin's so-called autobiography was published as early as 1916: *Charlie Chaplin's Own Story: Being a Faithful Recital of a Romantic Career, Beginning with Early Recollections of Boyhood in London and Closing with the Signing of His Latest Motion-Picture Contract* (Indianapolis, Ind.: Bobbs-Merrill Company, 1916).

3. Jane M. Gaines, "World Women: Still Circulating Silent Era Film Prints," *Framework* 51, no. 2 (Fall 2010): 295.

4. Hilary A. Hallett, "Based on a True Story: New Western Women and the Birth of Hollywood," *Pacific Historical Review* 80, no. 2 (2011): 177–210.

5. "Popular Player Contest," *Motion Picture Magazine* 12, no. 11 (December 1916): 15; "The Motion Picture Hall of Fame," *Motion Picture Magazine* 16, no. 11 (December 1918): 12; "Popularity Contest Closes," *Motion Picture Magazine* 20, no. 11 (December 1920): 94.

6. White, *Just Me*, 106.

7. Ibid., 151–52.

8. For a discussion on the collaboration between Hearst and Selig, see Jan Olsson, *Los Angeles before Hollywood: Journalism and American Film Culture, 1905 to 1915* (Stockholm: National Library of Sweden, 2008), 267–308.

9. Ads in *Moving Picture World* 19, no. 9 (February 28, 1914): 1056–57; *New York American*, March 1, 1914, Editorial and Dramatic section, 5.

10. See, for instance, "Pathe Stories in Hearst Newspapers," *Motography* 11, no. 5 (March 7, 1914): 177, and *New York American*, March 8, 1914, Editorial and Dramatic section, 6. In the mid-1910s, Hearst became an important name not only as a giant within newspaper publishing but also in the moving picture industry, producing weekly newsreels, serial films, and animated films. David Nasaw, *The Chief: The Life of William Randolph Hearst* (Boston: Houghton Mifflin, 2000), 237.

11. Fred J. Balshofer and Arthur C. Miller, *One Reel a Week* (Berkeley: University of California Press, 1967), 102–4.

12. See, for instance, *Motography* 11, no. 8 (April 18, 1914): 4.

13. Nasaw, *The Chief*, 235. To publish tie-ins in the Sunday editions was, according to Ben Singer, a way to target a female audience, so the promotional material most commonly was published on the "women's pages." Edison began this practice with its very first serial, *What Happened to Mary* (1912), teaming up in 1912 with the women's magazine *Ladies' World*. Ben Singer, *Melodrama and Modernity: Early Sensational Cinema and Its Contexts* (New York: Columbia University Press, 2001), 223. Shelley Stamp, too, discusses company strategies to reach a female audience by way of the serial format. In the United States, working-class women already by 1900 constituted a major proportion of the readers of dime novels and story papers, a tendency that continued with the serialized stories in monthly magazines. *Movie-Struck Girls: Women and Motion Picture Culture after the Nickelodeon* (Princeton, N.J.: Princeton University Press, 2000), 102–4.

14. *Motography* 11, no. 8 (April 18, 1914): 3. See also, for instance, *New York Dramatic Mirror* 71, no. 1841 (April 1, 1914): 26.

15. For a discussion of the American critique of Pathé Frères in the years 1907–1910, see Richard Abel, *The Red Rooster Scare: Making Cinema American, 1900–1910* (Berkeley: University of California Press, 1999).

16. "Pearl White's Message to Our Boys," unsigned article in *New York Star*, December 26, 1917, 78.

17. Ben Singer, "Female Power in the Serial-Queen Melodrama: The Etiology of an Anomaly," *Camera Obscura* 8, no. 1 (1990): 90–129; Singer, *Melodrama and Modernity*, 14.

18. Singer, *Melodrama and Modernity*, 223.

19. Hallett, "Based on a True Story," 185.

20. Eclectic Film Company's advertisement in *Motography* 11, no. 7 (April 4, 1914): 5.

21. Richard Abel, *Americanizing the Movies and "Movie-Mad" Audiences: 1910–1914* (Berkeley: University of California Press, 2006), 215–56.

22. Stamp, *Movie-Struck Girls*, 108.

23. Singer, *Melodrama and Modernity*, 276–79.

24. The Goat Man, "On the Outside Looking In," *Motography* 11, no. 2 (January 24, 1914): 49.

25. Ibid.

26. Stamp, *Movie-Struck Girls*, 110.

27. "Perils Pauline Didn't Forsee," *Motion Picture News* 9, no. 14 (April 11, 1914): 28.

28. Kalton C. Lahue, *Bound and Gagged: The Story of the Silent Serials* (New York: Castle Books, 1968), 11, 52.

29. Singer, *Melodrama and Modernity*, 217.

30. Ibid., 210.

31. Stamp, *Movie-Struck Girls*, 116–17.

32. "Serial Features," *Motography* 12, no. 8 (August 22, 1914): 273.

33. Ibid., 275.

34. Ibid., 274.

35. Stamp, *Movie-Struck Girls*, 116.

36. Ibid., 117.

37. "Thrills Increase in Pauline Series," *Motography* 12, no. 12 (September 19, 1914): 412.

38. Pathé was indisputably the leading production company during the heyday of the trick genre from 1906 to 1910 and later dominated the production of film serials. Its trick work was gradually integrated into narratives and was more realistically motivated. The spectacular events were no longer executed by a male magician with exceptional abilities; instead, an action girl at ease in dangerous and modern settings called the shots.

39. "Thrills Increase in Pauline Series," *Motography* 12, no. 12 (September 19, 1914): 412.

40. See, for instance, ads in *Motography* 11, no. 9 (May 2, 1914): 3, and (May 16, 1914): 4.

41. Stamp, *Movie-Struck Girls*, 142.

42. Jennifer M. Bean, "Technologies of Early Stardom and the Extraordinary Body," in "Early Woman Stars," Jennifer M. Bean and Diane Negra, eds., special issue, *Camera Obscura: Feminism, Culture, and Media Studies*, no. 48 (2001): 12.

43. Jane Gaines stresses the importance of Kalem's *The Girl Spy* series of 1909–1910, starring Gene Gautier, as a forerunner to the later action serials and serial queens. Gaines, "World Women," 286–91.

44. Bean, "Technologies," 12.

45. See, for instance, "Pearl White 'Doubled': Pathe Star Nearly Loses Her Life in Strenuous 'Iron Claw' Stunt," *New York Dramatic Mirror* 75, no. 1945 (April 1, 1916): 32. Also, the perils of the production team are discussed in "Perils Pauline Didn't Forsee," *Motion Picture News* 9, no. 14 (April 11, 1914): 28.

46. For examples of photographic tricks, see Lahue, *Bound and Gagged*, 120–22, 217.

47. "Fatal Film 'Stunt,'" *London Times*, August 16, 1922, 8.

48. White, *Just Me*, 160.

49. Louis Gasnier was to direct the serial with Donald MacKenzie.

50. White, *Just Me*, 157.

51. Ibid., 162.

52. Lahue, *Bound and Gagged*, 25.

53. Bean, "Technologies," 20.

54. "La femme la plus assassinée du monde," *Lectures pour Tous* (March 1920). Collection Rondel, Bibliothèque de l'Arsenal, Paris.

55. Singer, *Melodrama and Modernity*, 254–60.

56. Ibid., 198.

57. White, *Just Me*, 161.

58. Ibid.

59. Pearl White, quoted in Mabel Condon, "Sans Grease Paint and Wig," *Motography* 12, no. 8 (August 22, 1914): 279.

60. White, *Just Me*, 134.

61. Bean, "Technologies," 23.

62. For example, in Hervé Lauwick, "La vrai Pearl White," *Figaro*, May 1, 1921, 1.

63. Singer, *Melodrama and Modernity*, 224.

64. White, *Just Me*, last page.

65. Ibid., 12.

66. "Pathe's Own Convention: Exchange Managers Hold Three-Day Session in New York to Celebrate Million-Dollar Business of 'Elaine,'" *New York Dramatic Mirror* 74 (July 14, 1915): 23.

67. Kristin Thompson, *Exporting Entertainment: America in the World Film Market, 1907–34* (London: BFI Publishing, 1985), 28–60.

68. Ibid., 64.

69. Rapport du conseil d'administration, 1907–1908, 16, Collection Pathé, Fondation Jérôme Seydoux, Paris.

70. The numerous branches became part of Pathé's image and advertising. See, for instance, the ad in *Moving Picture World* 19, no. 9 (February 28, 1914): 1058.

71. For a discussion of Pathé's opening a branch in New Jersey, see Marina Dahlquist, "Becoming American in 1910? Pathé Frères' Settlement in New Jersey," *Quarterly Review of Film and Video* 22, no. 3 (2005), 29–38.

72. Later on, Pathé opened branch offices in two other Swedish towns, Malmö and Göteborg.

73. Ad in *Moving Picture World* 19, no. 9 (February 28, 1914): 1058. See also "Pathe Announces New Program," *Motion Picture News* 11, no. 2 (January 16, 1915): 27.

74. Ad in *New York Dramatic Mirror* 74 (July 14, 1915): back cover.

75. Richard Abel, *The Red Rooster Scare: Making Cinema American, 1900–1910* (Berkeley: University of California Press, 1999), 118–75.

76. "Exporting the American Film," *Motography* 6, no. 2 (August 1911): 90.

77. Ibid.

78. W. Stephen Bush, "Charles Pathe's Views," *Moving Picture World* 19, no. 4 (January 24, 1914): 390–91.

79. Ibid.

80. "Brevities of the Business," *Motography* 12, no. 6 (August 8, 1914): 215.

81. Lahue, *Bound and Gagged*, 105.

82. "Exporting the American Film," *Motography* 6, no. 2 (August 1911): 90.

83. Roland Robertson, *Globalization: Social Theory and Global Culture* (London: Sage, 1992); "Globalisation or Glocalisation," *Journal of International Communication* 1, no. 1 (1994); Roland Robertson and Kathleen E. White, eds., *Globalization: Critical Concepts in Sociology*, 6 vols. (London: Routledge, 2003); Miriam Hansen, "The Mass Production of the Senses: Classical Cinema as Vernacular Modernism," *Reinventing Film Studies*, ed. Christine Gledhill and Linda Williams (London: Arnold, 2000), 332–50.

84. Rudmer Canjels, *Distributing Silent Serials: Local Practices, Changing Forms, Cultural Transformation* (New York: Routledge, 2011).

CHAPTER 1

Changing Views and Perspectives

Translating Pearl White's American Adventures in Wartime France

RUDMER CANJELS

Near the end of 1915, the French surrealist writer Philippe Soupault witnessed an unprecedented force of cinematic inundation that flooded Paris and left distinctive markers in daily life.[1]

> One day you saw huge posters, as long as snakes, stretching out along the walls. At each streetcorner a man, his face covered with a red handkerchief, was pointing a revolver at the unconcerned passersby. You thought you heard galloping, a motor kicking over, screams of death. We descended on the cinemas and understood that everything had changed. Pearl White's smile appeared on the screen; this almost ferocious smile announced the upheavals of the new world. We finally understood that the cinema was not a perfected toy but the terrible and magnificent flag of life.[2]

The film to which Soupault was referring was an American serial that in France was called *Les Mystères de New-York*. The menacing revolver and the red handkerchief belonged to a criminal who terrorized the actress Pearl White for many episodes. However, this serial was, as will be discussed, not the same as the version previously released in America. This one was positioned quite firmly in its new French setting, not only acquiring a different structure but also an adjusted content. An important tool for accomplishing this was the tie-in, a novelization that appeared alongside the film, a tool that most likely was also noticed by Soupault. Namely, printed on the posters of *Les Mystères de New-York* that have survived, we find the words, "Grand Roman Cinéma Américain adapté par Pierre Decourcelle, publié par Le Matin." (Big American cinema novel adapted by Pierre Decourcelle, published by *Le Matin*.)

Present, past, and future episodes of a serial not only referred to and interacted with one another but were transformed into a new national context outside the cinematic space, that is, daily life in France. This article will examine how in two Pearl White serials in particular, French customs, speech, and views were used to create a connection between America and France, how patriotic undertones and anti-German slurs were used in a war-related context to accommodate and appeal to national sensibilities. A serial had the capacity to appear in different lengths and constructions (not only in the form of the short American serial of two reels), while at the same time it could absorb and integrate locality.[3] The use of seriality thus marked a different use of a global film form, one that could change and create a spontaneous mixture of globalization and localization. Homogeneity and heterogeneity as well as global and local were thus not necessarily each other's opposites.[4]

Elaborating Media Expositions

Marketing played an important role in the success of film serials, and the tie-in was among the most effective marketing strategies. The American tie-in published in weekly episodes in newspapers told the story of one film serial episode that at the same time could be seen at the cinema. The tie-ins created a resonating vibe of seriality that helped push film distribution and consumption in a rhythmic manner, as was first witnessed with the Edison serial *What Happened to Mary* in August 1912. It was only in 1915, when in America serials had already been popular for several years and tie-ins were widely publicized, that the European film market was introduced to the serial. As this volume makes abundantly clear, the most successful star of the American serial was without a doubt Pearl White, not only in the U.S. but in many other countries as well. Pearl White was not known in Europe before the release of her serials, but massive marketing campaigns soon remedied that.[5] Her early serials were produced by Pathé-Exchange, the American branch of the French Pathé, and directed by the Frenchman Louis Gasnier, who had left France in 1910. It was thus through a boomerang effect that the first American serial was released on a large scale in France by the French Pathé: *Les Mystères de New-York*.[6]

Les Mystères de New-York was not originally one Pearl White serial, but a combination of three Pathé-Exchange serials that in America had followed each other in succession in 1914 and 1915. Each starred the famous serial queen Pearl White: the fourteen-part *The Exploits of Elaine* (1914), the ten-part *The New Exploits of Elaine* (1915), and the twelve-part *The Romance of Elaine* (1915). The original episodes were re-cut in France and rearranged into a serial of twenty-two episodes. Each episode still had more or less the same length as the original, around six hundred meters, or twenty minutes. As the French episodes followed the original order of the three American serials, Elaine Dodge (Pearl White), with the help of Craig Kennedy (Arnold Daly), now successively had to deal with The Clutching Hand (Sheldon Lewis), the evil Wu Fang (Edwin Arden), and the international spy Marcus Del Mar (Lionel Barrymore). Pathé released the serial in at least forty-nine Parisian cinemas in France on December 3, 1915.[7] Up until early May 1916, a new episode could be seen in the Parisian cinemas every week, while during the previous week the corresponding story line, written by Pierre Decourcelle, could be read in the Paris newspaper *Le Matin*.[8]

Even though it is not mentioned in the advertisements or in the serial novel, Decourcelle did not start from scratch but relied heavily on the three American serial novels that had been written especially for the film serial by the well-known American detective writer Arthur B. Reeve. Reeve had already introduced the Craig Kennedy character in the December 1910 issue of the Hearst-owned *Cosmopolitan*. The fictional Kennedy, a professor at Columbia University as well as a scientific detective, quickly became known in America as the American Sherlock Holmes. Kennedy uses his knowledge of chemistry to solve cases, but he also invents numerous devices like a wireless telephone, a wireless fax machine, and a portable seismograph that could differentiate between the footsteps of various individuals. In the three Elaine stories, the character of Elaine obviously also gets a great deal of attention. She does not so much function as a sidekick, but more as an individualistic young woman whose doings and happenings assist and endanger Kennedy, while the two fall in love with each other. The serial novels that were connected to the Pathé films appeared in the Sunday editions of the Hearst syndicated press and were later published as a novel, also by Hearst.[9]

Like other American serials (including those of later date), the *Elaine* film serials cared little for developing character or deepening dramatic complexity. Sensation and shock were more important than psychological drama. Compared with several film episodes that have survived, the novelization of *The Exploits of Elaine* adds more insight into the relationship between Kennedy and

Elaine.[10] Their reflections on some of the dangerous situations are elaborated upon, while the various scientific experiments and gadgets Kennedy uses are more fully explained, and the coincidental happenings that often appear in these kinds of serials are given more connection. The serial novel was thus used for enriching and contextualizing the film.[11] The American tie-in, however, did not provide a very detailed story when compared with the elaborate French version.

American and French Crimes: Changing and Creating a Narrative

Each week for twenty-two weeks, an episode from *Les Mystères de New-York* could be seen in Paris, while the story by Decourcelle could be read daily in *Le Matin* as well as in French provincial newspapers. In addition to the story in the newspapers, the publishing house La Renaissance du Livre sometime later released a weekly booklet for twenty-five centimes. Each booklet corresponded to one film episode; later these could also be bought bound together as a book. From that moment on, a film serial was, because of its close ties to the serial novel, designated a ciné-roman in France.[12]

Pierre Decourcelle was a popular fiction writer who had written the successful novel *Les Deux gosses* (Two little boys), and in 1908 he, together with Eugène Guggenheim, founded the literary adaptation company, Société cinématographique des auteurs et gens de lettres (SCAGL).[13] *Les Mystères de New-York* probably benefited from Decourcelle's writing skills as well as his ability to translate a story from one medium into another. Decourcelle's *Les Mystères de New-York* elaborated much more on the story and its characters than did Reeve's novel. Sometimes, Decourcelle directly translated parts of Reeve's text, but often he developed and expanded the story. This expansion can be seen, for instance, with the minor secondary character of the gunman Limpy Red, one of the first characters introduced in the film and novel. In Reeve's novelization of *The Exploits of Elaine*, he is described only as "a red-headed, lame, partly paralyzed crook."[14] When Limpy Red, pressed by Elaine's father, snitches on his evil boss and gives the father an envelope with directions to The Clutching Hand's whereabouts, Reeve writes: "When Limpy Red, still trembling, left the office of Dodge earlier in the evening, he had repaired as fast as his shambling feet would take him to his favourite dive upon Park Row. There he might have been seen drinking with any one who came along, for Limpy had money—blood money—and the recollection of his treachery and revenge must both be forgotten and celebrated."[15] When Limpy continues to

A foldout booklet of *Les Mystères de New-York,* given away as an appetizer by the newspaper *Le Matin.* It told part of the storyline of the first episode.

another venue for more drinks, he is killed by means of a lead pipe, held by one of The Clutching Hand's associates.

In *Les Mystères de New-York,* Le Bancal Rouge (as Limpy Red is called) is a more interesting character, receiving an extended background. Le Bancal Rouge used to be a rifleman performing his feats in music halls and circuses but became addicted to alcohol and as a result came under the influence of

La Main Qui Étreint (The Clutching Hand). In *Les Mystères de New-York*, Le Bancal Rouge goes to the pub after revealing the whereabouts of the evil gang, not to drink away his blood money, but to be around people for safety and to wait to be accompanied to the port. In exchange for information on the whereabouts of the evil La Main Qui Étreint, Elaine's uncle (originally it was her father) had promised him a safe passage on the ship *La Lorraine* that would take him to France. Le Bancal Rouge had received enough money to build a new existence, perhaps opening a bar in Paris. While waiting, he has a drink and asks explicitly for the extra dry Pommery champagne instead of some German label.[16] After several hours of waiting in vain for his transport to arrive (Elaine's uncle in the meantime has been murdered), a rather slatternly, strong-armed, red-haired woman of German descent with a glass eye starts flirting with him, trying to profit from his apparent wealth. Getting restless and drunk, he tries to perform a William Tell trick on her, but she refuses. When the bar closes, Le Bancal Rouge leaves scared and full of doubt. Outside he is murdered with a cloth filled with sand by an accomplice of La Main Qui Étreint.

Through expansion and the deployment of his eye for detail, Decourcelle succeeded in making a more compelling story than the rather stilted and very basic version by Reeve, with its sparse details. Decourcelle took, in many instances, many more words to describe a setting (that fitted the film version rather well) and to relate that setting to the history of the characters. Decourcelle also inserted brief references that evoked the troubled world outside the film theater. *La Lorraine*, for instance, was an actual ship that had run between Le Havre and New York between 1900 and 1914. During the war the ship was used as an armed merchant cruiser renamed *Lorraine II*.[17] Lorraine was, of course, also a province of France that together with Alsace had been lost during the Franco-Prussian war in 1871 and which France wished to recover in World War I. Similarly, the reference to Pommery champagne can be linked to the Franco-Prussian war as well as to World War I. Champagne was a region in France that had often been invaded and ravaged, perhaps more than any other French province. At the time, the German front line was not very far from the soon-to-be-blown-up Pommery Chateau.[18]

As we shall see, the overall tie-in was frenchified and made explicitly anti-German; Le Bancal Rouge's rejection of German champagne was only the first and small sign of these changes. Fragments of text refer not only to a common French history but also to French clichés and habits. Therefore, it is possible that the tie-in might have made the transition from French films to American imports easier for the French audience to accept. French film production had received a very hard blow with the start of World War I. Many experts, actors, and workers left for the front, and film factories were abandoned. Pathé (as well as others) had already begun restructuring the company to be more of a distribution company than a firm regularly producing films. In 1915 American films were imported on a large scale to meet the product demand of exhibitors, creating an invasion of American products.[19] *Les Mystères de New-York* was, judging from advertisements and articles in film journals, probably the most well-known of the new American productions arriving at that time on the French market, except for the shorts by Charles Chaplin (known in France as Charlot).

Serialized War Relations Invading the Fabric of Life

It is fair to say that Le Bancal Rouge's extended exploits probably were due to the adjustment to a different tradition in France. Whereas in America, most novelized serials as well as film serial tie-ins were only published once a week (usually on Sunday), in France the very popular serial novel scheme was a daily one. Thus, to achieve a proper adjustment with regard to the film release pattern, a much longer story was needed for the serial novel. It is also possible that, like many other serial novel writers, Decourcelle was paid by the word, which might have made him more verbose. The richer world of his story expressed not only opposition to Germany but also the contrasts between France and America, between the Old World and the New World. The biggest adaptation that was made in the story, the change that was needed to bring opposition into the serial, involved changing the American character Craig Kennedy into the Frenchman Justin Clarel. However, the story remained situated in America. There is no mention of France in any of the original novels.

In the serial novel, Justin Clarel is quickly introduced as a famous and fearless Frenchman, holding a double job as both professor at Columbia University and crime detective. A flashback early in the tie-in explains why Clarel went to America. When Clarel tells his mentor, Alphonse Bertillon, that he wants to be part of the special Parisian police task force, Bertillon answers him: "Between you and me, the private police service in Paris and in the whole of France generally does not have a good press. It consists for the most part of former inspectors who left their job because of some bothersome affair or disagreement with their chief. Consequently, we do not hold the profession in the high regard that you rightly aspire to."[20] Apart from Decourcelle's obvious critique of the Parisian police force, other elements place the story in a realistic French contemporary setting. For instance, Clarel's mentor Alphonse Bertillon had really existed and had died a year prior to the start of the tie-in. He had been part of the Parisian police force and had developed the first scientific method of criminal identification.[21] Given his stature and his death, it is very likely the reading audience knew who Bertillon was. In the tie-in, Justin Clarel follows his advice, and within two years he is famous in America, as his mentor had predicted.

Though this instance of adding layers of connections that at the same time make statements about America and France is presented in a flashback scene, most connections and differences between the two countries that pop up now and then can be found in the dialogue between Clarel and Elaine. References to mutual relations between man and woman (including the cliché of the courteous, passionate Frenchman who easily can turn a woman's head); extensive comments on the deadening, dispiriting French bureaucracy; French expressions (e.g., "dont on dit en France" [as one says in France]); and other snippets of information about Parisian or French ways and habits are sprinkled throughout.[22] America is often presented as the land of opportunity and progress where one can easily advance one's career, though sometimes less positive sides of American culture are discussed. For instance, Elaine likes to spend large sums of money and often goes on shopping sprees, especially in search of antiques, which "many young American ladies" find irresistible (even though Elaine already possesses "many of those useless things with which the rich fill their lives and drawers").[23] The serial tie-in thus gives us a French view of French reality, a typical French perspective on America, and a rather conventional American perspective on France. However, the strongest connection to the world outside the serial were allusions to the world war that was going on outside the theater, threatening Parisian life.

The Romance of Elaine (1915), the third serial installment of the Elaine adventures, was one of the first film serials in America to deal extensively with a foreign threat (most so-called American "preparedness serials" would be made from 1916 on). In this serial, foreign spies have a secret submarine base in America, and Craig Kennedy's wireless torpedoes are stolen. In Reeve's serial novel the spies' nationality is never mentioned; they remain "foreign."[24] Only when the international spy Marcus del Mar (who is the head of the Anti-American League) gets torpedoed to the bottom of the sea in the last episode does it become clear he was probably German, as he writes a note saying, "Tell my emperor I failed only because Craig Kennedy was against me, Del Mar."[25] When *The Romance of Elaine* was released in the summer of 1915, American entry into the war was still nearly two years away. Reeve's

En haut des marches de marbre du perron il trouva Elaine.,
— Enfin!... murmura-t-elle, tandis qu'il la serrait tendrement dans ses bras... Mais tu as l'air tout soucieux... Est-ce encore cette maudite affaire?...

JUSTIN CLAREL

ELAINE

— Toujours!... répondit-il en pénétrant dans le salon... Il est dit qu'elle ne me laissera pas de repos...
Et se laissant tomber sur un fauteuil, il essuya son front, où perlaient quelques gouttes de sueur.
— Avez-vous du nouveau, mon oncle?... interrogea le jeune avocat.

A cutout from the giveaway newspaper booklet, with a drawing of Justin Clarel (Arnold Daly) and Elaine Dodge (Pearl White).

account recorded a growing sense of uneasiness but never mentioned France or Germany, saying only that a war was going on in Europe.

Thus, while the action of the American serial takes place during the war, the action in *Les Mystères de New-York* is situated almost entirely before the war. This becomes clearest when, in the last episode of *Les Mystères de New-York*, the outbreak of the war is built into the plot. In it the devious spies try to cut the Atlantic telegraph cable in order to prevent the United States from knowing about France's declaration of war. (In Reeve's version the spies try to cut it without any explanation of the objective, except that it would be a good idea.) References to the war that was at hand were included in the French serial from episode sixteen onward. At that point, Clarel's Frenchness is also taken to a higher level. Because in the first episode it had been suggested that Clarel had left France in search of fortune and fame, the question remained whether he was a true Frenchman or an assimilated American. At the time, but also well before, immigration to America had not been viewed favorably in France. It was considered a source of individual weakness, as the overwhelming majority of Frenchmen felt no need to emigrate. Immigration numbers confirm this: while between 1870 and 1914 more than twenty million immigrants from all over the world went to America, only a few tens of thousands of them were French.[26] With the addition of war to the story, the rupture between Clarel and France that perhaps had raised questions among readers and viewers about his loyalty to his native land was healed.

In episode sixteen it was made very clear that Clarel had remained French, and it was because of his Frenchness that he was successful in his work and life: "In all of his aspirations, hopes, and dreams, he had remained a son of French soil. And everything that harmed France, no matter how small the affront, struck his heart. The ups and downs of life had forced him to seek happiness abroad, but he had long wondered how in exile he could serve the country that had nurtured him and from which he was temporarily separated."[27] The reader is told that Clarel's knowledge and skilled deductive techniques had impelled him to search for ways to counteract the German might that he felt was at hand: "Years ago he had realized the insatiable desires of Germany and understood that despite a peaceful façade the predatory Kaiser was only waiting for the opportunity to unsheathe his concealed sword and throw himself on his enemies lulled in a false sense of security."[28] Thus, by going to America where he could find more opportunities to counteract Germany, Clarel could save France. He began working on a radio-controlled torpedo. He shared his invention with the American government (in gratitude for its hospitality) under the sole condition that upon completion, America would immediately share Clarel's invention with France, and only with France: "Only the two sister republics would have the monopoly over the remarkable machine, which would ensure them, from a maritime point of view, an incomparable advance and an uncontested superiority."[29]

The last episodes of *Les Mystères de New-York* concern the search for Clarel's torpedoes, which had been stolen by Julius Del Mar. In the end everything goes well, and together with the U.S. Navy he defeats the German enemy, which wanted to sink ships carrying reinforcements to France. As in the original, Clarel and Elaine reunite after these adventures, but where the American novel and film stop, the serial novel of *Les Mystères de New-York* continues.[30] Decourcelle has Clarel and Elaine leave for France on August 9, 1914, on *La Lorraine*, "exactly seven days after the declaration of war."[31] In France, Clarel would offer his torpedo invention to the government and Elaine would nurse the wounded until, with victory won, they would marry. The brilliant son of France thus returned to the country that needed him most immediately upon the outbreak of the war. Clarel brought with him help from America, not only in the form of Elaine, but also by way of the U.S. Navy, which together with

Clarel had tested and perfected the wireless torpedo. However, it was not a truly happy ending, because the reality of World War I had invaded the serial audience's pleasurable visions of heroics. The happy ending of marriage (an event that in the original novel is never mentioned) could only be fulfilled after the war with Germany had been won.

The war-related texts (the film and the tie-ins) of *Les Mystères de New-York* (as well as other serials that would follow) fitted cruelly into daily life in France. Episodes were announced in newspapers and film journals next to obituaries, remembrances, and funds for widows, while at the moving picture theaters, episodes were being screened right after special war bulletins. According to an unidentified American source reporting in June 1916, many French soldiers read Elaine's adventures in *Le Matin* (a figure of two million was cited) and were eager to see her exploits on the screen while on a six-day leave. As it would normally have been impossible to see all the episodes in such a short time (indeed, there were twenty-two episodes in circulation), "The War Office has asked Pathé-Frères to make arrangements to show the entire serial each week for the benefit of the soldier fans on furlough. Accordingly a circuit of screenings has been arranged, and Pearl White now plays to vast audiences of bearded uniformed men, fresh from the shock of war, who find in the great Pathe serial a much needed diversion."[32] Although America had not yet joined the war and specifically anti-German films (such as *The Kaiser, the Beast from Berlin* [1918]) had yet to be made, the serial was actively retrofitted to fall in line with changing opinion.[33] The French press, including *Le Matin*, which ran many serial tie-ins, began creating a false image of a United States that held France close to its bosom. A set of aims and views of the war comparable to those of France was projected onto the U.S. While before the war the Franco-American relationship had been a nonissue, now France's bond with its "sister republic" was made closer than it really was. From 1916 until the end of the war, the French press launched a deification of President Woodrow Wilson, published many articles on America's love for France (including stories about female American volunteers at the front), and indulged in a broadly pro-American perspective.[34]

Influential Confrontations

Though *Les Mystères de New-York* was the first extensively promoted and distributed American serial in France, it was not the first serial. Pathé and Gaumont had been competing to release the first one on a wide scale. While

Pathé restructured an already-existing American serial, Gaumont asked director Louis Feuillade to make a new one, which was to become the ten-part *Les Vampires* (1915–1916). Three weeks before the premiere of the first episode of *Les Mystères de New-York*, the first two episodes of *Les Vampires* were screened together (the two being of different lengths). The third episode was not released a week later but rather, and probably not coincidentally, on the date of the premiere of *Les Mystères de New-York*. The last episode was released on June 30, 1916; by then *Les Mystères de New-York* had already finished, and Pearl White would soon be seen again in a new serial.

The competition between the American and French serial products made their differences more noticeable. Perhaps the fact that Pearl White was featured prominently in advertisements led Gaumont to foreground Musidora as Irma Vep, even though her presence in the serial is, especially in the beginning, not noteworthy. Irma Vep, the female villain of *Les Vampires*, was presented in advertisements as a black-haired, mysterious, and morally depraved woman in it for the excitement and money, while *Les Mystères de New-York* was represented by the loving, blond, innocent, and high-spirited Elaine. Also, the episodes of *Les Vampires* were overall more deadly, gruesome, and disturbing than *Les Mystères de New-York*, a quality visible in *Les Vampires*' blood-drenched advertisements as well as in the lurid episode titles (such as La Tête coupée [The severed head], La Bague qui tue [The ring that kills], or Les Noces sanglantes [The bloody wedding]). Nevertheless, in spite of *Les Vampires*' exciting forms of crime and dubious morality (which the French previously enjoyed with the popular novels and films featuring the sadistic Fantômas), *Les Mystères de New-York* overshadowed *Les Vampires* in popularity.[35] One of the reasons might be the American film's massive advertising scheme using the serial tie-in. *Les Vampires* had (probably because of its hastened production and its very fluctuating lengths and release dates for each episode) failed to create a similar form of continuous marker; only when *Les Vampires* had almost disappeared from the theaters did a ciné-roman appear. Feuillade's next serial productions would be more like the American ones. With *Judex* (1917), *La Nouvelle Mission de Judex*, (The new mission of Judex [1918]), and *Tih Minh* (1919), all released by Gaumont, twelve episodes of more or less similar lengths were released in a weekly rhythm, while the novelizations appeared in newspapers and as booklets and novels.[36] Feuillade and others would continue this serial promotion and distribution scheme well into the 1920s, long after it had lost its charm in America.[37]

Germany and France in the House of Hate

Between Pearl White's first serial in France, *Les Mystères de New-York,* and her last wartime one, *La Maison de la haine* (*The House of Hate* [1918]), there were others that also had propagandistic components. Their French novelizations added plenty of anti-German propaganda that was absent in the original American story. In Marc Mario's *Les Exploits de Elaine* (*The Perils of Pauline* [1914]), Karl Summers sacrifices his life for Germany in an attempt to sink an American submarine; in Jean Petithuguenin's *Le Masque aux dents blanches* (*The Iron Claw* [1916]), Karl Legar pledges allegiance to the D.U.A. group (standing for Deutschland Über Alles); and in Marcel Allain's *Le Courrier de Washington* (*Pearl of the Army* [1916]), Major Brent kills himself after Pearl learns he was a German spy who tried to steal the defense plans of the Panama Canal.[38] References to French life were less present in these productions than in *Les Mystères de New-York,* perhaps because in these instances Pearl White's character had no French companion. Her concern for the war in France, as well as her love for that country, often nearly as strong as her love for America, thus suggested without Clarel an even more natural and common American point of view.

Almost eight weeks after the armistice with Germany that put an end to the actual fighting, the first episode of *La Maison de la haine* was released in Paris on December 27, 1918. It was the sixth Pearl White serial released in France. Pearl White plays Pearl Waldon, who inherits the Waldon arms factory after her father is murdered. She is continuously confronted and hampered by the evil deeds of the Hooded Terror, a German spy trying to get information about the factory's products. The adjusted twelve film episodes (the original American version had twenty episodes) were novelized by Guy de Teramond.[39] The story takes place before America's involvement in the war. In the U.S., no tie-in of *The House of Hate* seems to have been made, nor was it published as a novel, even though the script was partly written by Arthur B. Reeve. American film studios were at that time starting to question the use of the tie-in. It was argued that the exclusivity of the product and its story line was being bargained away. Also, newspapers began to ask higher prices and percentages from the studios. Thus, fewer tie-ins were made, though they did not disappear altogether, still popping up in the early 1920s. The French novelization seems to be the only tie-in of *The House of Hate* that was made.

The confrontation between France and Germany, one that in *Les Mystères de New-York* took some time to get into gear, was in this case made evident

Booklet cover of the final episode of *La Maison de la haine*, called "Sur la terre de France" (On French soil). The photograph shows the wedding of Pearl and Gresham.

from episode five. Then Pearl, as head of the arms factory, has to decide which party, the French or the Germans, will acquire supplies of a newly designed grenade launcher. She first meets with the French captain De Karguézec, who approaches her elegantly, with a "very French courtesy."[40] It has been made clear that Pearl, like her father, loves France, as it was "the land of freedom, where the conception of sacred science and dazzling art had influenced the whole world for several centuries."[41] Pearl immediately dislikes Baron Von Ratheim when he arrives to persuade her to accept his higher offer. Needless to say, Pearl accepts the lower offer of Captain De Karguézec. Confronted by other family members regarding her counter-commercial decision, she explains herself: "From now on the Waldon factory will only work for the defence of freedom, justice and civilization."[42] Pearl's reasons were very similar to those the French gave the United States for joining the war, which stressed the importance of French democracy and civilization to the world. In fact, in the press the American entry into the war was presented as a tribute to France, a misreading that ignored America's own national interest in helping France and the help offered to England and Belgium.[43]

The young chemist Harvey Gresham (Antonio Moreno), whom Pearl loves, exclaims in the fifth episode his love for France:

> I like your country, captain . . . if I was not an American citizen, I would have liked to have been French. . . . My most precious dream will be that, in this appalling war where the laws most sacred to humanity are violated, we will return the support that you brought to us in the past for the conquest of our liberty. . . . Have confidence, answered the officer with an assured tone . . . soon, I do not doubt it, your people will understand that to fight at our sides, is to defend the just and abused civilization, and they will rise as one man to help us![44]

While the French captain argues on behalf of France along the lines, expressed above, Gresham thus adds something new. Gresham, the American, expresses here the idea, presented in the French press at the time, that America was coming to France's aid in gratitude for the latter's aid in the Revolutionary War, when France helped America gain independence from Britain.[45] This misconstrued motive was also articulated in 1917 by French prime minister Alexandre Ribot, who implied as well that since the Declaration of Independence was inspired by French philosophers, America derived its morality from France.[46]

Unfortunately, as the original version is presumed to be lost, no American tie-in can be found, and no French re-edited film episodes seem to have survived, it is impossible to find out if this level of national bonding and admiration was also present in the original. The short episode descriptions in American film journals do not hint at it.[47] As *The House of Hate* was made after America's entry into the war, positive French characteristics probably were present in the original narrative. It nevertheless seems likely that the French version went further, including even more Francophile sentiments. For instance, the last chapter of the French serial, when after many adventures the sabotaging Hooded Terror is finally defeated, describes events that had not taken place at the time of its American release. At the end of the serial, the story continues in film what *Les Mystères de New-York*, as well as *La Reine s'ennuie* (*The Fatal Ring* [1917]), had only told in the tie-ins.[48] Unlike these serials, the story did not end with the couple's promise to join the Allied forces and marry when peace came. Both in the original and French versions, at the end (chapter 20 and chapter 12, respectively) Gresham goes fighting in France. When hit by a shell, he is transported by an American ambulance. Much to Gresham's surprise, he is attended to by his wife Pearl who, unbeknownst to him, had also come to France to work for the Red Cross. This final episode premiered in France on March 14, 1919, fifteen weeks before the Treaty of Versailles that officially ended the state of war between Germany and the Allied Powers.

The reader of the French tie-in learns that Gresham, who had arrived in France among the first American troops in May 1917 (in accordance with his request), unfortunately had to suppress his impatience and wait some time until he could fight for the cause. The American general John J. Pershing had insisted that his soldiers would not be used merely to fill gaps in the French and British armies, which in effect caused a delay until the American troops were sufficiently trained to perform in their own units. The novelist, de Teramond, thus situated the battle of the tie-in during the St. Mihiel offensive of September 12, 1918, when Pershing launched the first major American offensive in Europe with an independent American army. The offensive is extensively described, including many references to French regions and towns, with Gresham placed heroically on the frontline.[49] "Gresham marched in front of his soldiers, full of enthusiasm, giving an example and encouraging all of his forces: Forward, boys! he shouted to them. In front of them, he crossed the networks of barbed wire, jumped the holes filled with water, slipped along the craters of deep mines."[50] When he is injured and can not move forward, he continues to encourage the passing troops. Then, when Pearl appears and affirms that she is taking care of him, the novel suddenly ends.

Luckily, there is an epilogue, though de Teramond asks the reader: "Is it absolutely necessary, now, to give a conclusion to this story?"[51] De Teramond does so, duly summing up that Gresham recovers quickly, supported by his wife. Then he continues on a more personal note:

> As for readers, perhaps they have found that the adventures of the two young people were remarkably complicated and that sometimes even believability was not always respected, but the author will say that one should not take seriously a story written solely to distract for a moment. Living is fortunately much more simple! To be happy, it is not necessary for lovers to have escaped a series of a thousand of pitfalls and to have risked twelve times death in order to rescue that what one loves! It is enough to experience one day, to be satisfied, . . . to lean on the arm of another, and have confidence in the future.[52]

The serial, released just after the armistice, thus reiterated, with the help of the novelization, French ideas regarding American involvement and celebrated the French qualities of justice, democracy, and civilization that had been so much proclaimed in the years during the war. De Teramond's epilogue recognized and celebrated normal French lives, lives that were not up to the hectic standard of Pearl White. Her smile and many serial adventures had distracted

In the twelfth episode of *La Maison de la haine*, Pearl takes care of her husband Gresham, wounded during the St. Mihiel offensive in France.

audiences for many weeks during the difficult time of war. The novelizations had made the terrible and magnificent flag of life even more impressive.

While in the United States the content of the tie-in was used only to extend and elaborate somewhat on the screen image, in France it was used actively to fit the film into a different culture and make it a mouthpiece for French views of America. The introduction of American seriality in France showed how local adjustments to this film form were an important tool for the global dissemination of the serial format: serial content and format could be made to respond to national sensibilities, and seriality could influence local production and distribution as well as promotional techniques (as witnessed with Feuillade's serial productions). The transformation of a film serial in concurrence with a tie-in was a way to adjust to local discourses. It functioned as a steering mechanism in constructing local meanings when there first were none. By adding anti-German and pro-American views and adjusting the serial more to French reality and history, the serial integrated itself into daily public experience while perhaps also softening the distinctively American qualities of the original import from the U.S. The adaptation thereby went far beyond the more common aligning of promotional material or changing intertitles to accommodate viewership. Under the stress of war, localization transformed a supposedly national body of "foreign" films into a highly flexible transnational film form.

How much of the nationally specific storylines ended up in the film serials themselves and what effect these adaptations had on advancing Pearl White's extreme popularity in France remain unclear. It is, of course, likely that both during and after the war, the French admiration of Pearl White was boosted by the fact that in these serials, her love for France was often made apparent. With the Treaty of Versailles of 1919, unequivocal praise of America would come to an end, and severe criticisms of President Wilson's America could be read in the French press.[53] France, however, continued to love Pearl White and Pearl White loved France back.[54] In 1923 she left America for France and gave revue shows in Paris, where she also made her last film, *Terreur* (1924). She died in 1938 in the American hospital in Neuilly and was buried in the Passy cemetery in Paris.

NOTES

1. This article is based on chapter 3 of Rudmer Canjels, *Distributing Silent Serials: Local Practices, Changing Forms, Cultural Transformation* (New York: Routledge, 2011); a shorter version appeared in "Localizing Serials: Translating Daily Life in Les Mystères de New-York," in *Early Cinema and the "National,"* ed. Richard Abel, Giorgio Bertellini, and Rob King (New Barnet, UK: John Libbey, 2008), 215–25.

2. Philippe Soupault, "Le Cinéma USA," *Le Théâtre et comoedia illustré*, January 15, 1924. It is translated into English in Paul Hammond, ed., *The Shadow and Its Shadow: Surrealist Writing on the Cinema*, 3rd ed. (San Francisco: City Lights Books, 2000), 56.

3. Canjels, *Distributing Silent Serials*.

4. This relates to the concept of "glocalization," developed by American sociologist Roland Robertson. Robertson uses the notion of glocalization in his work to create more subtly "the dynamics of the production and reproduction of difference and, in the broadest sense, locality." Roland Robertson, "Glocalization: Time-Space and Homogeneity-Heterogeneity," in *Global Modernities*, ed. Mike Featherstone, Scott Lash, and Roland Robertson (London: Sage Publications, 1995), 29.

5. Around the same time *Les Mystères de New-York* was released in Paris, the serial *The Exploits of Elaine* opened in Britain. Pathé launched what was claimed at the time to be the greatest publicity campaign on record. See "The Vogue of the Serial," *The Bioscope* 28, no. 455 (July 1, 1915): 51, and "'Elaine' Makes Wonderful Showing in England," *Moving Picture World* 26, no. 4 (October 23, 1915): 637.

6. The claim that *Les Mystères de New-York* was the first American serial cannot hold up to close scrutiny. According to the English film journal *The Kinematograph and Lantern Weekly* and the American *Moving Picture World*, the serial *Trey of Hearts* (1914) could

be seen just prior to the release of *Les Mystères de New-York*; it, however, did not make an impact. See "'The Trey o' Hearts' in Paris," *The Kinematograph and Lantern Weekly* 19, no. 439 (September 23, 1915): 75, and "British Notes," *Moving Picture World* 26, no. 6 (October 30, 1915): 957.

7. Advertisement, *Ciné-journal*, 327 (November 20, 1915): 8–9.

8. The first installment appeared in *Le Matin* on Saturday, November 27, 1915. The tie-in was also published in several provincial newspapers.

9. In addition to the Elaine serials, Arthur B. Reeve also wrote the screenplays for other serials, such as *The Master Mystery* (starring Harry Houdini [1919]), *The Tiger's Trail* (1919), and *The Radio Detective* (1926) and the newspaper serialization of *Tarzan the Mighty* (1928). See John Harwood, "Arthur B. Reeve and the American Sherlock Holmes," *The Armchair Detective* 10, no. 4 (1977): 354–57; J. Randolph Cox, "A Reading of Reeve: Some Thoughts on the Creator of Craig Kennedy," *The Armchair Detective* 11, no. 1 (1978): 28–33.

10. I have viewed and compared episodes eight, nine, and ten of *The Exploits of Elaine*, previously (but no longer) available on video from Glenn Video Vistas.

11. In contrast to these purposes, the tie-in was less used as an essential tool for comprehension, as Ben Singer claims, comparing a film episode from a different serial with its tie-in. For more on the use of the serial tie-in, see Ben Singer, *Melodrama and Modernity: Early Sensational Cinema and Its Contexts* (New York: Columbia University Press, 2001), and Shelley Stamp, *Movie-Struck Girls: Women and Motion Picture Culture after the Nickelodeon* (Princeton, N.J.: Princeton University Press, 2000).

12. Richard Abel, *French Cinema: The First Wave, 1915–1929* (Princeton, N.J.: Princeton University Press, 1984), 72.

13. SCAGL, a Pathé affiliate, was set up to constitute a monopoly over film adaptations in order to diversify the activities of Pathé. Decourcelle would leave SCAGL around 1914. His *Les Deux gosses* was filmed in 1924 as an eight-part serial by Louis Mercanton. Richard Abel, *The Ciné Goes to Town: French Cinema, 1896–1914* (Berkeley: University of California Press, 1994), 40–41.

14. Arthur B. Reeve, *The Exploits of Elaine: A Detective Novel* (New York: Hearst's International Library Co., 1915), 6.

15. Ibid., 15.

16. Pierre Decourcelle, *Les Mystères de New-York* (Paris: La Renaissance du Livre, 1916), 20. All translations from French are made by the author unless otherwise attributed.

17. N. R. P. Bonsor, *North Atlantic Seaway: An Illustrated History of the Passenger Services Linking the Old World with the New*, vol. 2 (Prescot, UK: Stephenson & Sons, 1955), 213.

18. Frederic Coleman, *From Mons to Ypres with French: A Personal Narrative* (London: Sampson Low, Marston, 1916), 179.

19. William Uricchio, "The First World War and the Crisis in Europe," in *The Oxford History of World Cinema*, ed. Geoffrey Nowell-Smith (New York: Oxford University Press, 1997), 63. See also Abel, *French Cinema*.

20. Decourcelle, *Les Mystères de New-York*, 10–11. This scene from the first episode of the tie-in is not referred to in the first two episodes of the French film version.

21. The Bertillon system, based on the classification of skeletal and other body measurements and characteristics together with a mug shot, was officially adopted in France in 1888 and soon after in other countries. For more on Bertillon, see Henry Taylor Fowkes Rhodes, *Alphonse Bertillon, Father of Scientific Detection* (London: George G. Harrap, 1956).

22. Decourcelle, *Les Mystères de New-York*, 224, 460.

23. Ibid., 243, 338.

24. Arthur B. Reeve, *The Romance of Elaine* (New York: Hearst's International Library Co., 1916), 194.

25. Ibid., 350. His sympathies could indeed also lie with the Austrians or the Japanese. Though Japan was on the side of the Allies, several preparedness serials, such as *Patria* (1917), made use of a threat from the East.

26. Jacques Portes, *Fascination and Misgivings: The United States in French Opinion, 1870–1914* (Cambridge: Cambridge University Press, 2000), 343.

27. Decourcelle, *Les Mystères de New-York*, 364.

28. Ibid.

29. Ibid., 459.

30. Unfortunately, most of the episodes are lost or not available for viewing by researchers because of their fragile condition. In film episodes one, two, and fourteen of *Les Mystères de New-York*, which I was able to view (previously [but no longer] from Glenn Video Vistas), no references to war or patriotic subjects are made; the intertitles only mention that Clarel was French ("le célèbre détective scientifique français"). As noted, war-related material entered the print version only from episode sixteen on. Lobster Films may have more episodes of *Les Mystères de New-York*, but the film (a 28mm print) needs to be restored before it can be viewed.

31. Decourcelle, *Les Mystères de New-York*, 527.

32. "Pearl White the Idol of the French Soldiers," June 1916. Unidentified source found in the Pearl White clipping file, New York Public Library for the Performing Arts, New York City.

33. French serial novels with anti-German themes could be read as early as 1912. Hans-Jörg Neuschäfer, Dorothee Fritz-El Ahmad, and Klaus-Peter Walter, *Der französische Feuilletonroman: Die Entstehung der Serienliteratur im Medium der Tageszeitung* (Darmstadt, Germany: Wissenschaftliche Buchgesellschaft, 1986), 322–31.

34. Charles W. Brooks, *America in France's Hopes and Fears, 1890–1920* (New York: Garland, 1987), 320–72.

35. Abel, *French Cinema*, 71.

36. In addition to the daily and weekly rhythm that lasted several months, there also existed a yearly pattern. For several years a Feuillade serial, usually of twelve episodes, would be released around January, creating the ultimate form of seriality whereby audiences had a permanent incentive to be looking out for the next installment.

37. In France seriality was in flux, being employed for different genres and audiences, whereas some parts of its structure were changed to better fit the market. Canjels, *Distributing Silent Serials*, 156–65, 173–76. There is more on Feuillade in Francis Lacassin, *Louis Feuillade: Maître des lions et des vampires* (Paris: Bordas, 1995).

38. In the order of serials mentioned, the original American novelization can be read in Charles Goddard, *The Perils of Pauline* (New York: Hearst's International Library Co., 1915); weekly by Arthur Stringer in the *Atlanta Constitution*, from February 27, 1916; and in a weekly summarization by Guy W. M'Connell in the *Atlanta Constitution*, from December 3, 1916. The first two appeared as a French novelization in *Le Matin*, the last one in *Le Petit Journal*.

39. Unfortunately, it is unclear in which newspaper his novelization was published.

40. Guy de Teramond, *La Maison de la haine* (Paris: La Renaissance du Livre, 1920), 99.

41. Ibid.

42. Ibid., 102.

43. Brooks, *America in France's Hopes and Fears*, 354–55.

44. Teramond, *La Maison de la haine*, 117–18.

45. Brooks, *America in France's Hopes and Fears*, 418–20.

46. Ibid., 362.

47. As in *The Moving Picture World* (April 13, 1918), 285 (episode five), and (August 3, 1918), 716 (episode twenty).

48. Decourcelle's adaption of *La Reine s'ennuie* (released March 1918) contains hardly any reference to the war, as the story deals with an Egyptian priestess who tries to get a ring with the power of invisibility.

49. Teramond, *La Maison de la haine*, 284–87.

50. Ibid., 287.

51. Ibid.

52. Ibid., 288.

53. Brooks, *America in France's Hopes and Fears*, 601–72. Pearl White's love for France in her last American serial (before she tried her success in features) could unfortunately not be researched for this article. In August 1919 *Par Amour* (*The Lightning Raider* [1919]) was released, with a novelization written by Marcel Allain in *Le Petit Journal*.

54. Pearl White, "L'Histoire de ma vie," *La Liberté* (May 29, 1922–July 14, 1922).

CHAPTER 2

"The Best-Known Woman in the World"

Pearl White and the American Serial Film in Sweden

MARINA DAHLQUIST

When Pearl White arrived in Paris in April 1921, she was awarded massive attention by the press. Hervé Lauwick's article in the French newspaper *Figaro* bespeaks her fame: "Qui, en France, ne connaît Pearl White?" (Who, in France, doesn't know Pearl White?)[1] This question would not have been posed in such a rhetorical fashion in Sweden—a country often cited in connection with Pearl White and her serials' international success. Sweden is, of course, only mentioned to illustrate the extent of her stardom reaching even the most remote places imaginable—from an American perspective, that is. Despite all the hype concerning her international following, White was never perceived as a truly big star in Sweden. The main reason for the lack of recognition was that only a selected few of her films actually made it to Swedish audiences. Out of her eleven serial films, only *The Perils of Pauline* and the three *Exploits of Elaine* serials were screened in Sweden. And none of the Swedish copies have survived.[2] This text will explore the American serial film and Pearl White's somewhat eclipsed stardom on Swedish screens and in Swedish fan discourses.

The Swedish film scene was not very favorable to the American serial film format, mainly for two reasons. First, and most importantly, was the impact of Swedish censorship, established in late 1911. The American series and serials, as well as their French forerunners, constituted precisely the type of films that the Swedish national censorship body was set up to weed out from the market, aside from sexually tinged Danish melodramas. The censors imposed stringent regulations on crime serials, which minimized the opportunities for exhibition of the format in Sweden during the 1910s.

The second reason was marketing. In Sweden the promotion of the serials did not include cooperation with newspapers. Newspaper or magazine tie-ins simply did not exist. The marketing in Sweden, therefore, resorted to more traditional forms of promotion, namely, ads in newspapers and on billboards. The interactive aspect of the advertisements in the United States, including contests for authoring parts of the serials during the course of its production by answering plot questions of *The Perils of Pauline*, like "Where is Pauline Going?" or "What did the Mummy say?"[3] was lost in Sweden as in other countries where the serial format was reshuffled. It was, of course, pointless to arrange script contests and bring the audience into the production process, since the serials' narrative, even if re-edited, was firmly fixed after the American release.

The censorship problems, resulting in cuts and prohibited episodes, together with traditional forms of marketing, diluted the impact of the format and upset the chronology for the episodes. Combined, such vicissitudes undercut the popularity of the serial queens on a market already geared to features.

The Censors in Sweden

The serial films' success in Sweden paled in comparison with France or the United States, primarily as an effect of the censorship problems that both the French and the American serials encountered there. Action-saturated crime stories replete with modern technology both for perpetrating and combating crime did not sit well with the Swedish censors.

As the moving picture theaters began to make a mark on the cityscape around 1905, pedagogical groups in Sweden, and especially the elementary school teachers, launched a debate about the role of moving pictures in society. As elsewhere, many considered the moving picture theaters to be a threat to culture and pernicious to youth. The intense debate in the press was eventually instrumental in bringing about a government investigation and in its wake the establishing of a national censorship body in 1911, the Swedish Board of Film Censors—Statens biografbyrå. The conviction among local moving picture pedagogical authorities such as Walter Fevrell, Frans Hallgren, and Dagmar Waldner was that educational films, actualities, and ethnographical films had an immense educational potential.[4] The problematic film series were so-called dramatic images, sensational fiction films, and some of the "vulgar" comedies.

Jan Olsson has discussed and documented the debate leading up to the establishing of the Board of Censors, as well as the regulating of the Swedish film market due to the policies implemented by the Board.[5] The critical rationale for national censorship was the conviction that moving images exerted an immoral and detrimental influence on its audience—especially on the underaged and immature—and risked dimming their conceptions of justice and morality and thus ruining their character. According to the government ordinance regulating moving picture shows, "The inspector may not pass motion pictures, whose exhibition would conflict with common law or otherwise could have a brutalizing, exciting effect or would be contrary to all ideas of right and justice. Images depicting horror scenes, suicides or serious crimes in a manner or in circumstances that such an influence could be caused, should not be passed."[6] The American detective Nick Carter, in the spectacular series of books carrying his name, was singled out as the most notorious and emblematic character having brutalizing effects on youngsters. When deemed to be in the vein of Nick Carter, a film was more or less automatically banned for all audiences. The Board of Censors' classificatory protocols were the result of a long-standing debate in the daily press fueled by moral outrage launched by the "Nick Carter Books." In alarmist language, these were described as having "flooded" the Swedish market in 1908. Ulf Boëthius's study of the reception of the Nick Carter literature in Sweden maps the campaign against Nick Carter books and the campaign's offspring, targeting scandalous literature, moving pictures, postcards, and sensational journalism.[7]

Working-class youth and its entertainment choices provided the focal points for the debate. The overcrowded conditions under which the working class lived more or less forced children and young teenagers onto the streets, making them easy targets for the lure of cheap, sensational entertainment. Susceptible youths, readily attracted by garish book covers and thrilling movies, caused concern among reformers with a pedagogical background. They feared that the growing market for cheap booklets and films emulating Nick Carter "ideals" would turn young readers and viewers into criminals, a discourse that mirrored the U.S. debate on sensational representations, which often pegged nickelodeons as "schools of crime." Opposition to what was generically called *smutslitteratur*, putatively exerting a "filthy" and dangerous influence on its readers, was steadily growing in Sweden. The campaigns against *smutslitteratur* were broad in scope and targeted decadent literature with erotic overtones written by established authors, criminal and detective stories in cheap novelettes, sensational newspaper journalism, and moving pictures.[8]

According to Boëthius, Nick Carter emerged as the scapegoat because the character, with New York City as his major field of action, embodied the modern United States and the unsettling American mentality. Carter was not only sharp-witted but also strong, fast, and a man of action. Swedish booklet covers by intent looked very American, displaying large and colorful illustrations, taken directly from the American weekly magazine *Nick Carter Weekly* with the original titles and typeface still in place.[9] The Nick Carter books had become synonymous with cheap novels or *smutslitteratur* in general and would continue to be a symbol used every time a campaign against supposedly youth-corrupting material was mounted, from the beginning of the 1920s well into the 1970s and the video scare.[10]

Nick Carter's popularity peaked in the fall of 1908, at the same time as Swedish moving pictures theaters capitalized on the interest in detective stories by putting numerous detective titles on movie screens, including, for instance, Victorin Jasset's six Nick Carter films, based on the American Nick Carter booklets and produced by the French Écair, and Sherlock Holmes films. In February 1908 the Pedagogic Society, Pedagogiska sallskapet, and its film section, with Marie Louise Gagner as spokesperson, began a campaign against movie theaters and their "unsuitable" programs for children. In her initial speech, which drew marked attention and was published as a brochure under the title *Barn och biografföreställningar* (Children and moving picture exhibitions), she described three ills against which the fight should be aimed, one being scenes featuring murders, suicides, robberies, burglaries, and other brands of crimes.[11] From 1908 to 1911, Pedagogiska sällskapet conducted three studies documenting that children made up a considerable part of the audience. Gagner played a decisive role in the establishment of a national board of censors and was one of three censors appointed by the government in 1911. Dr. Walter Fevrell, earlier chairman of the moving picture committee at the Pedagogical Society, was appointed head of the Board. Dr. Jakob Billström and Professor Bror Gadelius had given the campaign leading up to the establishing of the Board a scientific legitimacy, and Dr. Billström was also appointed a censor. Pedagogical interests thus dominated the Board. Professor Gadelius emerged as an undisputed psycho-medical authority concerning censorship issues and was for decades affiliated with the Board as one of its experts.[12]

Three color-coded categories were established within the Swedish censorship system: (1) red—permission for public screening, including children; (2)

yellow—permission for screening for persons over the age of fifteen; and (3) white—not allowed for public screening.

Before the national Board was established, local police authorities were responsible for monitoring public amusements. According to Charles Magnusson—the general manager of Svenska Biografteatern (Svenska Bio), Sweden's most important production company at the time—this arrangement was far from satisfying, as the interventions at times were ridiculously capricious and inconsistent from district to district.[13]

Hard pressed, the major production companies as well as exhibitors reluctantly supported the idea of a national censorship body, which did not preclude them for severely criticizing several of the Board's decisions. In 1912 Charles Magnusson published the booklet *Några ord om Biografcensuren* (A few remarks on film censorship) in the name of Svenska Bio regarding its appeal of the ban against three films, among them Victor Sjöström's first film as director, *Trädgårdsmästaren/Världens grymhet* (*The Broken Springrose/The Gardener*; [1912]). Even though the importance of censorship was acknowledged by Magnusson and others, the overzealous ambition to protect even an adult audience was met with irony.[14]

In the Board of Film Censors' retaliatory booklet, Gustaf Berg zoomed in on the "depravity" of Danish films as well as the sensational Danish fictional world and the influence of both on domestic producers. According to Berg, as many as four out of five hour-long feature films examined by the Board, of which many were Danish, dealt with adultery or licentious eroticism against the backdrop of circuses, variety shows, and night cafés. In addition, detective stories brimmed with felonies and melodramas like Sjöström's *Trädgårdsmästaren*, which aestheticized suicide in the wake of a rape.[15] Berg also, somewhat ironically, responded to Svenska Bio's complaint about the film ban and the presumed influence the film could have by saying that it was hardly a common practice to "harden" boys against, for example, drinking, by placing numerous bars within easy reach. Hence, film depictions did not deter, but rather instructed susceptible audience groups by illustrating destructive or criminal behavior, he claimed.[16]

As a final installment in this particular debate, Svenska Bio published a second booklet accusing the censors of being gratuitous and inconsistent. Furthermore, the economic consequences that a ban incurred for film producers, distributors, and exhibitors, Magnusson argued, were devastating. Censorship decisions also affected promotion and advertising of titles in advance of their release, since marketing campaigns could not be launched until after a film was approved.[17] This was, of course, a major problem in promoting serial films, which gradually led film companies to have all the episodes inspected simultaneously. Alternatively, just one or two was submitted as a "test"; if banned, no other episodes were put up for inspection, as a serial would be screened in its entirety or not at all.

Pathé Frères and the Swedish Censors

Pathé Frères's Stockholm branch, the local distributor of Pearl White's serial films, repeatedly faced censorship problems. Its manager, Siegmund Popert, submitted a bevy of unsuccessful appeals to the government, hoping to overturn the censors' decisions to ban a number of Pathé films, while Svenska Bio, after its first campaign, refrained from appeals. In addition, Popert regularly wrote articles on censorship issues that appeared in the trade press. In 1917 the censors, somewhat irritated, even complained about what to their mind was Popert's overzealous penchant for writing appeals, which affected their work. Fearing Popert's pen, no inspector was, for instance, willing to individually shoulder the responsibility for inspecting a Pathé title. Allegedly, the working atmosphere was negatively influenced and much of the service's work was tied up in addressing the phalanx of complaints from Pathé.[18] Bans that attracted major concern at Pathé were those imposed upon *Två bröder* (Two brothers [1912]), directed by Georg af Klercker; *Fröken Napierkowska som Herodias dotter* (*La figlia di Erodiade* [1916]), directed by Ugo Falena; and the Pathé serial *Den röda cirkeln* (*The Red Circle* [1915]). Popert also appealed the Board's decision to prohibit Pathé's *Den vackra skogsjungfrun* (*The Maid of the Wild* [1915]) for children.

After the outbreak of World War I, Popert's non-Swedish background became a concern. Representing a French company, he was actually born in Germany, as his first name, Siegmund, suggested. In the eyes of some Swedes, his German origin aligned him with the enemy, which was extensively elaborated upon by *Filmbladet* in August 1915.[19] Although Popert applied for Swedish citizenship, Pathé decided to appoint G. M. Liedholm as head of the company branch in 1915. As *Filmbladet* put it, an "enemy cannot represent Pathé's Swedish branch."[20] Irrespective of the executive change, the trade paper surmised that Popert would remain a key player in the background, pulling the strings.[21]

Olsson has analyzed the censors' work during the three seasons of 1914–1915, 1915–1916, and 1916–1917 and the progressively escalating numbers of banned films. The number of yellow and white labels gradually increased during these years. In 1914–1915, 4,039 titles were inspected, out of which

353 were labeled yellow, or permitted for an audience over the age of 15, and 121 white, or completely prohibited. In the 1915–1916 season, a total of 4,306 titles were inspected, of which 618 were labeled yellow, an increase of 75 percent, while the white labels rose by 60 percent to 194. In 1916–1917, out of 3,829 titles inspected, 706 were yellow and 221 white. These figures are somewhat surprising, as the number of foreign films actually decreased during these years, while the amount of dramatic images during the seasons 1914–1915 and 1916–1917 remained more or less the same.[22] The figures are informative in considering the validity of Popert's claim that Pathé's films had been unfavorably treated by the censors compared to titles from other firms. Popert proposed an official survey to investigate a putative bias but received little response.[23]

Only a minority of Pathé's titles were fiction films. In a missive submitted to the government, Popert wrote on August 3, 1916, that out of 291 Pathé films that had been inspected by the censors, 113 were ethnographical, scientific films, or war films; 69 were actualities; and 109 were fiction films. In the latter group, 19, or 17.4 percent, had been banned. In comparison, 19 percent of the fiction films from the Danish Nordic Company had been banned during the same period.[24] Nationality was, however, less important for censors than genre. The casualty rate was staggering for the thrilling, fast-paced serial films, severely affecting the genre's exhibition history in Sweden.

The Serials and the Censors

Swedish censorship imposed stringent regulations on crime serials during the 1910s. A problem seriously harming the serial format came about when the individual episodes were not uniformly categorized by the censors. For example, some episodes were outright banned from screening, others categorized for adults only, and some approved for all patrons. In such cases, episodes could not uniformly target the same audience groups, at least not a young one. As a result, not only those serials banned in toto were excluded from the repertoire.

The French series and serials met with little enthusiasm from the Swedish censors. For example, the Nick Carter series by Victorin Jasset, directing for Éclair, was released before the establishment of the Board of Censors and was thus "safe." Six films were released in 1908 and four the following year due to their popularity and the general fascination with criminal fiction at this time. After the introduction of mandatory censor inspection, the climate turned frosty for crime films. Of Jasset's Zigomar series (Éclair, 1911) only the third and last episode, "Zigomar contre Nick Carter" (Zigomar versus Nick Carter) was chosen for inspection (in March 1912) and, not very surprisingly, banned from public screening, with the consequence that no episode of the serial was screened at all. Jasset's series *Protea* (Éclair, 1913), featuring a female spy as heroine, was likewise prohibited. Only two episodes of Léonce Perret's controversial *Main de fer* (*Iron hand*) series (Gaumont, 1912–1913, with the Swedish title *Järnhanden*) were inspected and, in fact, approved for an adult audience; the first episode was released October 7, 1912. Concerning the third episode, "L'Évasion du Baron de Croze" (The escape of Baron de Croze), even though it was inspected in February 1913 and passed for an adult audience, there is no documentation of any public screening.

Louis Feuillade's serials did not fare better. Only the second part, "Juve contre Fantômas" (Juve versus Fantômas) of the successful *Fantômas* serial, consisting of five episodes (Gaumont, 1913–1914), was inspected in August 1913. It was banned for all audiences, being considered by the Board as brutalizing and overstimulating, a "Nick Carter of the worst kind," according to the censors' remarks card.[25] Only the first three out of ten episodes of *Les Vampires* (Gaumont, 1915–1916), Feuillade's next serial, were inspected (in December 1915 and March 1916). The first two were labeled yellow while the third was banned. No document indicates any public screenings of the first two episodes. Feuillade's third serial, *Judex* (Gaumont, 1917), sports a more moralistic tone than the earlier serials and all episodes were thus permitted for public screenings for an adult audience; they were released in 1921.

When it came to the American serials, precious few were imported. Renowned serials like Edison's *What Happened to Mary* (1912), Kalem's *Hazards of Helen* (1914), or Universal's *Lucille Love, Girl of Mystery* (1914) were hence not even examined by the Swedish censors. Selig's *The Adventures of Kathlyn* (*Kathlyns äventyr*; [1913]) is one of the rare examples of a serial passed by the censors in its entirety. All twelve episodes were inspected in August 1916 and labeled red—permitted for children—more or less without cuts.[26]

The Iron Claw (Pathé, 1916), starring Pearl White, was for all practical purposes banned. Of twenty episodes, only the first was inspected (in June 1917). Similar fates befell *The Purple Mask* (Universal, 1917),[27] *Zudora* (Thanhouser, 1915),[28] *Graft* (Universal, 1915),[29] *The Million Dollar Mystery* (Thanhouser, 1914),[30] and *The Yellow Menace* (Serial Film Corporation, 1916).[31] Either all or only a few episodes were inspected of these serials—of which all were banned.

Serials with mixed censor labels that included some whites were usually not shown at all. An example is *The Adventures of Peg o' the Ring* (Universal, 1916). Of five episodes inspected in 1916, the first two were yellow and the other three white. Since the three white-labeled episodes were banned entirely, the yellow ones were never released. Another example is *The Red Circle*. Of eleven episodes inspected in May 1917, eight were completely forbidden and three passed for an adult audience.[32] Mixed categorizations of episodes from the same serial—some banned, some passed for an adult audience, and a few passed for all audiences—cut at the heart of the relayed serial phenomenon and precluded release.

In spite of the promotions' far from innocuous descriptions of its contents, *The Perils of Pauline* fared reasonably well with the censors. According to a four-page ad in *Motography*, "The action of the story includes flying machine accidents, thrilling rescues, fires at sea, train wrecks, automobile accidents. In fact, everything that can be introduced as a 'thrill.'"[33] Fifteen episodes of *The Perils of Pauline* were inspected in February 1915 and the remaining five the following May. All but four were labeled red, after some cuts of what was considered instructional criminal scenes, showing how crimes could be performed, fires, and scenes with brutality, especially against women—as when Pauline, with a sack over her head, is thrown to the floor, and when violence is highlighted with close-ups of Pauline in precarious situations as when she was bound and gagged.[34] Ads almost without exception specified when episodes were passed for children.

In France, Pearl White's next serial—or rather three serials—about Elaine's adventures was reworked into two parts by the writer Pierre Decourcelle. The serials *New-Yorks mysterier* and *De sju millionerna* were shown in Sweden in the late summer and fall of 1916, compiled from *The Exploits of Elaine* (1914), *The New Exploits of Elaine* (1915), and *The Romance of Elaine* (1915). The original thirty-five episodes was reworked and compressed to twenty-two in France for European distribution, excluding one episode. As Rudmer Canjels elaborates in his contribution to this volume, the serial was released in this format in France under the name *Les Mystères de New York*, once a week from December 3, 1915, to May 4, 1916. A Pathé ad in *Ciné-Journal* in November 1915 lists eighty-eight theaters in Paris and the provinces that had ordered the serial in advance.[35]

There were a number of cuts for *New Yorks mysterier* to exclude criminal activities or instructional scenes such as the manipulation of electrical cords, arrangements of false fingerprints, assaults, fighting, shooting, and so on. The serial was inspected in March 1916. Seven episodes passed, but about 8 percent or, more precisely, 338 out of 4005 meters, were eliminated by the censors.[36]

Popert did not appeal the censors' decision to ban six episodes in the Elaine serials, all from the early part of *New Yorks mysterier*. The episodes of

De sju millionerna were uniformly labeled yellow. Concerning *Den röda cirkeln* (*The Red Circle*), starring Ruth Roland, Popert put up a fight that would lead to an extensive exchange of harsh memos with the Board of Film Censors. This was the last standoff between Pathé and the censors, and as before, the government unfailingly upheld the Board's decision. Out of the eleven episodes inspected, only episodes 4, 6, and 10 were cleared for public screening for adult audiences, while eight were labeled white and thus totally prohibited. The only comment made by the censors concerning the episodes was a distinct and dismissive remark, "Brutalizing, due to its Nick-Carter character."[37] As Olsson has shown, the censor cards were often used for expressing subjective opinions and comments during the first years of censorship. These opinions soon turned more succinct, sometimes very laconically giving the reason for a ban or for cuts.[38] The first five episodes of *Den röda cirkeln* were inspected on May 1, 1917, and the remaining six in early June. As many as three censors inspected some of the episodes; Marie Louise Gagner partook in all of the inspections.

According to Pathé Frères, *Den röda cirkeln* had not faced censorship problems in any other country than Sweden; here, it was argued, its moral was not understood. In his appeal to the government, Popert therefore proposed that the serial should be regarded as one film, and that all episodes be considered together as the overarching moral otherwise could not be judged.[39] The cliff-hanging serial form, without the closure of "good triumphs over evil" in the separate episodes, made it difficult to tease out the film's moral value. Critic Artur Möller was in step with Popert when arguing, after half of *De sju millionerna* had been released in Stockholm, that it did not matter how many crimes a film depicts, or how violent they are, so long as the forces of good eventually conquer.[40]

According to Shelley Stamp, the serial format also encountered censor skirmishes in the United States from a similar perspective. The moral impact was difficult to evaluate, as criminals were seldom brought to justice in the same episode as their crimes were perpetrated. The Standards and Policy adopted by the film industry's National Board of Censorship in the U.S. in 1916 stated that all episodes in a serial should be considered together and the total moral effect be judged.[41] According to Kalton C. Lahue, the serials became the primary targets in censorship discussions in the U.S., as the villains often remained unpunished until the very last episode and thereby could carry on their criminal activities week after week.[42]

Popert's request that the episodes of *Den röda cirkeln* be considered as one entity did not convince the Swedish government, per advice from the censors.

Poster for *De sju millionerna* (The seven millions), episodes 1–3. Lund University Library.

After having inspected six more episodes and banned four of them, the censors concluded that their judgment would not have been different had they inspected all the episodes together. According to the censors, *Den röda cirkeln*'s flagrant depiction of criminal acts outdistanced *New Yorks mysterier* and *De sju millionerna*, two serials they had passed only after considerable hesitations and numerous cuts. To support the censors' argument, the Board of Censors, in its collective report, mentions an incident in small-town Västerås where a gang of juvenile delinquents, actually too young to legally watch the serial, pointed to *New Yorks mysterier* as the source of inspiration for their crimes. According to the censors, this and similar incidents made it even more urgent to be conscientious when inspecting serials.[43]

Pathé and the Board of Film Censors had additionally locked horns in an involved legal dispute in 1916 concerning a title change made by Pathé after inspection, which violated the censorship laws. Pathé lost this case. All the while, the interaction between Pathé and the Board was profusely reported upon in the daily press.[44] This dispute partly explains the hostile tone of subsequent skirmishes. Furthermore, the Board even singled out Popert and Pathé for their foreignness, as they were supposedly seeking only to maximize profit at the expense of local interest safeguarded by the Board. In a patronizing manner, the Board dismissed Pathé's complaints.[45] In his reply, Popert contested this line of reasoning, saying he was merely requesting the same legal protection under the Swedish law as received by any other company—foreign or not.[46]

Marketing and Seriality

In contrast to the exhibition model in the United States—that of screening each episode of *The Perils of Pauline* at a number of theaters simultaneously in order to coincide with the publishing dates of the tie-ins and advertisements—the release in Stockholm was based on exclusive rights for theaters. Only one film copy was available on the Swedish market. Advance notices prior to the actual release were few and far between and merely informed the readers tersely that *Paulines äventyr* (*The Perils of Pauline*), the world's biggest hit, was to appear.[47] The claim of "biggest hit" should not be understood literally, as the word hit, or *slagnummer* in Swedish, was used indiscriminately in ads. Gustaf Berg, the head of the Board of Censors, criticized this inflated form of film marketing in an article some years later. According to Berg, superficial, specious homage in the ads was perceived as ridiculous and left audiences cold.[48]

On the day of *Paulines äventyr*'s release—Monday, February 22, 1915—large ads were published in all the Stockholm newspapers for the exclusive screening at the Star Theater.[49] Gustaf Gooes, a Swedish American and former traveling showman, owned the Star. With its 315 seats, it was not one of the largest or most important venues in Stockholm.[50] The limited size of this theater recalls Ben Singer's claim in the U.S. context that the serials were rarely screened in large, first-run theaters but rather at small neighborhood venues.[51] The twenty Pauline episodes were released twice weekly—at first on Mondays and Fridays, but after the fourth episode, two new episodes were released every Monday (with the exception of the ninth episode). According to an ad for the Star Theater, this change was the result of requests from the audience to see longer blocks of the serial. The screening time thus approached the feature format. Also, aligning the exhibition with the features met the audiences' wish to be spared summaries of the earlier episode at the beginning of each new installment.[52] The serial's release span was thus highly compressed in comparison with the biweekly releases in the United States.

Paulines äventyr was often labeled a cinematographic short story.[53] Many of the Stockholm reviews of the first episode commented upon the phenomenon of seriality in relation to the length of the serial's release span in the United States—six months—and the feat of keeping audiences in suspense throughout these months, eagerly waiting for the next episode every other week.[54] The first episode was screened for three days at the Star between 5 P.M. and 11 P.M. up until the release of the second episode on Friday, February 26.[55] If the initial showtimes corresponded to those for the second episode, advertised for four shows per night, the maximum audience for the serial in Stockholm would have been 3,780. The reviews of the first episode were overall appreciative and focused on the thrills and excitement offered by the serial.[56]

The ad for the third and fourth episodes in the *Stockholms-Tidningen* stressed that each episode formed a self-contained narrative unit. A quotation from *Moving Picture News* in the same ad elaborates on the frustrating effects of serials when episodes end just when they are most exciting, leaving audiences hanging after an intertitle stating that the story will continue two weeks later.[57] Similarly, the advertisement for the ninth episode in *Aftonbladet* also mentions that every episode formed a finished story. Audience members could therefore easily follow the narrative even if they had missed earlier episodes.[58] The Swedish advertising strategy, emphasizing narrative clarity and closure rather than thrills and cliff-hanging excitements, in a sense dismantles the serial format, perhaps to gloss over the shortcomings of a fragmented narrative to an audience that might have missed an episode or more.

Apart from using the same quotations and headlines, the ads were rarely identical across newspapers. The immense success the serial had garnered in the U.S. was stressed and demonstrated by quotations not only from the leading American trade organs—*Moving Picture World*, *New York Dramatic Mirror*, and *Moving Picture News*—but also from major American newspapers, such as the *Chicago Examiner*, the *New York Times*, and the *New York Evening Journal*. More than fifty posters and photographs were offered to Swedish exhibitors.[59] A few episodes into the screening, Swedish newspaper reviews were quoted in the local trade press. Local pens seemingly had more clout than praise from afar. An ad in *Filmbladet*, for example, reprinted part of a review in *Social-Demokraten* of the fifth and sixth episodes, which featured Pauline's balloon adventures. According to the critic, "a more exciting experience can hardly be imagined."[60] The sixth episode, ending with the heroine trapped in an onrushing car bound to hands and feet, was concluded with the matter-of-fact comment that her dire straits would be put on hold until the following Monday. The ads repeatedly focused on the high costs of production, the exciting narrative, the thrilling effects, the prize money delivered in script contests, and in this case the fact that the renowned Lady Duff Gordon had designed Pearl White's wardrobe of ninety-four different costumes. Habitually, readers were reminded of the serial's immense popularity in the U.S.[61] Not all critics were in tune with the one writing in *Social-Demokraten*. A review of the third episode in *Stockholms-Tidningen* expressed concerns regarding a scene in which a boy strangles a pirate who, in turn, had tried to kill him. That the children in the audience nervously laughed during the scene evidenced, for the critic, that the youngsters were not mature enough to experience such intense imagery.[62]

On March 29, the Star Theater posted an ad announcing that the upcoming episodes of *Paulines äventyr* could not be released according to schedule due to a delay in shipping. For a format predicated on a returning audience, this was of course devastating. When the serial resumed on May 10, ads were smaller and reviews virtually nonexistent.[63] Surprisingly, neither Pearl White's nor any other star's name was used in the headline of the advertisement and were only mentioned a few times in quotations from American newspapers. *Paulines äventyr* was, however, still very successful in screenings outside Stockholm. As late as February 1916, exhibitors' profits for the serial were mentioned in advertisements to illustrate the overall successes of Pathé's films.[64]

Pearl White's name was again promoted as a main attraction of an upcoming American serial, no title mentioned, in fifteen episodes. It was advertised in August 1915 in the trade paper *Filmbladet*, a year in advance of the actual release of the Elaine serial.[65] As mentioned above, the Board of Censors banned six episodes of *New Yorks mysterier*, leaving only seven episodes available for public screenings for audiences over fifteen years old. Pathé released the seven episodes but refrained from further editing to get the banned episodes approved at a reinspection. Since the Swedish copies no longer exist, it is impossible to evaluate how the exclusion of almost half of the episodes affected the narrative at large. Furthermore, the first round of revision in France did not completely follow the serial's chronology; instead, the three serials were intertwined.[66] For example, the first episode of *De sju millionerna*, "Spökhuset," was actually episodes 13 and 14 of *The Exploits of Elaine* ("The Devil Worshipper" and "The Reckoning"), while the second and third episodes, "Ringens hemlighet" ("The Cryptic Ring") and "Luftpiraterna" (combining "The Saving Circles" and "Spontaneous Combustion") were episodes 2, 5, and 6 from *The New Exploits of Elaine*. The episodes banned by the censors were supposed to have been numbers 2, 5, 6, 7, 9, and 11 out of a total of thirteen episodes from *New Yorks mysterier*.[67] In contrast, the censors passed all nine episodes of *De sju millionerna* for an audience over the age of fifteen.

New Yorks mysterier was even more widely and aggressively advertised than *Paulines äventyr*, with large ads appearing in most of the important Stockholm newspapers. Some ads were as big as half a page.[68] The serial was advertised in *Aftonbladet* as an "unsurpassed, exciting, [and] sensational detective film."[69] According to the ad, it was screened in 543 theaters in New York alone. The ad also stated that in Paris, the serial's immense popularity made getting tickets almost impossible during the first days after the release, but easier when the serial was taken up by more theaters.[70] In Stockholm, *New Yorks mysterier* was released in sixteen episodes on a weekly basis, starting out with three episodes on Monday, August 13, 1916. As with the exhibition of *Paulines äventyr*, the rights were granted exclusively for one theater—this time Stora Teatern. Owned by John A. Bergendahl, one of the important theater owners in Stockholm, the theater had opened early in 1916. It was advertised as being one of the largest and most elegant moving picture theaters in Stockholm, with 855 seats.[71] *New Yorks mysterier* elicited considerable praise: *Dagens Nyheter* deemed it a "first class film product" and Pearl White's performance and cold-bloodedness admirable,[72] while *Stockholms-Tidningen* considered it "an unusually thrilling detective film."[73] In *Aftonbladet* the critic, likewise, found the detective drama "very thrilling and worth seeing, with a magnificent setting and exceptional photography."[74]

In the marketing, Pearl White was still not presented as being on a par with stars featured in contemporary Swedish titles: Lili Beck, Lars Hanson, Maja Cassel, and Carl Barcklind. And many international stars were more prominently marketed, among them the Europeans Asta Nielsen, Clara Wieth, Lauritz Olsen, Sarah Bernhardt, Francesca Bertini, and Marie Jacobini and the American stars Mary Pickford, Clara Kimball Young, Vivian Martin, Douglas Fairbanks, and Robert Warwick. Pearl White's participation in the serial is not singled out as its main attraction; often, she is mentioned in the reviews only in passing as a featured player together with Arnold Daly and Justin Clarel.[75] As the episodes appeared over time, the reviews grew more and

Poster for *New-Yorks mysterier*, episode 5, "Den giftiga kyssen" (The life current), Lund University Library.

more succinct. At its most minimalistic, *Aftonbladet*'s "review" of the fourth and fifth episodes mentioned only that the serial is still running.[76] Some of the slightly more elaborated reviews of the sixth and seventh episodes—the last ones of the serial—expressed confusion, since the final episodes only resolved a few of the pending plot points from earlier in the serial.[77] This is not surprising, as the episode supposed to be shown before was missing for censorship reasons, as were five other episodes from earlier in the serial. Irrespective of this calamity, the serial seems to have been popular, drawing full houses.[78]

On Monday, September 4, 1916, the week after the *New Yorks mysterier* was finished, Stora Teatern released *De sju millionerna*, advertised as a sequel to *New Yorks mysterier*.[79] The two serials were—although having different names—almost considered as one in the advertisements promoting all the sixteen episodes together. The new serial followed the previous release model: two episodes every Monday down to the last three episodes, which opened together on Monday, September 25.

Reruns began before the serials had ended with the early episodes of *New Yorks mysterier* screened at the Orientaliska Teatern on Monday, September 11, 1916, and the following Monday at the smaller Bostock-Biografen.[80] Thus, three theaters screened different episodes of the serial at the same time since there was only one copy of each serial in circulation, according to the censorship cards. All three theaters adhered to the same exhibition formula, with weekly releases on Mondays of two or three episodes. *De sju millionerna* was exhibited in a similar manner. The serials were shown the entire fall, gradually moving to smaller theaters such as Södra Kvarn, Vanadis-Biografen, Sirius, Aténa-Biografen (in this theater eight episodes ran the first week, later two per week),[81] and Katarina-Biografen.

Kathlyns äventyr (*The Adventures of Kathlyn*) was released on December 3, 1916, after *Paulines äventyr* and the Elaine serials and also after the multiple but little-noticed Stockholm reruns had come to a close. Screened at Götiska Teatern (333 seats) and hardly advertised in the daily press,[82] the serial attracted even fewer reviews than the earlier serials. All twelve episodes were released in blocks of two or three on Sundays until December 31.

The War and the Future

In December 1916, *Filmbladet* reported the finding of a trunk on the west coast of Sweden containing film reels, flotsam from a sunken ship.[83] The trunk had been sent from Pathé Frères in Paris to its branch in Stockholm. According to *Filmbladet*, it contained episodes from *New Yorks mysterier* to be shipped from Stockholm to Russia. This was a unique incident in regards to the traffic in film prints. For the Swedish market, the release of the last six episodes of *Paulines äventyr* was delayed for several weeks, but not for such perilous vicissitudes of transportation. In May 1915, Popert declared that currently Pathé had no difficulties in acquiring titles from Paris, London, as well as the

United States. No film shortage was expected due to the war, at least not for the upcoming season.[84]

For reasons other than transportation difficulties or war, Pearl White's later productions had problems reaching Swedish screens; only three of them were released in Sweden. *Mayblossom* (*Den gamla visan*, dir. Edward José [1917]) was on May 17 allowed by the censors for an adult audience. The film was released at the Bostock-Biografen theater on Monday, October 29, 1917. In the ad, Pearl White is promoted as a famous actress known from *Paulines äventyr* and *New Yorks mysterier*. A review in *Göteborgs Morgonpost* is quoted as praising the acting, the directing, and the settings.[85] The acting was, however, less appreciated in a Stockholm review after the opening.[86] Theatrically released only one week apart, *Know Your Men!* (*Svindlarens dotter*, dir. Charles Giblyn [1921]) and *The Thief* (*Fåfängans offer*, dir. Charles Giblyn [1920]) premiered for an adult audience on March 12 and 19, 1923, respectively. Neither of them, however, was released in Stockholm but rather in Örebro and then Gävle, two rather small-size towns, which attested to the films' expected lack of drawing power.

On rare occasions, Pearl White was treated as a celebrity in Sweden, as when the trade paper *Filmen* in 1919 published interviews with the American screen actresses Fanny Ward, May Allison, Maurguerite Clark—and Pearl White—on the subject what the ideal man would be for them. The serial queens' importance for ushering in a new, modern, female protagonist is totally ignored here, as all of them are presented as feminine, fashionable, and at times even domestic. Claiming she was too busy to think about men, Pearl White highlighted one key quality for an ideal man: courage—mentally, morally, and physically. A tint of subordination colored her remarks, similar to what Singer finds in the serials. Here she claimed that a man must have the strength to deny her what he considered she should not do or have. He should have both moral strength enough to convince her as the case might be and commanding physical strength to effectively overpower her, albeit never using it.[87]

In a Swedish trade article from 1919 addressing perilous working conditions in American cinema as well as the actors' huge incomes and focusing on actors like Douglas Fairbanks and William Duncan, the serial queens are not even mentioned.[88] The dangers of toying with wild animals—a specialty of prominent serial actresses like Kathlyn Williams and Marie Walcamp—were, however, acknowledged by *Filmen* in 1918.[89] The phenomenon of female prowess in dealing with ferocious felines and the urban risk taking that was indicative of modernity, so salient in the U.S. advertisements for serials, was

Swedish poster from 1923 for *Fåfängans offer* (*The Thief*, 1920), designed by Eric Rohman, Lund University Library.

discursively muffled in Sweden. The serial film seems to have reached Sweden too late to achieve a profound impact in the wake of the feature film format, which already dominated the screens. The serials were thus neither important as a transitional format, nor were they as culturally significant as in the United States.

Swedish poster from 1923 for *Svindlarens dotter* (*Know Your Men!*, 1921), designed by Eric Rohman, Lund University Library.

Notwithstanding the lack of éclat for the serials, Pathé's impact on the Swedish film industry was considerable: early on as a prime supplier of films in the burgeoning nickelodeon era and later as an active force for production and distribution. In March 1913, *Aftonbladet* said that "in the moving picture business Pathé Frères is the international firm that without doubts or comparisons is the largest and most widespread one and has always been a forerunner in the field."[90] Pathé's establishment and activities in Sweden during the first years of the 1910s were highly significant for distribution, programming, and exhibition practices in Sweden at a time when multireel feature films increasingly dominated exhibition. Furthermore, due to Popert's interventions, Pathé was in the foreground of the Swedish film debate. The battle for the company's most significant genre in the mid-1910s—the film serial—was, however, somewhat of a lost cause. Vocal protests apart, even Pathé, a once-unrivaled film company, eventually had to surrender to unyielding local forces at a time when its former might was gradually eroding.

Interviewed in 1914 during a stay in the United States, Charles Pathé was invited to speculate on the future of moving pictures. "'It is very great,' he replied. 'It will tend toward the adaptations of books and plays by celebrated authors.'"[91] Looking at the ensuing history of the medium, this can be seen as an accurate prediction, a prophetic observation bearing on changes that were to reorganize film production, including that of Sweden. Soon enough, canonical literature and national settings dominated a downsized domestic production, and Swedish films gradually found an international market and much praise to boot. In the Swedish discursive arena, sensationalism continued to be a bone of contention, and Nick Carter and the American serial format remained scapegoats for the vigilant censors. In the process, the serial queens' brand of cinematic modernity was put on hold as peasant films reigned, and Pauline and her sisters only peripherally graced the screens.[92]

NOTES

1. Hervé Lauwick, "La vrai Pearl White," *Figaro*, May 1, 1921, 1.

2. Other nonserial films shown in Sweden featuring Pearl White were *Mayblossom*, from 1917 (*Den gamla visan*, released October 29, 1917), *The Thief*, from 1920 (*Fåfängans offer*, released March 19, 1923), and *Know Your Men!*, from 1921 (*Svindlarens dotter*, released March 12, 1923). The censors banned *The Iron Claw* (1916) and *Tiger's Cub* (1920).

3. See, for instance, ads in the *San Francisco Examiner*, March 15, 1914, City Life section, 5; *New York Dramatic Mirror* 71, no. 1842 (April 8, 1914): 26; and *Motography* 11, no. 7 (April 4, 1914): 6.

4. Frans Hallgren, *Kinematografien, ett bildningsmedel: Pedagogiska Skrifter* (Lund, Sweden: Sveriges Allmänna Folkskolelärareförenings litteratursällskap, 1914); Dagmar Waldner, *Filmen som kulturfaktor: En inblick i kinematografiens värld* (Stockholm: Ivar Haeggström, 1915); Dagmar Waldner, *Filmen: Dess framställning, inspelning och förevisning* (Stockholm: Chelius, 1921).

5. Jan Olsson, "Magnified Discourse: Screenplays and Censorship in Swedish

Cinema of the 1910s," in *Celebrating 1895: The Centenary of Cinema*, ed. John Fullerton (London: John Libbey, 1998); Jan Olsson. "Svart på vitt: film, makt och censur," *Aura Filmvetenskaplig tidskrift* 1, no. 1 (1995): 14–46; Jan Olsson, *I offentlighetens ljus* (Stockholm: Symposium, 1990).

6. "Granskningsman må ej godkänna biografbilder, hvilkas förevisande skulle strida mot allmän lag eller goda seder eller eljest kunna verka förråande, upphetsande eller till förvillande af rättsbegreppen. Bilder, som framställa skräckscener, självmord eller grofva förbrytelser på sådant sätt eller i sådant sammanhang, att dylik verkan kan åstadkommas, må sålunda icke godkännas." Kungl. M:ts nådiga förordning angående biografföreställningar. All translations are by the author.

7. Ulf Boëthius, *När Nick Carter drevs på flykten* (Uppsala, Sweden: Gidlunds, 1989).

8. Ibid., 20–30.

9. Ibid., 8, 41.

10. Ibid., 325.

11. Marie Louise Gagner, *Barn och biografföreställningar* (Stockholm: Hökerberg, 1908).

12. Olsson, "Svart på vitt," 21, 24.

13. Charles Magnusson, *Några ord on Biografcensuren* (Stockholm: Wilhelmssons Boktryckeri, 1912), 3.

14. Ibid., 3–4.

15. Gustaf Berg, *Några ord från biografcensuren* (Stockholm, 1912), 6.

16. Ibid., 10.

17. Charles Magnusson, *Ett Gemäle: Ytterligare några ord i biografffrågan* (Stockholm: Aktiebolaget Svenska Biografteatern, 1912), 11–12.

18. Statens biografbyrå's report of June 9, 1917, National Archives of Sweden, Stockholm, Statens Biografbyrås arkiv.

19. "Film- och biogubbar: IV. S. Popert," *Filmbladet* 1, no. 15 (August 15, 1915): 185–86.

20. "Inrikes biografnytt: Pathé Frères filial i Stockholm," *Filmbladet* 1, no. 15 (August 15, 1915): 183.

21. "Film- och biogubbar," 185.

22. Olsson, "Svart på vitt," 38.

23. Popert, Appeal to the Swedish Government, May 25, 1917, National Archives of Sweden, Stockholm, Statens Biografbyrås arkiv.

24. Popert, Letter to the Swedish Government, August 3, 1916, National Archives of Sweden, Stockholm, Statens Biografbyrås arkiv.

25. "Förråande, upphetsande, Nick Carter av värsta slag," Censor card no. 8742. National Archives of Sweden, Stockholm, Statens Biografbyrås arkiv.

26. Apart from *The Perils of Pauline* and the Elaine serials, Swedish audiences were treated to such other serials as *The Lion's Claws* (Universal, 1918), *The Lure of the Circus* (Universal, 1918), *The Master Key* (Universal, 1914), *The Master Mystery* (BA Rolfe Productions, 1919), *Patria* (International Film Service, Pathé and Wharton, 1917), *The*

Red Ace (Universal, 1917), *The Scarlet Runner* (Vitagraph, 1916), and *The Trey o'Hearts* (Universal, 1914).

27. All six episodes were inspected in August 1917, and all were labeled white.

28. Three episodes were inspected in February 1918, and all were labeled white.

29. Five episodes were inspected in September 1916, and all were labeled white.

30. Only one episode was inspected in December 1916, and it was completely prohibited.

31. Two episodes were inspected in February 1917, and both were prohibited.

32. Other examples are *The Black Box* (Universal, 1915) of six episodes, inspected in January 1916, with three labeled white and three yellow; *The Broken Coin* (Universal, 1915), with five episodes inspected in April 1916, three labeled white and two yellow; *The Secret of the Submarine* (American Film Company, 1915), with five episodes inspected, of which three were labeled white and two yellow; and *Liberty—A Daughter of the USA* (Universal, 1916), of which four episodes were inspected in February 1917, two being labeled white, two yellow, and one red.

33. Ad for *The Perils of Pauline*, *Motography* 11, no. 7 (April 4, 1914): 6.

34. Censor card no. 12034. National Archives of Sweden, Stockholm, Statens Biografbyrås arkiv.

35. *Ciné-Journal*, no. 325/21 (November 6, 1915).

36. Censor card no. 15053. National Archives of Sweden, Stockholm, Statens Biografbyrås arkiv.

37. "Förråande på grund av sin Nick-Carter karaktär." Censor card no. 17.670. National Archives of Sweden, Stockholm, Statens Biografbyrås arkiv.

38. Olsson, "Svart på vitt," 36.

39. Pathé Frères's appeal of May 25, 1917, National Archives of Sweden, Stockholm, Statens Biografbyrås arkiv.

40. Artur Möller, "Filmkultur," *Stockholms-Tidningen*, September 22, 1916, 7.

41. Shelley Stamp, *Movie-Struck Girls: Women and Motion Picture Culture after the Nickelodeon* (Princeton, N.J.: Princeton University Press, 2000), 113.

42. Kalton C. Lahue, *Bound and Gagged: The Story of the Silent Serials* (New York: Castle Books, 1968), 47–48.

43. Statens biografbyrå's report to the Swedish Government, June 9, 1917, National Archives of Sweden, Stockholm, Statens Biografbyrås arkiv.

44. "Målet om den ändrade filmen åter före," *Stockholms-Tidningen*, August 29, 1916, 7; "Den ändrade filmtiteln," *Aftonbladet*, August 8, 1916, 8; "Den ändrade filmtiteln," *Stockholms Dagblad*, August 29, 1916, 9.

45. Statens biografbyrå's report to the Swedish Government, June 9, 1917. National Archives of Sweden, Stockholm, Statens Biografbyrås arkiv.

46. Response from Pathé Frère's Stockholm Branch by way of Popert, to the Swedish Government, June 27, 1917. The appeals, together with reports, were published in *Filmbladet*. See, for instance, "Pathé Frères klagar ånyo" 3, no. 11 (June 1, 1917): 168;

"'Den röda cirkeln' och den 'partiska' censuren" 3, no. 12 (June 15, 1917): 176–78; "Pathé Frères nyaste klagomål" 3, no. 14 (July 15, 1917): 195.

47. For example, in *Stockholms-Tidningen*, February 13, 1915, 3, February 15, 1915, 2; *Dagens Nyheter*, February 20, 1915, 8, and February 21, 1915, 13.

48. Gustaf Berg, "Synpunkter på biografsäsongen 1917–1918," *Filmbladet* 4, no. 13 (1918): 230.

49. See, for instance, *Stockholms-Tidningen*, February 22, 1915, 4; *Dagen*, February 22, 1915, 2; *Dagens Nyheter*, February 22, 1915, 8; *Stockholms Dagblad*, February 22, 1915, 2; and *Social-Demokraten*, February 22, 1915, 2.

50. Kurt Berglund, *Stockholms alla biografer* (Stockholm: Svenska turistföreningen, 1993), 317. The theater was located at Klarabergsgatan 40, at the city center of Stockholm.

51. Ben Singer, *Melodrama and Modernity: Early Sensational Cinema and Its Contexts* (New York: Columbia University Press, 2001), 203.

52. Ad in *Stockholms-Tidningen*, March 8, 1915, 3, and *Dagen*, March 9, 1915, 2.

53. See, for instance, ad in *Dagen*, February 22, 1915, 2.

54. NN, "På biografparkett," *Stockholms-Tidningen*, February 24, 1915, 6. See also ad in *Aftonbladet*, February 22, 1915, 2, and *Dagens Nyheter*, March 1, 1915, 12.

55. Ad in *Stockholms-Tidningen*, February 25, 1915, 3.

56. See, for instance, *Social-Demokraten*, February 23, 1915, 6.

57. Ad in *Stockholms-Tidningen*, March 1, 1915, 3. See also *Dagens Nyheter*, March 1, 1915, 12, and March 6, 1915, 11.

58. Ad in *Aftonbladet*, February 25, 1915, 2.

59. See, for instance, Pathé's ad in *Filmbladet* 1, no. 5 (March 15, 1915): inner front cover.

60. "mer spännande upplevelser, kan inte tänkas," in "Veckans biografprogram," *Social-Demokraten*, March 10, 1915, 6.

61. See, for instance, ads in *Stockholms-Tidningen*, February 26, 1915, 3, and March 1, 1915, 3; *Dagen*, February 22, 1915, 2; *Social-Demokraten*, March 1, 1915, 2; *Dagens Nyheter*, February 26, 1915, 11, and March 1, 1915, 12; and *Filmbladet* 1, no. 4 (March 1, 1915): back cover.

62. "På biografparkett," *Stockholms-Tidningen*, March 4, 1915, 7.

63. Ad in *Stockholms-Tidningen*, March 29, 1915, 3, and May 10, 1915, 3.

64. Ad in *Filmbladet* 2, no. 4 (February 15, 1916): cover.

65. Ad in *Filmbladet* 1, no. 15 (August 15, 1915): 179.

66. Rolf Lindfors and Bertil Wredlund, *Långfilm i Sverige 1910–1919* (Stockholm: Proprius förlag AB, 1991).

67. The episodes banned were "The Twilight Sleep," "The Poisoned Room," "The Vampire," "The Hour of Three," "The Bells of Darnemouth," and "The Serpent Sign."

68. See, for instance, *Stockholms-Tidningen*, August 13, 1916, 2.

69. "oöverträffad, spännande, sensationell detektivfilm," ad in *Aftonbladet*, August 14, 1916, 3.

70. Ibid.

71. See, for instance, the ad in *Aftonbladet*, August 21, 1916, 3, and *Stockholms-Tidningen*, August 16, 1916, 3. Like the Star Theater, Stora Teatern was centrally located at Götgatan 49 in Stockholm.

72. *Dagens Nyheter*, August 15, 1916, 7.

73. X.X.X., "På biografparkett," *Stockholms-Tidningen*, August 16, 1916, 6.

74. "mycket spännande och sevärt, storslaget iscensatt samt framför allt utomordentligt väl inspelat," in "Från bio till bio," *Aftonbladet*, August 15, 1916, 10.

75. Ibid.

76. Kamé, "Från bio till bio," *Aftonbladet*, August 22, 1916, 10.

77. Kamé, "Från bio till bio," *Aftonbladet*, August 29, 1916, 10.

78. X.X.X., "På biografparkett," *Stockholms-Tidningen*, August 23, 1916, 6.

79. See, for instance, the ad in *Aftonbladet*, September 4, 1916, 3.

80. See the ad in *Stockholms-Tidningen*, September 11, 1916, 3, and *Aftonbladet*, September 18, 1916, 4.

81. See ad in *Stockholms-Tidningen*, October 25, 1916, 2.

82. See a rare ad in *Stockholms-Tidningen*, December 3, 1916, 3.

83. "En koffert innehållande film," *Filmbladet* 2, no. 23 (December 1, 1916): 315.

84. S. Popert, "Läget gynnsamt, deklarerar Pathé Frères hr Popert," *Filmbladet* 1, no. 8 (May 1, 1915): 109. See also "Filmtillförseln och U-båtsblockaden," *Filmbladet* 3, no. 4 (February 15, 1917): 50–51.

85. Ad in *Dagens Nyheter*, October 29, 1917, 12, and *Stockholms-Tidningen*, October 29, 1917, 5.

86. Marfa & Co, "Från veckans biografpremiärer," *Dagens Nyheter*, October 30, 1917, 6.

87. "Min idealman," *Filmen* 2, no. 2 (1919): 20. There is a rare image of her in *Filmen* 2, no. 11 (1919): 13.

88. "En riskabel sysselsättning," *Filmen* 2, no. 1 (1919): 8–9.

89. "Vilddjur på scenen," *Filmen* 1, no. 3 (1918): 25.

90. "Pathé Frères är den världfirma i biografbranschen som utan allt tvivel eller jämförelse är den största och mest vittutbredda och som städse varit föregångaren på området," in "Pathé Frères," in a special issue, "Biograf-nummer," of *Aftonbladet*, March 9, 1913, 11.

91. "The Future of the Motion Picture," *Motion Picture News* 9, no. 3 (January 24, 1914): 17.

92. See, for example, Oscar Hemberg, *Några ord om filmens framtid* (Stockholm, 1917), and Gustaf Berg, "Synpunkter på biografsäsongen 1917–1918," *Filmbladet* 4, no. 11 (1918): 206–8.

CHAPTER 3

Pearl, the Swift One, or the Extraordinary Adventures of Pearl White in France

MONICA DALL'ASTA

The social blueprint for Pearl White's film persona has often been identified in the figure of the American New Woman as it emerged in the popular press during the 1910s. For instance, Pauline Marvin's craze for adventure and thrills in *The Perils of Pauline* (1914) stands as a perfect equivalent for the bravery exhibited by those famed "plucky girl reporters" whose daring exploits were offered in the form of first-person, highly sensational articles in contemporary newspapers.[1] In the same vein, in an intertitle in the first episode of the serial, Pauline Marvin declines her guardian's request that she marry his son Harry, not because she is not in love with him, but because she is unwilling to renounce her "adventurous spirit" and her "desire to live and realize the greatest thrills so that I can describe them in a romance of adventures." There is no doubt that for the American audience, Pearl White simply represented a hyperbolic transfiguration of an already familiar, but still quite novel, feminine type that was emerging in both society and popular media.

But what if the most immediate model of her character was not American, but French? Consider that when *The Perils of Pauline* was put in production, the American branch of Pathé was still under the management of Louis Gasnier, a French director who had been sent to New Jersey in 1912 by Charles Pathé to commence production in the United States.[2] Though the story of the serial is attributed to Charles Goddard (who was also the author of the tied-in novelization that was published in the Hearst syndicated papers)[3] and the screenplay to George B. Seitz, it does not seem unrealistic to think that Gasnier himself might have contributed some hints to the character's design. The director's active role in contriving the serial's plot is described in his own reconstruction of his work on *Pauline*, as reported by Georges Sadoul, when Gasnier recalled how he not only was "to direct the installments, but also to concoct all those quite improbable adventures. Each episode ended in an anguishing way for the spectator. I was forced to always imagine what 'was going to happen,' which was not easy."[4]

In any event, the all-sport record-holding woman and pioneer aviator, Marie Marvingt—also known as "the fiancée of danger," "the most important woman in France since Joan of Arc," and "the universal sportswoman"—had already become familiar to the American audience when *The Perils of Pauline* was released in 1914.[5] In 1911, *Collier's* weekly magazine published an article in which she described "the intoxication of flight," recalling, with almost ecstatic accents, the "very unusual and strange sensation" and the "uneasiness," soon "turned into joy unalloyed," which she had experienced on the occasion of her first flight in her monoplane, *Antoinette*.[6]

Born in 1875, Marie Marvingt was from a tender age trained in a wide variety of sporting disciplines, first in swimming, then by "studying at the local circus and learning rope work (slack and tight), trapeze, horseback riding, juggling, and rifle shooting. She excelled in all sports she attempted, spending the most time in those which were the most dangerous."[7] What is peculiar in the case of Marie Marvingt is the astounding range of her sporting skills. Beside swimming (in 1905 she was the first woman to swim across the Seine), she could canoe and sail; she played tennis, golf, and polo; she was a skilled cyclist, automobile driver, and fencer; she excelled in all winter sports, from skiing and ski jumping to ice speed skating, luge, and bobsledding; and she set records in hard rock alpinism as early as 1903 by climbing mountains no woman had climbed before. She participated in several all-male sporting events: in 1907 she received the Prize of Honor at an international military competition for shooting a Flobert carbine; a year later she completed the Tour de France on her bicycle, *Zéphirine*, a feat achieved by only 36 out of the 114 male contestants. As David Lam points out, "After the end of the Tour de France that year (in which women were of course not permitted to participate), she rode the entire course alone, simply to show that a woman could do so, covering more than 4,000 km and 8 passes, while averaging more than 150 km per day."[8]

Marie Marvingt on balloon *La Lorraine,* Hippodrome de Longchamp, Grand Prix de l'Aéro-club de France, June 26, 1910. Courtesy Bibliothèque Nationale de France.

At the beginning of the new century, Marvingt was attracted by the new technology of flight. Defiant of danger (as reported by David Lam, no less than "87% of those who learned to fly before World War I died in accidents"),[9] by 1907 Marvingt was piloting balloons, and in 1910 she became the third woman in the world to earn a pilot's license. Like her fellow "plucky girl reporters," she often recounted her exploits in articles and interviews where the major attraction was the description of the various risky situations she had managed to survive. In the fall of 1909, for instance, she personally reported in *Le Petit Journal* on the perilous journey across the North Sea, from Nancy to England, which she had recently traversed in her own balloon, *L'Etoile filante*, with Colonel Emile Garnier as passenger and assistant.[10] The flight had been seriously life threatening, as during the night the balloon had been driven by air turbulence into a storm and consequently made heavier by ice and snow. As a result, it plunged rapidly downward until it came dangerously close to the sea, whose high waves drenched the basket and its contents. The sacks of sand carried to control the balloon's elevation were thrown out as rapidly as possible until the balloon finally rose to a safer altitude. Yet it remained difficult to control, so even the landing was quite eventful, with the balloon stranded in a tree and Marie tumbling from the basket. She immediately regained her energies and ran for help to free Garnier from his uncomfortable position in the tree.

One can only wonder whether the scenarists of *The Perils of Pauline* had chosen the name of Pauline Marvin as an explicit homage to this incredible woman, but there is no doubt that Marie Marvingt's exploits could be an ideal

Pauline Marvin's balloon adventure
in *The Perils of Pauline* (1914).

source of inspiration for a feminine-oriented action serial. In fact, the cinematic qualities of her balloon adventure can be seen in the episode in which Pauline experiences a similar situation, riding in an out-of-control balloon until she manages to stop it by dropping the anchor and catching a rock.[11] Though in this instance Pauline has to wait for Harry to be saved, she nonetheless proves she can care for herself even in a difficult situation such as this one by climbing down the anchor rope with the pure strength of her muscles.

In the following years, both the real and the fictional heroine became involved with the war. Eager to contribute to the effort of the French Army, Marvingt disguised herself as a man and managed to reach the front where, for several weeks, she was able to serve as an infantry(wo)man in the 42nd Bataillon de Chasseurs à Pied before being discovered and discharged. She wrote about the experience and kept reporting on the war later on, after she was finally formally invited (apparently by Marechal Floch himself) to use her skiing skills to take supplies to the troops who remained encircled in the Dolomite Mountains. She then served as a nurse in the Red Cross, but her plan to develop an aerial ambulance service was too innovative for the times and was rejected by the French government. The realization of this project was to become her lifelong mission, and she successfully devoted the next forty years to promoting the concept of "l'Aviation sanitaire," or aero medical evacuation.[12]

Following the trail of Marvingt's military feats, Pearl White also found her way to the war. In the role of Pearl Dare, she enlisted in the ranks of the

American army in 1916, wearing a uniform and burning all her energies in the fight against the enemy. It is notable that in *Pearl of the Army*, her character acquires a much greater autonomy than in previous narratives, especially in comparison to the *Elaine* serial trilogy.[13] No longer is she the impatient, reckless young woman who rushes into danger simply to satisfy her craving for thrills, always escorted by a loving and much savvier male defender, as in *Pauline*; nor is she the vulnerable ingénue who gets involved in the most terrible adventures against her will, to be regularly saved by her fiancée, as in *Elaine*. In the only serial with her name in the title, Pearl unleashes extreme, even threatening, energies. Always in movement, disconcerting with her long, uncombed hair floating on the uniform, she carries a pistol, pilots an airplane, wrestles against her tough male enemies in close combat. Since her fiancée gets killed in one of the first episodes, she is left alone to care for herself, but she never looks like she needs any help; in fact, it is now her turn to become the helper and the defender, to contribute to the safety of her nation. Interestingly, as Rudmer Canjels has discovered, the French novelization of the *House of Hate* (*La Maison de la haine*, dir. George B. Seitz [1918–1919]) elaborates on Pearl's involvement in the war, with Pearl Grant completing her adventures as a nurse in a Red Cross ambulance in France.[14]

The parallels between the stories of Pearl White and Marie Marvingt may be no more than a coincidence, yet still it is enough to suggest that Pearl's enormous appeal to French audiences was not simply due to some exotic fascination for the peerless modernity of the American New Woman, but was instead rooted in some very familiar experiences of feminine heroism. For French audiences, in other words, and especially for women spectators, Pearl's character was not simply a foreign novelty, but an image that resonated acutely with the deep transformation of gender roles and stereotypes that they were experiencing in their everyday lives. She may have been an American product, but she was soon to become a distinct French icon.

Protéa and Irma Vep, *Filles changéantes*

In fact, an amazing figure of a fearless, vigorous, and athletic woman had already appeared on the French screens a couple of years before Pearl White's triumphal presentation in *Les Mystères de New York*. First introduced by Victorin Jasset in the role of an accomplice of Zigomar in the last film of that series (*Zigomar peau d'anguille*, 1913), Josette Andriot did so well in the stunt scenes that she was soon chosen to play the lead in another spirited action movie, *Protéa*, which was, in turn, to initiate a long and very popular series of sequels.

Shown in many venues across the United States at the end of 1913, the film may represent another French source for the character of Pauline.

The concept of Protéa was at once original and well tried: Jasset simply turned the obscure figure of the elusive bandit in black famously attached to the names of Zigomar and Fantômas into a woman, thus offering for the first time in French film history the image of an invincible heroine, endowed with almost supernatural resources, mysteriously strong, undaunted, and ever-changing. Unlike her predecessors, Protéa was not exactly a bandit: she was a spy from the imaginary country of Messénie who fought to take possession of a secret treaty between Messénie's two enemies, the nations of Celtia and Slavonia. She was then marked by an enthralling ambiguity: as a secret agent, she situated herself on the border between the law and the lawless; she operated on behalf of Messénie's police but made large use of illegal methods; she stood on the right side but was nonetheless pursued by crowds of foreign gendarmes. In other words, the transgressive aspects of the character were an important component of its appeal and placed a stress upon the super womanly nature of its behavior.

Like Fantômas and Zigomar, Protéa unceasingly shifted between an extremely graphic figure, wearing a tight bodysuit when she appeared in the role of "herself," and the swarm of identities and costumes she assumed when she worked undercover. Her prodigious ability to disguise and substitute herself for whomever else is described by Francis Lacassin:

> Businesswoman in the Police headquarters of Messénie, where she is charged with the mission of recovering a secret treaty, she is also the two-faced worldly woman who gets on the Orient-Express to get hold of diplomatic documents belonging to her pursuer, Count Varello; the burglar acrobat attempting to rob the offices of the Foreign Affairs Ministry of Celtie; the old lady who comes to present a petition to the Minister; aide-de-camp to the same Minister; director of a feminine gipsy orchestra during an official ball; spouse of the Albanian ambassador, whom she has locked in a closet with his wife; fire-fighter running to put out a fire . . . lit by her own hand; lion tamer in a circus menagerie; country girl ready to carry the luggage of an officer travelling without carriers. Which, thanks to the content of the luggage, allows her to disguise herself as an officer of the Celtian army, and to get back to Messénie.[15]

All of these frenzied metamorphoses, and the euphoria of change they clearly express, take on a particular undertone in the case of Protéa, quite distinct from that which occurs in the films of Zigomar and Fantômas. As an allegory of the potential body, the all-black bodysuit acquires a whole series of new meanings when worn by a woman. By neatly exposing the forms of the female body, it points to femininity as difference and provides that difference with a specific potential. As the ultimate costume, it stands for the infinity of all possible costumes, for all the exciting new identities, opportunities, adventures, the still-unknown spaces and forms of experience that modernity was then opening up for women. In fact, it is a figure of freedom, a visual condensation of women's wish of agency, of their curiosity and desire.

Different from the looser costumes worn by Zigomar and Fantômas, which seem to be exclusively functional for the purpose of concealment in the night, Protéa's very tight bodysuit looks more like a garment specially conceived for sporting activities. "An older French sister of the American serial queens," as Annette Förster has dubbed Josette Andriot,[16] in the films of the series she performed all sorts of stunts with enviable energy and athleticism. Well-skilled in many sports—swimming, diving, horseback riding, cycling, and so on—Andriot proved to be ideally fit for the role of Protéa, a character that a publicity text described as being

> a Nature long experienced to the sports, a will imposing itself on the strongest monsters, a Sphynx . . . [who] goes overwhelming over everything in her path, in the name of her duty . . . , implacable, deadly, . . . a power who knows her strength, at every moment she can be "another one," and yet she is still the "same!" . . . She feels she is strong enough to crush destiny as she has been crushing men and beasts![17]

To portray Protéa's phenomenal physical powers appropriately, Jasset did not hesitate to make use of special effects, as in the sensational scene that ends the opening episode of the series. Protéa is desperately riding her bike to flee from the police cars that are pursuing her when, suddenly, the bridge in front of her is blown up by her enemies: "Head to the handlebars, Protéa soars like an arrow, bounces, and carried by her vertiginous jump, lands on the opposite side of the river, under the policemen's stunned eyes."[18]

In her following adventures—packed with "infernal automobiles," treacherous manors, pursuits, explosions, poisoned gas, horseback riding, fencing, "and furthermore: staircases heaving upward, floors falling downward, whirling columns and squeezing walls!"[19]—the character of Protéa was slightly reworked and adjusted to the ideal of an avenging heroine. Sometimes presented as a woman detective, she found herself ready to fight the band of the "Blue Marigolds" (in *L'Auto infernale*, or *Protéa II*, dir. Joseph Faivre [1914]), to protect a defenseless young couple from the mischievous ends of their enemies (in what would be her only serial, *Les Mystères du château de Malmort—Protéa IV*, six episodes, dir. Gérard Bourgeois [1917]), or to solve the case of a classical "locked-room mystery" (in *L'Intervention de Protéa—Protéa V*, dir. Jean-Joseph Renaud [1919]).

Ahead of Pearl White and paralleling her exploits during the 1910s, Protéa was, then, an all-exciting, early incarnation of the French *femme nouvelle* (new woman), a self-reliant, energetic woman determined to take hold of all the opportunities the new century had begun to reveal on the horizon of feminine desire. Her elusive and enigmatic nature is simply a function of her ceaseless mutability, both the physical mobility that allows her to transcend the normally anticipated feminine behavior and the feverish process of identity shifts that put her in situations that test her over a wide variety of subject positions, both male and female. By representing the still-unexplored potential of the female body, her bodysuit functions as a black mirror to reflect the paramount transformation of women's condition in early-twentieth-century France. On the one hand, as a sporting garment it points to freedom of movement, to the ability of taking an active initiative in newly opened spaces. On the other, as the ultimate un-dress, the clothing that remains when Protéa removes her disguises, it stands for the virtual multiplicity of all dresses, obviously hinting at the all-modern experience of fashion. This identification between Andriot's transformist heroine and the woman of fashion is made explicit in the first episode of the series, in the scene where Protéa, already stylishly dressed, disappears for a second behind a curtain only to immediately reappear in different, equally elegant attire.

After Andriot's Protéa, the black bodysuit would be worn by an even more popular actress who was to become Pearl White's most direct competitor in France. In the role of the vicious Irma Vep (an anagram of Vampire)—the female criminal who plays the lead in Louis Feuillade's *Les Vampires*—Musidora offered a new and more troubling interpretation of the French *femme nouvelle*, one that sharply captured the contradictory emotions, concerns, and anxieties provoked by the ongoing process of women's emancipation. She was at once beautiful and mischievous, seductive and calculated, courageous and profoundly selfish. She was part of a gang and adopted the black uniform of her confederates, but her stronger temperament was constantly singled out, as was her bodily difference. For in fact, her costume was not exactly identical to that of her male fellows: made of a very thin silk fabric and somewhat translucent, her *maillot de soie* (silk bodysuit) exposed her bodily forms in the most enticing way, clearly evoking an erotic subtext that was repeatedly made explicit in dozens of lyrical homages written by a number of male authors.

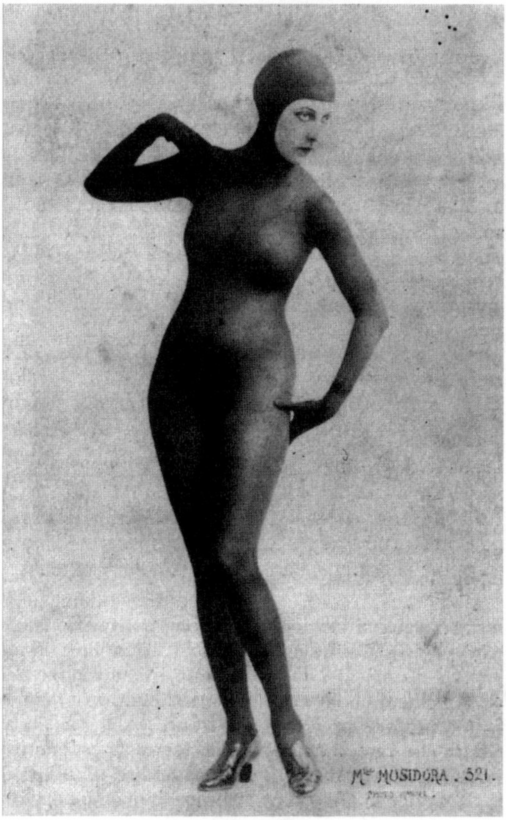

Portrait of Musidora wearing Irma Vep's intriguing catsuit.

In the case of Irma Vep, the bodysuit's relation to the universe of fashion is obvious, as it appears that it was designed and produced in the atelier of Pierre Poiret, the famous stylist who as early as 1908 had dared to remove the corset from all of his models.[20] To be sure, Irma Vep's costume was a celebration of the modern style in women's fashion, the whole garment being made of a fabric—the same used for silk stockings—that was about to become the very symbol of change in feminine costume. Moreover, Irma, not less than Protéa, was a genius of disguise, able to shift from alias to alias, from the identity of a spirited *vedette* (star) in a cabaret to that of a servant, of a clerk, and even of a young male viscount. In Musidora's own words, she was the *fille changéante* (ever-changing girl),[21] and the easiness with which she could become another was both fascinating and profoundly uncanny.[22]

Much less athletic and frenzied than Protéa and Pearl White, Irma represented the most disturbing side of the new woman, the dark side of the modern woman as a person "out of control." When *Les Vampires* was released during the winter months of 1915–1916, the same time as the appearance of Pearl White's star vehicle, *Les Mystères de New York*, the Parisian audience found itself haunted by the vision of two opposed heroines, one blonde and joyful, one black and threatening, who seemed to chase one another in an endless quest. As Robert Desnos would later recall, "This one was blonde. She disappeared, and the beautiful novel that had begun with her was finished with the one who followed her, and who was brunette. They were dying only to be reborn. . . . They were women, real women. Their life was not ordinary, it was precious and they risked it. . . . All of Klondike nuggets could not suffice to buy the magic of their marvelous existence. A hundred lives would not be enough to live their lives."[23]

Pearl Vite, a Socialist

In France the name Pearl White meant freshness, modernity, speed. As Louis Aragon observed in an emotional homage to her screen persona, in the French pronunciation her name was transformed into an involuntary pun, Pearl Vite—the Swift One.[24]

The Pearl White craze first exploded in France in the winter of 1915–1916, when the three serials in which she starred as Elaine (*The Exploits of Elaine*, *The Romance of Elaine*, *The New Exploits of Elaine*) were distributed in a condensed version of twenty-two episodes under the title *Les Mystères de New York*.[25] What Georges Sadoul meant by his neologism *serialomanie*[26]—or chapter-play fever—was profoundly bound up with the war. As Henri Fescourt recalled in his memoirs, several Parisian studios had been converted to war production since the beginning of the conflict, thus causing a drastic reduction in national film production that facilitated foreign imports.[27] With national production half paralyzed, Pathé had an easy time reinforcing its already dominant position in the domestic market through the import of its American films, particularly the Pearl White and Ruth Roland serials. In an effort to compete with Pathé, Gaumont—the other major French company of the period, whose leading director, Louis Feuillade, had just rejoiced at the extraordinary success of his *Fantômas* series—set out to produce *Les Vampires*, thus initiating a strategy of domestic resistance to the American serials that would soon be taken up by a number of smaller studios. At the same time, and also in imitation of the Pathé example, all the major distributors began to import a whole variety of foreign serials. As a result, by the end of the decade the French film market was literally flooded with a host of both national and international episodes.[28]

However, there was another side to the rapid proliferation of serials in France that was also closely related to the war. Due to the recruitment of a great many men into the army, film audiences came to be composed primarily of women and children. Witness Paul Gilson's words when he recalled the screenings of Pearl White's serials at the Ciné-Magic theater, where a public of "female workers and children" appeared to be more frightened by the vicious exploits of the Masque-aux-dents-blanches (the Laughing Mask of *The Iron Claw*) or the Main-qui-étreint (the Clutching Hand of *Les Mystères de New York*) than "from the explosions of the *Grosse Bertha* [a World War I cannon]."[29] As a consequence, the film industry suddenly found itself obliged to appeal almost exclusively to the female taste in order to achieve the successful positioning of its products. Though sources are thin regarding this, the role played by female audiences in commanding Pearl White's triumph in France can convincingly be inferred from the revolutionary impact of war on women's lives during this period.

As has been repeatedly pointed out, World War I represented a unique opportunity for women to extend their experience beyond the domestic sphere, in France as elsewhere. Not only did the number of jobs available for women increase, but their salaries were no longer subject to men's control and administration. Moreover, a whole series of traditionally "masculine" occupations became accessible to women. As François Thébaud writes, "the war broke down age-old barriers and opened many prestigious professions to women," so that suddenly "France had its *financières* (bank ladies) and *cheminottes* (railway ladies); women punched tickets in the Metro, worked in sales, collected bills, and even drove trolleys."[30] Many women enjoyed an improvement in their economic conditions, as "wartime work was well paid, particularly in munitions factories, where women could often earn twice what they made in the traditional female occupations."[31] Though certainly working mothers had to face severe labor overloads, the absence of fathers and brothers and a new economic autonomy gave younger women the opportunity to experience a totally unprecedented freedom.

No wonder, then, that Pearl White would soon become their idol. Even more than in *Les Mystères de New York*, where her knack for movement and athleticism was restrained by the presence of a male protagonist in charge of her safety (the scientific detective Craig Kennedy, promptly renamed Justin Clarel and transformed into a French patriotic hero),[32] the exciting potential of her frenetic body was fully revealed with the next releases. Immediately following *Les Mystères de New York*, *The Perils of Pauline* was distributed in 1916 under the title of *Les Exploits d'Elaine* so as to cash in on the tremendous popularity of her previous vehicle. Also in 1916 came *La Masque aux dents blanches* (*The Iron Claw*), soon followed by *La Reine s'ennuie* (*The Fatal Ring*) in 1917, *Le Courrier de Washington* (*Pearl of the Army*) and *La Maison de la haine* (*The House of Hate*) in 1918, *Par amour* (*The Lightning Raider*) in 1919, *Par la force e par la ruse* (*The Black Secret*) in 1922, and finally *Pillage* (*Plunder*) in 1924.

Female spectators thus became ever more familiar with the image of this lively and restless heroine, an undaunted creature who seemed to replicate in the fictional realm both the enthusiasm and the anxieties they were experiencing at the moment of their entry into the public sphere, a social space that remained fundamentally male oriented. Pearl White was acclaimed as the symbol of the unfettered modern woman, a brave, strong, and dynamic female individual who simply acted like a man—pretty much in the same way as the women workers who attended her films did every day in the much more concrete reality of their lives. Not surprisingly, she soon became a model to imitate. As Marcel Lapierre recalls, "with her tartan wool skirt, her ample shirt and big velvet beret, she summarizes the ideal of a whole generation in love with adventure. The teenagers—and sometimes even men of a mature age—dream in front of her picture. Working class girls reproduce her hairstyle and adopt the beret 'à la Elaine.' It is the first time—it is worth noting—that a film actress induces an important process of imitation among Eve's daughters."[33] Quite strangely, of the numerous homages paid to Pearl in France, none, as far as I know, was written by a woman.[34] This might, hopefully, change when research extends beyond the more traditional film sources to embrace the still-underexplored territory of women's magazines. Meanwhile, we can nonetheless measure the sheer impact of her sporting personality in the words of several male authors whose writings are vividly expressive of an ardent, unconditioned admiration. Witness, for instance, Louis Delluc, the main film critic of the time:

> I like Pearl White a lot.
>
> She is just perfect for the screen. Her pace and gestures—her minimal expressions—which do not amount to impotence—and her sporting personality—boxing, horses, autos, etc.—there are many aspects that make her precious for the cinema.
>
> Young and attractive, she has a young and attractive style of dressing. Posters of two continents have popularized the black dress, sober skirt,

> white spats and the little hat that are just one of the thousand and one compositions of this full-tilt heroine. Only a few actresses have understood the costuming technique of the screen. Most of them end up looking cumbersome and pretentious while trying to look nice. No action movie actress had yet obtained Pearl White's almost synthetic silhouette.[35]

Unfortunately, Delluc does not cite, along with Pearl White, those French actresses like Musidora and Josette Andriot who greatly contributed to simplify the style of female costuming in film, to the extent of removing all garments that could encumber their movements beyond the minimal and quite "synthetic" coverage of their bodysuits. But it is known that Delluc did not appreciate Feuillade's cinema,[36] which he considered to be representative of an older aesthetic, and most often his judgment of French popular cinema was no less ironic than severe. In the end, his concept of *photogénie* (photogenic) clearly favored Pearl White over Musidora, the dynamism of the American urban melodrama over the oddments of nineteenth-century French *roman-feuilleton*. For Delluc, Pearl's costuming style was photogenic to the extent to which it was thoroughly functional for the mobility that permeated her films, a truly cinematographic quality of which she was the personal emblem. Far beyond her influence on female costume, Delluc observed, the vision of her restive body was contagious, at once a cure for the nerves and a healthy model for the audience, able to induce an uncontainable need for physical action.

> The spectacle of her exploits does better for neurasthenia than Chaplin's bitter genius, and even better than Douglas Fairbanks' vitality, at once sentimental and shy. I am not thinking either of William Hart's energy, which always seems a bit desperate. Pearl White is just energy and vitality, and that is all. But what am I saying? She is just health with no afterthought. . . .
>
> These kind of heroes have always been fascinating for the French. Their flair, gracious strength, success has been and is adored. Then it is not surprising that Pearl White, who can do everything, and does it so well, transports the audience. No doubt she is doing much for accustoming the audience to the hygienic ideal of sports. At the end of her films one feels like driving cars and airplanes, riding a horse, shooting like Eagle Eye, dancing, skating, swimming, diving, and everything, everything else, and the desire is not far from realization. Thanks to her, many workers have now come to think they can regularly train their muscles, through sports they had previously considered as just reserved for the rich. Equality in physical culture, oft-claimed but never put in practice, has found quite a support in

> her films. Did Pearl White ever suspect she was doing socialist work with her innocent movies?[37]

Again, there is no mention of the specific impact that such cinematographic education to a sporting lifestyle could have on women spectators. Yet Delluc's words certainly take on a peculiar significance in relation to that audience, composed of women who only a few years before had still been required to wear girdles and corsets. Going so far as to call her a socialist, Delluc clearly attests to the extent that Pearl White had been adopted and appropriated by French culture, to the point of becoming a champion of national health and, no doubt, equality for women. Her cinematographic exploits were in perfect timing with the efforts of so many pioneer activists of physical education for women such as Alice Milliat, the founder of the Fédération des sociétés féminines sportives de France in 1917; Thérèse Brulé, high jumper and record breaker in 1919; Suzanne Liébrard, sprint champion in 1917–1918 and advocate of physical exercise for all women; and, of course, the extraordinary Marie Marvingt. The socialist aspects of these women's point of view can easily be seen in Milliat's comment that "we are fully aware that we have been working for the improvement of women's well being, no matter which social class they belong to,"[38] as well as from Liébrard's claim that "sports should not be reserved to just the most endowed girls; on the contrary they should be addressing all girls, including those who show a weaker physical complexion."[39]

Pearl White's celebrated "sporting science"[40] was the most joyful endorsement of their belief that "women should be given the right to enjoy sports."[41]

Pearl White and the Surrealists

In the wake of the phenomenal success of *Les Mystères de New York*, many other serial queens found their way from the United States to France. Among the first were Ruth Roland with *Le Cercle rouge* (*The Red Circle* [1914]) in 1916, Marie Walcamp with *Suzy l'américaine* (*Liberty, a Daughter of the USA* [1916]) and Grace Cunard with *Le Domino rouge* (*The Purple Mask* [1916]) in 1917, Irene Castle with *Coeur d'héroine* (*Patria* [1916]) and Mollie King with *Le Mystère de la double croix* (*The Mystery of the Double Cross* [1917]) in 1918, followed by Juanita Hansen with *L'Avion fantôme* (*The Brass Bullet* [1918]) in 1919 and Marguerite Courtot with *Globe-trotter par amour* (*Bound and Gagged* [1919]) in 1920. Yet none of these actresses ever managed to reach the popularity Pearl White enjoyed in France during the serial's golden age. Once more, Delluc's explanation for

Pearl White, portrait with autograph dedication.

her success pointed to the unique photogenic rendering of her image on the screen. For instance, when compared to the "intensité quasi mathématique" (almost mathematical intensity) she was able to express in her movements, Ruth Roland appeared inexorably "artificial."[42] Moreover, Pearl's "grâce photogénique" could attain sheer lyrical apexes, her films being pervaded with a silent, extremely touching "poésie acrobatique."[43]

In other words, she was a poet: not just an object, but a subject of poetry. In the eyes of the surrealists, she proved to be touching to the extent to which she was constantly in motion, so captured by the urge to act for the sake of acting that she managed to achieve a perfect freedom from all bounds of consciousness, thus actually attaining in the easiest and most joyful fashion that sort of oneiric condition of existence the surrealists strove to nurture with their poetry and lifestyle. See how Louis Aragon summarized the concept: "These lines are a hymn to the one whom, in an involuntary pun, the big audiences called Pearl Vite, paying homage to her swift energy and rich beauty. What makes the theater dead for us is no doubt that its unique subject and rule of action is morality. Our era can no longer have any interest in morality. In the movies, speed appears in life, and Pearl White never acts to obey her conscience, but only for the sake of acting, as in a sporting exercise."[44] "Our era" was certainly a discovery and a big challenge. It was the excitement of modernity, the destruction caused by war, the subversion of all traditional values, and the hope in a new era in which life would no longer be subjected to "the rules of Economy and Exchange" and therefore to "the enslavement to work."[45] It was a fight for change made in the name of poetry, which is freedom, or love. All these motifs were inextricably and paradoxically intertwined in the surrealists' appraisal of Pearl White. What has to be noticed in this regard is the retrospective character of these writings, which regularly took on a reflective aspect, even when they were written only a few years after the period—the middle teens. For the surrealists the image of Pearl White stood for the mythical period of their youth, or more generally for the historical collective experience of a whole generation. It was imbued with a paradoxical sense of awakening, leading not to the espousal of adult, reasonable values, but to the realization of the unsurpassed values of youth and unconsciousness.

In recalling his own experience as a fifteen-year-old spectator, Robert Desnos quite unexpectedly described Pearl White as "the blueprint of the beloved woman, the mother figure of the heart winning heroine," or in other words, the archetypal erotic ideal cultivated by the young males of "la génération de 1900."[46]

> Pearl White was the symbol of the sensual desires of a whole generation, one that was deprived of its necessary and legitimate pleasures because of the war, I am speaking of the generation of 1900. . . .
>
> Did she ever know how many young men in love evoked her in their loneliness? And awakening in the morning, did she not feel her flesh exhausted from so many embraces and imaginary kisses, and from the countless adventures she had experienced at the side of those lovers of whom, without knowing, she had been the slave?
>
> Marvelous figure of love, exalting evocations, multiplied ad infinitum, Pearl White reigned upon the world. She haunted all those new minds, she agitated those senses in fusion.[47]

The fantasy of Pearl's erotic subjugation evoked in these words is more than interesting, being a typical example of the surrealists' contradictory approach to the female image. While on the one hand it could be aligned to the long gallery of sadistic fantasies that characterize their representations of the female body, on the other it is also revealing of the crisis of masculinity that is the basis of such a misogynist attitude. It shows a shift in male desire from a traditionally passive female figure to an active and independent one, an indocile body that was inviting inasmuch as it was challenging. Pearl's enslavement in the realm of night and dream is thus the clearest admission of male weakness in the face of the new, uncanny sensuality of the *femme nouvelle*, one that no longer was a synonym for poise and composure but instead sprang out from the lively behaviors of a wholesome, dynamic body. This was enough to credit Pearl White with the merit of provoking a silent revolution simply by virtue of a sentimental education, or a sheer "propaganda of love." With Pearl White, love became "the master to whom it was compulsory to obey, whom it was honorable to serve and the unique justification for a creature."[48]

In sum, through the celebration of *Les Mystères de New York*—considered to be not less than a capital moment "in human evolution,"[49] or a condensation of "the great reality of this century"[50]—the surrealists wanted to reaffirm their unconditioned faithfulness to the values of their youth, to the memorable discoveries made during the terrible, and yet so very exciting, period of war: "All we could grant of fidelity used to go to those serials previously so decried. . . . Beginning on Saturday, on this screen, episode XIX: 'The Creeping Glove'—You can count on us."[51] The nostalgic tone of their reminiscences has certainly to do with the recognition that what they had then perceived as the subversive potential of cinema, even and especially in its most popular and artistically "unconscious" forms, had soon been defeated by its transformation into a big economic empire, driven exclusively by the laws of Capital. Of course, Pearl White's films were also profoundly implicated in this metamorphosis, but the surrealists quite honestly recognized, as one of them said, "We did not understand what was happening. We lived at speed, with passion."[52] In the naive, frantic adventures of the American serials, they had envisioned the possibility of a new vitalist aesthetic, and maybe even of a surrealist cinema. Only later did they come to realize that a *nouveau maître* (new master) had emerged on the scene: "Money. It took possession of the screens and the film studios. Greedy and gouty as it was, it was frightened by the existence of those free lovers."[53]

What remained was the sense of an intense revelation, the perception of a whole new field of virtuality that waited to be brought to expression—the realm of surreality, imbued with an exciting threat to the reasonable logic of the everyday world. Not to equivocate, this poetic revelation was thoroughly permeated with violence. In 1923 Philippe Soupault recalled,

> We used to walk the cold, deserted streets in search of an accident, an encounter, life. To distract ourselves we had to hitch our imaginations to sensational dreams. Still more colorful than maps of the world, the newspapers used to distract us for a moment or two. For a few cents you could travel the world and witness the marvelous and bloody dramas that momentarily illuminated some dot on the globe. We were thirsty, terribly thirsty for that strange and powerful life, that life we drank like milk.
>
> One day you saw huge posters, as long as snakes, stretching out along the walls.
>
> At each street corner a man, his face covered with a red handkerchief, was pointing a revolver at the unconcerned passersby.
>
> You thought you heard galloping, a motor kicking over, screams of death.
>
> We descended on the cinemas and understood that everything had changed.
>
> Pearl White's smile appeared on the screen; this almost ferocious smile announced the upheavals of the new world.[54]

The sentimental attachment to Pearl White as an allegory of modern love, on the one hand, and the appraisal of her as a queen of destruction, on the other, were equally strong. She was both desirable and menacing, ravishing and sinister. She came forward as the emblem of a welcomed disruption of habits and values that also incorporated a crisis of traditional masculinity and a transformation of heterosexual relationships that the surrealists were ready to record, if often in reactive and contradictory terms. This may help explain why, in their bewildering description of wartime, they came to align themselves with those feminists who, as Françoise Thébaud recalls, would not hesitate to define the period as a very "happy time," a "good time," a "fine time." In Aragon's words, "above and despite all," Pearl White serials gave access to "the poetry of our age," offering the unforgettable experience of "une très belle époque" (a very beautiful era).[55]

Pearl's Pupil

With so many fans in France, no wonder Pearl White would be willing to move there. During her promotional trips to Paris, she was invariably received as an important personality, a great star, or even a heroine. For instance, on the

Graphic portrait of Pearl White on the
cover of *Le Petit Journal ilustré*, May 8, 1921.

cover of *Le Petit Journal illustré* of May 8, 1921, she was portrayed in front of the airplane about to take her to France wearing a pilot costume, holding a colorful bouquet in her hands, and wearing the most charming smile on her face—a touching image of happiness. The caption read, "Popular film artist Pearl White [is portrayed] just about to go from England to France, using the fastest and most enjoyable means of locomotion."[56]

When her appeal for the American audience began to fade, she set out to live in Paris, where she found herself enfolded within the warmth of an extraordinary affection. She was apparently already quite rich; she had made a fortune by rolling and racing, jumping, and riding through several dozens of episodes, shorts, and features, acquiring worldwide fame but also a chronic back injury. Still, she was not yet ready to stop working. In the spring of 1923, she publicly refuted the news circulated by some newspapers that she was about to retire into a convent.[57] She appeared on the stage of a cinema, wearing a red velvet dress to reassure her fans that her rest in a convent would last only three weeks, after which she intended to go on "shooting more films in France, and with French artists." As a journalist commented, "It is hard to imagine Pearl White retired in a convent if one remembers her films, or the way how, just lately, she walked on the stage, so young and sporting, with the ease of an American boy. All French film buffs will rejoice in learning that after a period of both physical and spiritual rest, Pearl White will certainly go back to the film career that gave her—and still holds for her—so much success."[58] Pearl's announcement proved to be more than just publicity. She returned to the French screens one last time in 1924 with the feature *Terreur* (ironically, released in the U.S. under the title *The Perils of Paris*), directed by Edward José and based on a script written by a longtime French serial specialist, Gérard Bourgeois. Somehow, fatefully, both the Belgian-born José, who had directed her in a number of her American episodes (notably in *The Iron Claw* and *Pearl of the Army*), and Bourgeois, the director of Josette Andriot's only serial, *Protéa IV*, in 1917, were also to end their careers just after this film. No doubt it was a sign that—as the surrealists were giving witness to in their retrospective memories—the golden age of the serial was gone forever. Yet her film was warmly welcomed in the pages of all major film magazines, obtaining very good reviews. While there is no way to document how well the film was received by audiences, there is no reason to suppose the spectators had a different reaction than the critics, who spoke enthusiastically of "an extremely interesting film, which Pearl White interprets from beginning to end with a liveliness, a good humor and a spirited verve that no doubt will captivate the audience,"[59] going so far as to define *Terreur* "the best movie ever created by the protagonist of *Les Mystères de New York*."[60]

If one believes Pearl's own statements to the press, she should certainly be credited with a major role in the production. In a short announcement published by both *Le Cinéopse* and *Mon Ciné*, she explained how, following her decision to make a film in France, she had looked for a script "that would be suitable to my genre" and talked some French friends into contributing to the financing of the film, chosen the actors, found a studio, and arranged that the studio's lighting be maximally effective for shooting. "The studio was too bright, and I managed to persuade its owner that it had to be darkened. He agreed and I went on working to provide the lighting, all the lighting that was necessary for perfect photography."[61] She also recalled her effort to apply "the American mode of production" yet was keen to insist that "this is a French film on all levels," utilizing "French personnel and French financial capital."[62] Produced by Fordys, an independent company that does not appear to have made any more films after this one, *Terreur* transposed the usual nervous, fast-paced style of American serials into a typical French setting, from the countryside to Parisian rooftops and sewers, telling the story of an intrepid French heroine, Hélène Lorfeuil, who fights, and regularly wins, against the murderers of her father, the inventor of a death ray. All the serial's classical ingredients were concocted to produce a wondrous fantasy from which Pearl White emerged "in all the glamour of her star personality": "supple, elegant, sporting, and infinitely lovable."[63]

Beyond her declarations in the course of the film's promotional campaign, there is at least one other indication that Pearl was seriously considering the possibility of continuing to produce in France. In September 1923, an article in the magazine *Comœdia* reported her announcement that she was looking for "a pupil whom she will teach the secrets of her art."[64] After referring to her surprise at the fact that "France has never had actresses specializing in . . . the 'Pearl White' genre," the article went on to quote a letter she had addressed to the editor of the magazine's regular film column, Jean-Louis Croze:

> As you wrote so well, I really like France a lot. Yes, I am very fond of it. I love your country and all your people. But I would like to see in your theaters a young lady of a quite special kind that is now missing. . . .
>
> I would be truly glad to have a pupil whom I would teach this job of which I think I know everything.
>
> The only requirements I ask for are patience, a lot of work, and no useless shyness. And finally . . . how should I say? . . . sports, a lot of sports. . . .
>
> I dare hope that with my help she will easily find a way to ensure her future.[65]

Despite the critical success of her French production, however, Pearl White's active involvement in the French film industry would not last beyond here. The generalized *retour à l'ordre* (backlash) that characterized the 1920s—best represented by the reaction against feminism starting in this period[66]—did not encourage more fantasies of women's empowerment as suggestive and physically enthralling such as those evoked by Pearl White in her films. Also, as recorded by Desnos, French cinema was already steadily moving in the direction of so-called French quality, with large capital investments, extreme technical precision, and a whole rhetoric of cinematographic artistry. As a consequence, Pearl's effort to make her legacy a part of French film history was doomed to fail, and her pupil would soon be forgotten.

She made two further appearances on the stage, both in 1925, first in a Montemartre revue titled *Tu perd la boule* (You lose the ball), then in a London music hall, but her back injury worsened, and she had to give up acting. The rest of the story is more or less known: she cleverly invested her funds in stocks, property, and commercial activities in Paris and Biarritz, married for the third time (to a wealthy Greek businessman), and traveled around the world before her ailment deteriorated so much that she became addicted to drugs and alcohol. At any rate, she never returned to the United States, dividing the rest of her brief life—she died at just forty-nine—between Paris and Cairo.[67] She is buried in the Parisian Cemetery of Passy.

NOTES

1. Ben Singer, *Melodrama and Modernity: Early Sensational Cinema and Its Contexts* (New York: Columbia University Press, 2001), 248–53.

2. Richard Abel, *The Red Rooster Scare: Making Cinema American 1900–1910* (Berkeley: University of California Press, 1999), 173.

3. Charles Goddard's novelization was first issued in serial format during 1914 in the Hearst newspapers and then published the following year in book form as *The Perils of Pauline* (New York: Hearst International Library [1915]). The text is now available online through Project Gutenberg, at http://www.gutenberg.org/ebooks/6065 (accessed December 12, 2012).

4. "Mettre en scène ces serials mais encore imaginer ces abracabrantes aventures. Chacun de ces épisodes se terminait d'une façon angoissante pour les spectateurs. J'était toujours obligé d'inventer 'ce qui devait arriver' et cela n'était pas facile." Quoted in Georges Sadoul, *Histoire général du cinéma*, vol. 3 (Paris: Denoël, 1951), 334. All translations are mine unless otherwise indicated.

5. David Lam, "Marie Marvingt and the Development of Aeromedical Evacuation," *Aviation, Space, and Environmental Medicine* 74, no. 8 (August 2003): 863.

6. Marie Marvingt, "The Intoxication of Flight," paragraph in an article titled "The Sky Women," *Collier's* 8, no. 2 (September 30, 1911): 15.

7. Lam, "Marie Marvingt," 863.

8. Ibid., 864.

9. Ibid.

10. Marie Marvingt, "Comment la Mer du Nord fut traversée en ballon, en pleine tempête, au milieu de la nuit," *Le Petit Journal*, no. 17,132 (November 22, 1909): 1–2.

11. In the only surviving version of the serial, this adventure takes place in the second half of the first episode. Yet according to Shelley Stamp, "There are considerable discrepancies between the original episodes of *The Perils of Pauline* and those that survive in Blackhawk editions released by Grapevine Video. Surviving prints are based not on the original 35mm 1914 release version of *The Perils of Pauline* but on a 28mm version that Pathé recut and rereleased after the initial run. The original twenty

installments were pared down to nine episodes, some of which integrate material from two or three of the original chapters; other material is left out entirely." *Movie-Struck Girls: Women and Motion Picture after the Nickelodeon* (Princeton, N.J.: Princeton University Press, 2000), 228–29n98. An examination of secondary sources shows that Pauline's balloon exploit in fact originally took place in the sixth episode.

12. For this information, and more generally for Marie Marvingt's life, see Rosalie Maggio and Marcel Cordier, *Marie Marvingt: La femme d'un siècle* (Sarreguemines, France: Editions Pierron, 1991), and Eileen F. Lebow, *Before Amelia: Women Pilots in the Early Days of Aviation* (Washington, D.C.: Brassey's, 2002), 35–45. It is noteworthy that in 1934–1935, Marie Marvingt apparently tried her hand at directing two documentary films, *Les Ailes qui sauvent* and *Sauvés par la colombe*, both devoted to the development of the air ambulance service.

13. For an analysis of Elaine's ambiguous heroic status in comparison to that of other female serial characters, see Stamp, *Movie-Struck Girls*, 135–36.

14. See Rudmer Canjels's contribution to this volume, 39.

15. "D'abord femme d'affaires dans le Cabinet du préfet de police de Messénie lorsque lui confie la mission de rapporter le traité secret, femme de monde sous deux visages différents dans l'Orient Express pour s'emparer des papiers diplomatiques du comte de Varello lancé à sa poursuite, acrobate cambrioleuse lors d'un raid nocturne manqué au ministère des Affaires étrangères de Celtie, vieille dame venue presenter une supplique au ministre, aide de camp du même ministre, chef d'un orchestre tzigane féminine lors d'un grand bal, épouse de l'ambassadeur d'Albanie qu'elle a enfermé dans un placard avec sa femme, pompier venu éteindre un incendie . . . allumé par elle-même, dompteuse de lions dans une ménagerie foraine, paysanne prête à porter le bagages d'officier en panne de porteurs. Ce qui lui permet, grâce au contenu desdits bagages, de se travestir en officier de l'armée de Celtie pour regagner la Messénie." Francis Lacassin, *A la poursuite de Protéa* (Saint-Denis-la-Plaine, France: Conseil général de Seine-Saint-Denis, 1995), 4.

16. Annette Förster, "Histories of Fame and Failure—Adriënne Solser, Musidora, Nell Shipman: Women Acting and Directing in the Silent Cinema" (PhD diss., Utrecht University, Netherlands, 2005), 241.

17. "Nature dès longtemps rompue à tous les sports, volonté qui s'impose aux monstres les plus forts," a "Sphynge . . . [qui] va, broyant tout, au nom de son devoir . . . implacable, mortelle, . . . elle est une 'puissance'—et qui sait son pouvoir—à chaque instant, 'une autre,' et pourtant, toujour 'telle'! . . . En se sentant de force à courber le Destin ainsi qu'elle à courbé les hommes et les fauves!" Quoted in Jacques Deslandes, "Victorin-Hippolyte Jasset," in *Anthologie du cinéma*, vol. 9 (Paris: L'Avant-scène du cinéma, 1975), 285.

18. "Protéa, tête baissée sur son guidon, s'élance comme une flèche, bondit, et emportée par son vertigineux élan, franchit la rivière d'un bond fantastique, sous les yeux des policiers ahuris." Ibid.

19. Pier Da Castello, "Protea e l'automobile infernale," *La Vita cinematografica* (July 22, 1914), repr. in "I film della Eclair in Italia," ed. Vittorio Martinelli, special issue, *Immagine*, no. 21 (1992): 22.

20. Jacques Champreux, "Les Films à épisodes de Louis Feuillade," *1895*, special unnumbered issue (October 2000): 140.

21. Musidora's own definition is reported in Sadoul, *Histoire général*, vol. 3, 342.

22. For an analysis of the figure of Musidora/Irma Vep in light of the anxieties raised by the appearance of the *femme nouvelle*—that is, "the modern woman, the career woman, the female shopper, and the working-class woman" as "objects of interest but also distrust"—see Vicki Callahan, *Zones of Anxieties: Movement, Musidora, and the Crime Serials of Louis Feuillade* (Detroit: Wayne State University Press, 2005), 82–83.

23. "Celle-ci était blonde. Elle disparissait et le beau roman commencé avec elle s'achevait avec celle qui la suivait et qui etait brune. Elles ne mouraient que pour renaître. . . . Elle étaient des femmes, des vraies femmes. Leur vie n'était pas médiocre, elle était précieuse et elles la risquaient . . . toutes les pepites du Klondyke n'auraient pas payé la magie de leur fantastique existence. Cent vies n'auraient pu suffire à vivre leur vie." Robert Desnos, "*Les Mystères de New York*" (1929), repr. in *Les Surréalistes et le cinéma*, ed. Alaine Virmaux and Odette Virmaux (Paris: Seghers, 1976), 127.

24. Louis Aragon, "Anicet ou le panorama" (1921), repr. in *Les Surréalistes et le cinéma*, 127.

25. For more information on the editorial operation, see Jean Mitry, *Histoire du cinéma: Art et industrie*, vol. 2 (Paris: Encyclopedie universitaire, 1969), 26–27, and Canjels, *Distributing Silent Serials*, 49–59.

26. Sadoul, *Histoire général du cinéma*, vol. 3, 335.

27. Henri Fescourt, *La Foi et les montagnes* (Paris: Paul Montel, 1959), 137.

28. Between 1915 and 1925, the French market demonstrated a unique receptivity toward foreign serials. Besides the several dozens of American titles, many Italian, German, and British serials were screened during those years. The serial craze of the French film industry was so great that sometimes foreign originals in two or four parts were further divided into a greater number of episodes, such as happened to Fritz Lang's *Die Spinnen*. Originally made in two chapters and transformed for the French market into a ten-episode serial, it was released under the title of *Mysteria*. For more information, see Roger Icart, "Serials et films français à épisodes," in Fédération Internationale du Film, *Le Cinéma français dans le monde: Influences reciproques: Actes du Simposium FIAF 1988* (Toulouse, France: Cinémathèque de Toulouse/Institut Jean Vigo, 1989), 215–25, and Roger Icart, "*Mysteria*: Version française du film de Fritz Lang *Les Airagnées*," *Archives*, no. 74 (1998): 1–15.

29. Paul Gilson, "*Les Mystères de New York*" (1946), repr. in *Les Surréalistes et le cinéma*, 134.

30. Françoise Thébaud, "The Great War and the Triumph of Sexual Division," in *A History of Women in the West*, ed. Françoise Thébaud, vol. 5, *Toward a Cultural Identity in*

the Twentieth Century (Cambridge, Mass: Belknap Press of Harvard University Press, 1994), 39–40, 30.

31. Ibid., 40.

32. On the frenchification of Justin Clarel, and more generally on the complicated operation through which *Les Mystères* was adapted to the French market (by rewriting the intertitles and by offering an original tied-up novelization written by a veteran *feuilletoniste* like Pierre Decourcelle), see Rudmer Canjel's contribution in this volume.

33. "Avec sa jupe de lainage ecossais, son ample chemisette et son grand béret de velours, elle résume l'ideal de toute une jeunesse éprise d'aventures. Les adolescentes—et même des messieurs d'age mûr—rêvent devant sa photographie. Les midinettes copient sur elles pour s'arranger les chevaux et adoptent le béret 'à la Elaine.' C'est la prémiere fois, notons-le, qu'une artiste de cinéma provoque chez les filles d'Eve un important mouvement d'imitation." Marcel Lapierre, *Les Cents Visages du cinéma* (Paris: Grasset, 1948), 136.

34. With the single exception of a poem by Irène Hillel-Erlanger, *Par amour*, after the title of the French edition of *The Lightning Raider*, in *Voyages en kaléidoscope* (1919) (Paris: Allia, 1996), 137–41: "**Joie / d'être soi** / d'être compris / épanoui / *en* / l'atmosphère d'amour! / Don de Sympathie / O génénereuse affectueuse / impétueuse / Inspirée / **Pearl!** / . . . O / donnez-nous / donnez / ce **Rythme** / encore . . . / encore. . . ." "**Joy of being yourself** / understood / blossomed / *in* / a loving atmosphere! / Gift of Sympathy / Oh generous loving / impetuous / Inspired / **Pearl** / Oh give us / give / that **Rythm** / once more . . . / more."

35. "Pearl White me plaît beaucoup. . . . Cinégraphiquement elle est très au point. Son allure et ses gestes—son minimum d'expression—qui n'est pas de l'impuissance—et sa personalité sportive—boxe, cheval, auto, etc.—la rendent tout à fait précieuse pour l'écran. Jeune et jolie elle a une façon de s'habiller qui est jolie et jeune. Les affiches de deux continents ont popularisé le veston noir, la jupe sobre, les guêtres blanches et le petit chapeau qui ne sont que l'une des mille et unes compositions de cette héroine à toute vapeur. Très peu d'actrices ont compris la technique vestimentaire de l'écran. La plupart ont de la prétention et de la lourdeur, pour avoir voulu trop d'agréement. Personne, dans un film d'action, n'a obtenu cette élégante silhouette quasi synthétique de Pearl White." Louis Delluc, "Pearl White" (1918), in *Ecrits cinématographiques II*, ed. Pierre Lherminier (Paris: Cinémathèque Française, 1986), 78–79.

36. See, for instance, the note of July 6, 1919, in which Feuillade's serials are defined as "des crimes encore plus graves que ceux dont les auteurs sont condamné par le Conseil de Guerre" (even greater crimes than those condemned by the War Tribunal). Louis Delluc, untitled review of some of Feuillade's serials, July 6, 1919, in *Ecrits cinématographiques II*, 92.

37. "Le spectacle de ses exploits est meilleur pour la neurasthénie que le génie amer de Charlot [Charlie Chaplin] ou même que la verve—sentimentale et pudique—de

Douglas Fairbanks. Je ne parle pas de l'energie de William Hart où il y a toujours du désespoir. Pearl White, c'est de l'energie et de la verve, et c'est tout. Mai non, qu'est-ce que je dis? C'est de la santé sans arrière-pensée. . . . Ce genre d'héros a toujours charmé les Français. Le panache, la force gracieuse, le succèss ont été et sont adorés. Il n'est donc pas étonnant que Pearl White qui sait tout faire et qui le fait si bien, transporte les spectateurs. Elle aura beaucoup fait pour acclimater l'idée hygiénique du sport dans le public. Au sortir de ses films on a envie de conduire autos et avions, d'aller à cheval, de tirer comme Oeil-de-Faucon, de dancer, de rinker, de nager, de plonger, de tout, de tout, de tout, et l'envie n'est pas très loin de l'exécution. A cause d'elle, beaucoup d'ouvriers songent à l'entretien normal de leur muscles par des sports qu'on les avait habitués à laisser aux riches. L'égalité de la culture physique, déjà proclamée mais guère mise en pratique, a eu là un appui sérieux. Pearl White s'est elle jamais doutée qu'elle faisait oeuvre de socialiste avec ses films innocents?" Delluc, "Pearl White," 78–79.

38. "Nous avons conscience d'avoir travaillé au mieux être de la femme, à quelque classe sociale qu'elle appartienne." Cathérine Louveau, "Inégalité sur la ligne de départ: Femmes, origines sociales et conquête du sport," in "Le Genre du sport," ed. Thierry Terret and Michelle Zancarini-Fournel, special issue, *Clio*, no. 23 (2006), at http://clio.revues.org/document1877.html (accessed December 6, 2012).

39. "Le sport ne doit pas être réservé aux jeunes filles les plus douées, mais au contraire s'adresser aussi à toutes celles plus faibles dans leur constitution physique." Suzanne Liébrard, quoted in Nathalie Rosol, "Le Sport vers le féminisme: L'engagement du milieu athlétique féminin français au temps de la FSFSF (1917–1936)," *STAPS*, no. 66 (Fall 2004): 69.

40. Ernest Coustet, *Le Cinéma* (Paris: Hachette [1921?]), 117.

41. "La femme a le droit d'avoir le goût du sport." Suzanne Liébrard, quoted in Rosol, "Le Sport vers le féminisme," 69.

42. Delluc, "Pearl White," *Ecrits cinématographiques II/2: Le Cinéma au quotidien*, ed. Pierre Lherminier (Paris: Cinémathèque Française, 1990), 66.

43. Delluc, "Par Amour" (1919), in *Ecrits cinématographiques II/2*, 110.

44. "Ces lignes sont un hymne à celle que le grand public appelait par un involontaire calembour *Pearl Vite*, rendend homage à son énergie rapide et à sa riche beauté. Ce qui fait que le théâtre est mort pour nous, c'est sans doute que sa matière unique est la morale, règle de toute action. Notre époque ne peut plus guère s'intéresser à la morale. Au cinéma, la vitesse apparaît dans la vie, et Pearl White n'agit pas pour obéir à sa conscience, mais par sport. Elle agit pour agir." Aragon, "Anicet ou le panorama," 127.

45. "La Révolution d'abord et toujours!," surrealist manifesto, *La Revolution surréaliste*, no. 5 (October 1925): 31–32.

46. "Le type initial de la femme aimée, la figure mêre de l'héroine qui accable les coeurs." Desnos, "*Les Mystères de New York*," 130.

47. "Pearl White fut le symbole des désirs sensuels de toute une géneration que la guerre sevrait de joies légitimes et nécessaires, je parle de la géneration de 1900. . . . A-t-elle su que tant d'amoureux l'évoquaient dans leur solitude? Et, au matin, quand elle s'éveillait, n'avait-elle pas la chair lourde de tant d'étreints idéales, de tant de baisers imaginaires e de la formidable quantité d'aventures que lui avaient fait courir ces jeunes hommes dont elle était à son insu l'esclave? Figure merveilleuses de l'amour, évocations exaltantes, Pearl White multipliée à l'infini régnait sur le monde. Elle hantait toutes ces cerveilles neuves, elle agitait ces sens en fusion." Ibid.

48. "Le maître auquel il fallait obéir, qu'il était honorable de servir et la seule justification de la créature." Ibid., 131.

49. Ibid., 130.

50. Louis Argon and André Breton, quoted in Sadoul, *Histoire général du cinéma*, vol. 3, 344.

51. "Tout ce que nous pouvions accorder de fidelité allait aux films à épisodes dejà si decriés. . . . A partir de samedi, sur cet écran, xix:—*Le Gant qui rampe*—Comptez absolument sur nous." Andre Breton, "Comme dans un bois" (1951), repr. in *Les Surréalistes et le cinéma*, 279. English translation in *The Shadow and Its Shadow: Surrealist Writings on the Cinema*, ed. Paul Hammond (London: British Film Institute, 1991), 73.

52. "Nous ne comprenions pas ce qui se passait. Nous vivions avec rapidité, avec passion." Philippe Soupault, "Le Cinéma U.S.A." (1923), in *Ecrits de cinema, 1818–1931*, ed. Alain Virmaux and Odette Virmaux (Paris: Plon, 1979), 42. English translation in Hammond, ed., *Shadow and Its Shadow*, 56.

53. "L'argent. Il pris possession des écrans et des studios. Il s'effraya, lui, le podagre et le goinfre, de ces amoureuses en liberté." Desnos, "*Les Mystères de New York*," 131.

54. "Nous marchions dans les rues froids et désertes à la recherche d'un accident, d'une rencontre, de la vie. Il fallait pour se distraire atteler l'imagination aux rêves sensationnels. Les journaux qui son plus colorés encore que les cartes géographiques nous distrayaient un instant. On parcourait pour quelques sous le monde entier et on assistait aux drames merveilleux et sanglants qui illuminent un instant certains points du globe. Nous avions soif, terriblement soif de cette vie étrange et fort, de cette vie que nous buvions comme du lait. . . . Un jour on vit de grandes affiches longues comme des serpents s'étaler sur les murs. A chaque coin de rue, un homme, la figure couverte d'un mouchoir rouge, braquait un revolver sur les paisibles passants. On croyait entendre des galopades, des ronflements de moteur, des vrombissements et des cris de mort. Nous nous précipitâmes dans les cinémas et nous comprîmes que tout était changé. Le sourire de Pearl White apparut sur l'écran; ce sourire presque féroce annonçait les bouleversements du nouveau monde." Soupault, "Le Cinéma U.S.A.," 42. English translation in Hammond, *Shadow and Its Shadow*, 55–56.

55. Soupault, "Le Cinéma U.S.A.," 42.

56. "Pearl White en avion," *Le Petit Journal illustré*, no. 1585 (May 8, 1921), 1.

57. According to Eve Golden, the false news had been reported to the American

press by Pearl's friend Texas Guinan, but unfortunately Golden did not provide the source for this information. Golden, *Golden Images: 41 Essays on Silent Film Stars* (Jefferson, N.C.: McFarland, 2001), 203.

58. "Il est difficile d'imaginer Pearl White au couvent, après l'avoir vue dans ses films d'abord, et dernièrement encore, si jeune, si sportive, s'avançant sur la scène avec la désinvolture d'un boy américain, et tous les cinéphiles se réjouirant de cette certitude, qu'après un repos physique et moral, Pearl White reprendra la carrière cinématographique qui lui valut et lui réserve encore tant de succès." GLYM, "Eclipse d'étoile: Pearl White ne quitte le studio que momentanément," *Mon Ciné*, no. 55 (March 8, 1923), 11.

59. L. d'H., "*Terreur* avec Pearl White," *Le Cinéopse*, no. 55 (March 1924): 261.

60. James Williard, "Un film attendu: *Terreur*," *Cinémagazine*, no. 13 (March 23, 1924): 15. See also "Pearl White dans *Terreur*," *Cine Miroir*, no. 49 (May 1, 1924): 17–19. Unfortunately, I did not have a chance to see this film, which apparently still survives in a fragmentary version, as referred by Eve Golden, who defines it as "more amateurish than *The Perils of Pauline*." See Golden, *Golden Images*, 203.

61. "C'était un studio 'clair' et j'arrivais à persuader son propriétaire qu'il fallait le noircir. Il acquiesça à mon désir et je m'occupais dès lors d'avoir la lumière, toute la lumière nécessaire à la confection d'un film dont la photographie serait impeccable." Pearl White, "Comment j'ai tourné *Terreur*," *Mon Ciné*, no. 110 (March 27, 1924): 17.

62. "Il s'agit d'un film français sous toutes ses formes," based on "des élements français et des capitaux français." Ibid.

63. "Dans tout l'éclat de son ascendant de star: souple, élégante, sportive, infinitement sympathique." L. d'H., "*Terreur* avec Pearl White," 261.

64. "Une élève à laquelle elle apprendra les secrets de son art." G. A., "Miss Pearl White demande à *Comœdia* de lui procurer une élève à laquelle elle apprendra les secrets de son art," *Comœdia*, no. 3927 (September 18, 1923): 1.

65. "J'aime beaucoup la France, comme vous l'avez si bien écrit. Oui, réellement, je l'aime beaucoup. J'adore votre pays et tous vos compatriotes. Mais je voudrais voir dans vos théâtres cinématograhiques une miss qui serait speciale. . . . Je prenderais volontiers une élève, à laquelle j'apprendrais un métier que je crois posséder à fond. . . . J'exige seulement beaucoup de patience, beaucoup de travail et surtout pas de timidité inutile. Il faudrait aussi . . . comme dire . . . des sports, beaucoup de sport. . . . J'ose espérer qu'avec mon appui, elle trouvera facilement à assurer son avenir." "En France il n'y eût pas d'interprète cinématographique *specialisée* dans . . . de créations à la 'Pearl White.'" Ibid. See also the following article in the coverage thread: J.-L. C. [Jean-Louis Croze], "L'Elève de Pearl White," *Comœdia*, no. 3968 (October 29, 1923): 3.

66. See Karen Offen, *European Feminisms 1700–1950: A Political History* (Stanford, Calif.: Stanford University Press, 2000), 251–56.

67. For a well-informed overview of Pearl White's life, see Golden, *Golden Images*, 198–204.

CHAPTER 4

"The Most Assassinated Woman in the World"

Pearl White and the First Avant-Garde

CHRISTINA PETERSEN

In the final moments of the first segment of Jean Epstein's film, *La Glace à trois faces* (The three-sided mirror [1927]), the wayward and cruel protagonist pens a dismissive note to his current love interest. "Pearl," he writes, "for my peace of mind, I need a change of scenery. You are as old-fashioned as your first name. I've had enough. I'll see you the day after tomorrow." Although Epstein lifted this dialogue wholesale from Paul Morand's original story, it aptly sums up the filmmaker's own thoughts about another Pearl, perhaps the most famous in film history: the serial star Pearl White.[1] Epstein's negative reaction to White's famous "blood-and-thunderish" serial melodramas, which included *The Perils of Pauline* (1914), *The Exploits of Elaine* (1914), and *The Romance of Elaine* (1915), could simply be explained as a function of the first European avant-garde's more general interest in futurism and antitraditionalism, since by 1921 serials represented a style and type of film that was already passé, even for commercial filmmaking.[2] Such a generalization, however, does not account for fellow impressionist filmmaker Louis Delluc's praise for White as a photogenic icon of cinematic socialism and the surrealists' later valorization of White as a marvelous emblem of modernity who possessed the uncanny ability to realize dream images on the screen. Epstein's retention of Morand's dialogue, then—that the young protagonist will see Pearl "the day after tomorrow"—also points to White's dual status as a figure the first avant-garde would both relegate to the past and return to as a symbol of cinema's forgotten future.

At first glance, much like Epstein's and Delluc's differing takes on White, the avant-garde's reactions to her appear to have vacillated according to each theorist's position on the role of narrative in the art of cinema. However, upon further examination they prove to fall largely along movement lines. At once the embodiment of a low-culture narrative mode and a spectacular star object who transcended any particular plot line (as well as a paradoxical representation of "healthy" modern human existence defined by a perpetual state of mortal peril), Pearl White's pejorative status as "the most assassinated woman in the world" may have been more revealing than Epstein originally intended. Although Epstein decried her constant near-death experiences and numerous last-minute escapes as unrealistic pulp fiction, for Delluc and the surrealists, White's continual success in cheating death on the screen typified exactly what made cinema an art in its own right: the camera's ability to discover the inner life of objects and enliven the inanimate. Delluc and Epstein would term this general uncanny quality *photogénie*, while the surrealists celebrated Pearl White as a "marvelous" apparition. From these responses, it is apparent that White's extraordinary star body could not be wholly divorced from her body of work. Although she constituted both a narrative and a photogenic object for the avant-garde, she was never merely objectified, a consequence of her dichotomous status as singular female star who stood in for both an entire genre and helped to define the first European avant-garde's relationship to American film culture.

Pearl's Impression on the Impressionists

While film historians Jennifer Bean and Ben Singer have noted the resonances between serial queen melodramas of the 1910s and futurism's call for the construction of an entirely new subject (in which the quotidian imbrication of life with death was a necessary component of survival in the modern world), the French impressionists took up White herself as a critical object who illustrated the movement's most famous concept: *photogénie*.[3] In "Pearl White," published in *Paris-Midi* (June 8, 1918), Delluc waxed lyrical about White's film persona as a young, pretty, and athletic girl who knew how to dress for the screen to emphasize her youth and vigor.[4] This sartorial enhancement reinforced Delluc's view that White's daring escapades served to underscore her intrinsic morality, where White's physicality functioned as an outward sign of her "moral power," just as "the spectacle of her exploits is better for neurasthenia than the bitter genius of Chaplin or the verve . . . of Douglas Fairbanks."[5] White's ever-constant ability to cheat death, often represented by modern means (railroad locomotives, hot air balloons, and airplanes, to name a few), thus offered a healthy vision of how to deal with the shocks and horrors of the "hyperstimulating" modern world teeming with the excessive stimuli of overcrowding, increasing urbanization, and mechanization and the general rapidity of modern life.[6]

Delluc here echoed Georg Simmel's, Siegfried Kracauer's, and Walter Benjamin's views on the neurological and nervous effects of modernity on the human subject, as well as Singer's argument that the "popular sensationalism" that typified serial queen melodramas "both compensated for and mimicked the frenzied, disjointed texture of modern life."[7] However, Delluc discounted the filmic image's mimicry of the experience of modern existence in favor of Pearl White's mimetic effect on the serial spectator. For Delluc saw White as an innocent who braved the treacherous modern world "without an ulterior motive. Here is a young girl who carries herself well: she does all that she can to make us feel better, she does all this to prove that we may as well."[8] Much like Bean's assertion that the White serials engendered a mimetic rather than desiring spectatorial relationship to the star, Delluc lauded White for depicting a social type usually thought to be powerless—"a young girl"—as able not only to survive, but thrive in the modern environment, thereby giving spectators an image of agency in a world in which things seemed increasingly out of their control.[9] Delluc took this claim one step further, asserting that White's onscreen agency served as an identification point not only for the individual spectator but for an entire social class. He discerned an underlying socialist message in her films, since "because of her, many workers consider the normal maintenance of their muscles through sports that one had become accustomed to leaving to the rich. Equality in physical culture, already proclaimed but hardly put into practice, had, in her, serious support."[10] In this sense, Delluc appears to have considered the inherent moral message of Pearl White and her films to be their subversive potential to suggest something other than the capitalist system that produced them and that they purported to uphold.

From this brief consideration, Delluc's view of Pearl White is strikingly similar to Bean's much more recent argument concerning serial stars of the 1910s. In his focus on White's spectacular modern body and its effect on the spectator, Delluc also invited us to ask, as Bean puts it, "whether the subject's relations with others, its encounter with the screen, and its position in the modern world may be better understood in corporeal rather than conscious terms."[11] Both Delluc and Bean argue that spectators identified with White not because she transcended her body, but rather because she fully inhabited and reclaimed it for the modern subject. Delluc then drew on this initial consideration of White in his later work on the concept of *photogénie*. In "Masked Faces" (1918), appearing only four months after "Pearl White," Delluc discussed the overall transformative aspects of cinema, describing film as "an impenetrable mask that covers the face."[12] This film-mask did not conceal so much as it revealed what was inherent within the object filmed. For Delluc, such masks "only give character to those which already possess it. According to the type chosen, they only show or attenuate this character."[13] He then gave the specific example of Bessie Love and the cinema-mask's ability to "transform her just enough so that she is *completely* herself."[14] Along with Pearl White's wardrobe and her spectacular stunts, Delluc now attributed to the cinema in general the ability to discern the intrinsic character of the filmic object. He ended the essay with the invocation, "Mary Pickford, Fanny Ward, *Pearl White*, Bessie Love, Mae Murray are, do not forget, masks."[15]

Two years later, Delluc would expand this idea to include objects other than the face and would reconceptualize these "masks" as *photogénie*. In his 1920 essay of the same name, Delluc defined *photogénie* as "the science of light schemes for the recording eye of the cinema,"[16] that is, how light falls on certain objects and how we respond to their registration on film. According to Delluc, this "science" constituted the very essence of the art of film. He even granted the art of the cinema ancient roots when he dated the phenomenon of *photogénie* from the moment humans first looked at their reflection in a pool of water.[17] In this vein, Delluc faulted the choices of misguided film directors, rather than their filmic objects, for the fact that not everything depicted on film offered moments of *photogénie*, since so many directors attempted to alter the underlying character of the people and objects placed before the camera rather than allow the camera to discover their innate traits. Such attempts at conscious transformation were "wasteful of the beautiful subject," since they usually failed where *photogénie* succeeded unconsciously. *Photogénie* thus replaced "masks" as Delluc's new term for film's ability to reveal what the naked eye alone could not discern. Delluc himself reinforced such a reading when he repeated, almost verbatim, his declaration from "Masked Faces" in "Photogénie": "Believe that Pearl White, Mary Miles, Mary Pickford, are what they are."[18]

In this formulation, White's photogenic qualities stemmed from the fact that the camera enhanced her true nature, and for Delluc, she became representative of the American cinema's triumph in this area. As opposed to Italian film, the Americans "made portraits as beautiful and more beautiful, and they discovered, understood, realized the *photogénie* of things: the lifeless things of nature and inanimate objects made by man."[19] In the case of White, the camera's ability to give life to the lifeless—to animate—through *photogénie* was twofold: not only in the way her youthful and energetic body became animated on the screen as she constantly cheated death, but also in the way her performances enlivened filmic spectators deadened by modern existence.

By contrast, Epstein took a relatively dim view of Pearl White, since for him she failed to transcend the serial narratives that Delluc viewed as merely opportunities for her athletic escapades. In "The Senses (b)" (1921) he warned, "There's a dreadful danger in not knowing chalk from cheese. And duped the sages were in not realizing sooner that those popular, foolish (that goes without saying), novelettish, blood-and-thunderish, serialized Exploits of Elaine characterize a period, a style, a civilization. No longer, thank goodness, in vogue. Good yarns that go on endlessly and then start all over again. *Les Trois Mousquetaires, Fantômas, Du côté de chez Swann*, and this one with the extra-dry American flavor. The most assassinated woman in the world."[20] Epstein considered White and her oeuvre hopelessly out-of-date, much like Louis Feuillade's *Fantômas* (1913) and Henri Diamant-Berger's *Les Trois Mousquetaires* (1921), as "good yarns that go on endlessly and then start all over again."[21] For Epstein, the repetitive nature of White's perilous stunts represented the interchangeability of these narratives and thus signaled their antiquated status. As "the most assassinated woman in the world," Pearl White's body became not spectacular but mundane, since one could predict the cliffhanger climaxes of her serials. The rote quality of White's films was further reinforced by the fact that their plots were published in weekly episodes that appeared in advance of each film chapter's debut. Such fictional tie-ins constituted a large part of serial queen melodramas' popularity in the United States in the 1910s, since rather than functioning as spoilers for the films, they served as complementary intertexts for the film viewer, often reiterating backstories from previous chapters that the films eschewed.[22] In 1915 Pathé imported this practice for the French market along with three of White's most famous serials—*The Exploits of Elaine, The New Exploits of Elaine* (1915), and *The Romance of Elaine*—and repackaged them as the twenty-two-episode *Les Mystères de New York* (The mysteries of New York [1915–1916]), concurrently serialized by Pierre Decourcelle (with illustrations from the film) in the Paris daily *Le Match*.[23]

White's association with narrative form therefore extended well beyond the film screen and, for Epstein, tainted her films since they mixed art forms.

He in fact pointedly mentioned Decourcelle's print version of *Les Mystères de New York* to highlight White's films' failure to adhere to the specificity of the medium as he defined it.[24] As opposed to Delluc's valorization of White for transcending the narrative significance of her films to represent the essence of cinema, Epstein decried the importation of the literary narrative form into film and called for casting it aside to create a tabula rasa of "a new poetry and philosophy. We need an eraser to efface such styles, and then start constructing afresh. But are we capable of so much amputation? Neither wit, nor plot, nor theater. *The Exploits of Elaine*—it is easier today to admit that one did see a few episodes—is not simply a farrago of cliff-hanging semidenouements, or Monsieur Decourcelle would happily have buried it. Generally speaking, the cinema does not render stories well."[25] Epstein's aversion to narrative in film struck at the heart of what he considered the "truth" of art, whereby "the cinema is true; a story is false" because narratives are not true to life.[26] Epstein argued that stories were unrealistic to the way that life in general, and especially that in modernity, actually unfolded. Rather than the linear development of a single plot line toward a definite ending, Epstein emphasized the multiplicity of angles from which one could look at a single event. For him, "there are only situations, having neither head nor tail; without beginning, middle, or end, no right side or wrong side; they can be looked at from all directions; right becomes left; without limits in past or future, they are the present."[27] We can see this at work both in his own filmmaking practice, in his efforts to sideline a conventional melodramatic plot in *Coeur fidèle* (1923), as well as in his own theorization of *photogénie*.

Later, in "The Senses," Epstein turned from his dislike for action-packed melodramas to those films he did enjoy. Further underscoring his interest, in the name of realism, in the mundane rather than the spectacular. Epstein declared his desire for "films in which not so much nothing as nothing very much happens."[28] Chaplin and Sessue Hayakawa stood out in this regard for their ability to suspend narrative through performance, and in particular, how Hayakawa "sweeps the scenario aside" with the expressive movements of his body, not just his face.[29] Such a view observed the same lines as Delluc's theorization of *photogénie*, and Epstein published his own ruminations on the concept three years later. In "On Some Characteristics of *Photogénie*" (1924), Epstein further defined the term as "any aspect of things, beings, or souls whose moral character is enhanced by filmic reproduction."[30] This definition closely followed Delluc's in its emphasis on the camera's power to discern a different quality than the naked eye as well as its ability to uncover a new visual aspect of a commonplace object. However, while Delluc argued that such defamiliarization allowed filmed objects to demonstrate their true qualities masked by the naked eye, White failed as a photogenic object for Epstein for the same reason that he considered her as a filmic object best left in the past: her unfaithful affiliation with print narrative.

In general, Epstein argued, "the cinema should avoid dealings, which can only be unfortunate, with historical, educational, novelistic, moral or immoral, geographical, or documentary subjects. The cinema must seek to become, gradually and in the end uniquely, cinematic; to employ, in other words, only photogenic elements. *Photogénie* is the purest expression of cinema."[31] Based on this declaration, Epstein then attempted to chart what he considered would be the future of cinema as a medium purified, not of all other artistic influences, but of those of the representative arts. Epstein saw film's future not as an art aimed at depicting reality as one encountered it in the everyday, but to expose a new reality, "a reality for a special occasion, which is untrue to everyday reality just as everyday reality is untrue to the heightened awareness of poetry."[32] Like fellow avant-garde filmmakers Germaine Dulac, Hans Richter, and Viking Eggeling, Epstein looked to the abstract arts of poetry and music as models for film to emulate, since both revealed a new way of looking at things through their use of metaphor and rhythm.[33] Metaphor became an important concept in this regard, as Epstein emphasized *photogénie*'s supernatural ability to confer life on the inanimate by discovering its inherent personality, or for Delluc, its underlying character. In Epstein's formulation, a revolver captured on film became not just another object for use but a "revolver-character" that represented "the impulse toward or remorse for crime, failure, suicide. It is as dark as the temptations of the night, bright as the gleam of gold lusted after, taciturn as passion, squat, brutal, heavy, cold, wary, menacing. It has a temperament, habits, memories, a will, a soul."[34]

For Epstein, the camera could not transform White in the same way as a revolver, since the spectator who read Decourcelle's print serial encountered not only the film serial's narrative but also White's image in conjunction with the text. In fact, the complete, novelized version of Decourcelle's serial advertised it as "adapted by Pierre Decourcelle and illustrated by the film" and included an image of White as protagonist Elaine Dodge, which suggests the power of these images embedded within the text as well as those on the film screen to draw an audience. Singer further notes that such fiction tie-ins often achieved "a kind of photo-novella effect" due to the prevalence of filmic illustrations that doubled rather than supplemented those in the film.[35] For Epstein then, White came to exemplify the deplorable narrativized filmic image as well as an iconic nonphotogenic image of narrative. Yet his reference to her only further serves to underscore her important role in defining both Epstein's and the impressionist movement's concepts of *photogénie* and the cinema as an art form.

A Warm Surrealist Serial Reception

While Epstein ended his 1924 essay on *photogénie* by invoking Apollinaire's term *surreal* in relation to cinema's status as "poetry's most powerful medium," later adherents of surrealism received Pearl White much differently than Delluc and Epstein, although they considered her along the same lines.[36] Like Delluc, the surrealists registered White in relation both to her actual film image and the spectator's reception of it, and like Epstein they viewed her as a representative of cinema's past who existed concurrently in print and on the screen. Yet the surrealists differed from both Delluc and Epstein in that they did not prize her as a star who transcended any particular film's plot or denigrate her as an emblem of the cinematic art's derailment through narrative. Instead, the surrealists loved White as a narrative and theoretical star object but in a different fashion than male stars like Chaplin or Buster Keaton. In "On Decor" (1918), poet Louis Aragon gave *photogénie* a surrealist twist, acknowledging not only the power of the camera to transform objects into characters but also to transform characters (especially those played by stars) into automata. He viewed the decor of a Chaplin film as more than merely the setting and props in and around which the comedic action took place, but as "Charlie's very vision of the world which, together with the discovery of the mechanical and its laws, haunts the hero to such an extent that by an inversion of values each inanimate object becomes a living thing for him, each human person a dummy whose starting-handle must be found."[37] In addition, the surrealists, like Delluc, adored White not as an erotic object, like fellow female serial star Musidora, but rather as an apparition from the past, a cinematic dream image who haunted the present of a society revolutionized by the death machines of mechanized warfare. Indeed, the greatest difference between the impressionists' and the surrealists' reception of Pearl White lay in the latter's exploration of World War I's influence on modern society as demonstrated in her films.

Seen through the lens of World War I, White's death-defying stunts became not just representative of a more general modern "new heroic personhood freed from the laws of physics" but also of a new generation that, according to Benjamin, "had gone to school in horse-drawn streetcars [and] now stood in the open air, amid a landscape in which nothing was the same except clouds and, at its center, in a force field of destructive torrents and explosions, the tiny, fragile human body."[38] For Benjamin as well as the surrealists, the Great War had brought with it a general devaluing of past life experience due to the vast upheavals in the social, economic, and political world that were registered on the visceral level. White figured prominently in this new world for surrealist poet Robert Desnos, who noted that "across the deserted streets of Paris, then in the grip of a bellicose madness, under a sky lacerated by searchlights and artillery shell explosions, as we sought the privilege of shadowy adventures of love, did you know that, in our desire for escape and evasion, we rediscovered that privilege in the wake of Pearl White, in the touring cars of *Les Mystères de New York*, and the mock battles between bogus policemen and stupendous bandits?"[39] The surrealists followed Delluc in viewing Pearl White as a symbol of humanity's successful struggle with modern existence, as her films afforded the chance to experience "the shadowy adventures of love." They also saw her as a representative of the marvelous, mysterious, and fantastic aspects of cinema due to the outdated nature of the episodic serial queen melodrama after World War I, with its cliffhanger endings and athletic female stars. While Delluc praised the life-affirming aspects of White's serials, the surrealists, by contrast, focused on her supernatural qualities as the star of an old-fashioned cinematic form that represented a different path film might have taken before the feature's single-showing narrative structure took hold.[40]

In "The Marvelous Is Popular" (1963), filmmaker and critic Ado Kyrou followed André Breton in describing the surrealist notion of the "marvelous" as a form of nostalgia as well as kitsch, in which "those privileged in the marvelous exist no more," suggesting that the early surrealists' love for White and the serial queen melodramas of the 1910s was perhaps predicated more on resurrecting her as an icon of film's forgotten future rather than on solely celebrating her ability to animate both her own body and that of the spectator.[41] Such revivals were often literal—Desnos discussed the effect of a showing of *Les Mystères de New York* in a Paris movie theater in 1929—as well as figurative, but they both represented the avant-garde's interest in registering the war's influence on modern society from within popular culture.[42] In the wake of the rise of the feature film and the Hollywood studio system, the surrealists lauded that which transcended the mundane, which because of their temporal cushion included the French and American serials from their youth. Serials became "marvelous" for the surrealists for their "hint of other-worldliness," not only of other places and other ways of living, but of the earlier time in which they were produced.[43] In particular, though, the surrealists "began to idolize everything that went against the standards of bourgeois morality," such as Delluc's "socialist" Pearl White serials, which simultaneously signified the past while also commenting on the present.[44]

In one of the earliest surrealist invocations of White, "Cinema U.S.A." (1924), the poet Philippe Soupault likened the experience of watching a film to that of a "sensational dream" in which, among other images, "Pearl White's smile appeared on the screen; this almost ferocious smile announced the upheavals of the new world."[45] For Soupault, White was not only a representative of the modern "New Woman" marked by "energy, self-reliance, [and] direct contact with the extradomestic world" but also the harbinger of a new era in which newspaper stories about "crimes, departures, wonders" became the "poetry of [the] age."[46] In this sense, Soupault's reception of White's serial queen melodramas became not a means to reconnect with one's own modern alienated body; rather, her films themselves represented this decorporealization. Soupault prized White's smile as opposed to her entire body, suggesting a fragmentation not just of the modern subject but also of the modern body that the cinema could best represent specifically through its use of close-up and montage. This emphasis on fragmentation typified the surrealist approach to moviegoing in general in which the mood of the individual images of a particular film or serial episode outweighed the narrative whole. Soupault himself reported in 1931 that he "liked *Fantômas* a great deal. But what attracted me in these works was much more the strange poetry, the mysterious atmosphere they expressed than the 'elevated' deeds and exploits of policemen."[47]

André Breton further described the well-known surrealist version of moviegoing as dropping "into the cinema when whatever was playing was playing, at any point in the show, and leaving at the first hint of boredom—of surfeit—to rush off to another cinema where we behaved the same way."[48] Nevertheless, while Soupault and Breton both emphasized that they went to see any film at all (and no film in particular) and left whenever the images began to make sense, they also singled out certain films that held the surrealists' attention. For both Soupault and Breton, the serials of the 1910s were privileged texts: "All we could grant of fidelity used to go to those serials previously so decried (*The Exploits of Elaine*, *The Laughing Mask*, *Les Vampires*): 'Beginning on Saturday, on this screen, episode XIX: "The Creeping Glove"—You can count on us.'"[49] What drew the surrealists to serials, in addition to the serial queen melodrama's ability to represent the upheavals of modern life in the modern medium of film, was that they offered the experience of disruptive surrealist moviegoing within a single text. For serials' very episodic and paratactic nature allowed the surrealists to experience a film that was already fragmented before they entered the theater. Breton considered serials marvelous for their representation of the power of cinema in general to disorient the viewer, since "the marvel, besides which the merits of a given film count for little, resides in the devolved faculty of the first-comer to abstract himself from his own life when he feels like it" when he set foot into the movie theater.[50]

Aragon further linked the surrealist practice of dropping into movie theaters with Pearl White in his 1921 novel, *Anicet ou le panorama*, in which the main characters Anicet (modeled on Aragon himself) and Baptiste (based on Breton) go to the movies on a weekday afternoon and loudly voice their opinions about the images onscreen.[51] Not unlike Delluc, Anicet prefers film to theater because it eschews morality, since "in the cinema, speed appears in life, and Pearl White does not act to obey her conscience, but for sport, for hygiene: she acts to act."[52] Anicet considers White's films as sites where movement—both on-screen and off—is paramount, where White's actions excite and impassion the spectator, who barely has time to think, let alone to discuss. For him, Pearl White's films constitute "the spectacle that is appropriate to the century."[53] By contrast, Baptiste argues that the spectacles offered by White's films are debilitating because they place the spectators in a passive position, thereby sapping their life force. He claims that Pearl White acts so that Anicet doesn't have to: "You search for the elements of lyricism by accident, the spectacle of intense action that you give yourself the illusion of accomplishing; under the pretext of satisfying your modern need to act, you passively satiate by placing yourself in the most grievous school of inaction in the world: the screen before which, everyday, for a tiny sum, the young people of this time come to waste their energy watching others live."[54] However, while Baptiste takes a dim view of serials in this regard, his description of their function in the lives of their spectators is very much a surrealist one. For the passivity of the spectators who give themselves over to their onscreen surrogate in a darkened room parallels that of a subject dreaming.[55] As Breton himself discussed in "The Manifesto of Surrealism" (1924), one of surrealism's primary goals was to dissolve the barrier between dreams and reality, in which one was not merely an interval in the absence of the other, but rather a "future resolution of these two states, dream and reality, which are seemingly so contradictory, into a kind of absolute reality, a *surreality*, if one may so speak."[56] In the case of the surrealists, White and her oeuvre became a model for the type of conscious hallucination that the surrealists were attempting to achieve in other arts. The serial queen melodrama's ability to eschew logic in favor of visual stimulation therefore allowed spectators to regress, not only to a state of passivity as for Aragon's Baptiste, but also to an earlier time both in their lives and film history in which the relationship between narrative and logic was still fluid.

"Love and Poetry": Putting Pearl into Practice

Desnos in particular was taken with the revolutionary potential of the cinema located in its oneiric qualities, not only in film's ability to represent the unconscious, but also as a dream for the future state of the world. In "*Fantômas, Les Vampires, Les Mystères de New York*" (1927), he likened the darkened theater to a bedroom and the potential of the screen to become "the equal of our dreams." He went on to state that "three films fulfilled this mission: *Fantômas*, for revolt and liberty; *Les Vampires*, for love and sensuality; *Les Mystères de New York*, for love and poetry."[57] Desnos loved these three serials for the fact that they possessed the ability, perhaps due to their narrative openness and spectacular elements, to invade the spectator's dreams. In particular, he privileged *Fantômas* for its evocation of the modern streets of Paris, both in reality and "in the depths of our dreams" and extolled the charms of Musidora in *Les Vampires* for visiting the bedrooms of the spectators who dreamed about her as well as the bedrooms she literally infiltrated in her films.[58] However, in the case of Pearl White, Desnos saw an image of life and love that allowed the surrealists to rediscover a sensuality long thought lost to the horrors of war. Such a view recast White as a dream image, not only of the past but of the future, whose constant brushes with death could innervate the film spectator. The sensual became for Desnos the most radical alternative to modern life that the cinema could offer, since "to the sensual . . . belong the deepest revolutionary pleasures, the legitimate perversions of love and poetry" that he found in *Les Mystères de New York*.[59]

Desnos's view of White's serial queen melodramas, as opposed to *Fantômas* and *Les Vampires*, was therefore oriented more toward the production of a new life praxis, following Peter Bürger's recounting of the primary goals of the European avant-garde, since the surrealists refused "to consider the spectacle of the screen other than as the representation of the life we desire, with the same status as our dreams."[60] Desire here took on a different valence than that which Desnos professed for the beautiful Musidora; following Bean, it became mimetic, although not solely on the corporeal level. Desnos suggested that the mimetic desire engendered by *Les Mystères de New York* was also a desire for mimesis that would bring the world of the cinema and the world outside of the theater closer together, in which movies should "exalt what is dear to us and only what is dear to us; why we wish that the cinema would be revolutionary."[61] However, what shape such a "revolutionary" cinema would take thirteen years after serial queen melodramas ruled the screen remained the real mystery of New York.

Two years later Desnos took up this question again, only this time concerning himself solely with Pearl White and her films. In "*Les Mystères de New York*" (1929), Desnos continued his consideration of cinema as the best means of representing the modern era, in which the hero "vanquished yesterday, vanquished tomorrow, resuscitates each day through his own blood and tears" in search of the love that seemed to have been eradicated by modernity.[62] He traced this sensual rebirth directly to White, whom he considered the "figurative mother of the heroine who overwhelms the heart of the ravaged Don Juan" in contemporary cinema.[63] In Desnos's estimation, White not only constituted a mother figure for the thirty-year-old men who learned to love from watching her image on the screen; she also served as a stand-in for other female stars for whom the surrealists professed a markedly more erotic love.[64] Desnos viewed White and her international contemporaries, Musidora and Nazimova, as three representations of the same dream image on the screen for whom the normal rules of life, law, and love did not apply. These female stars lived life to the fullest as "true women" who truly appreciated the precious nature of life and did not concern themselves with conventional morality and traditional ideas of femininity.[65] However, while the films of White, Musidora, and Nazimova offered a different depiction of women, in the case of White and Musidora especially, their films also represented a different form for cinema itself.

For Desnos the serial did not simply signify a cinematic form best left in the past as it did for Epstein, but rather an alternate path for film that obeyed the "master" of love rather than capital. Like Delluc, Desnos deplored the rule of capital in cinema, citing it as the reason for the demise of the serial queen melodrama. For, in the place of love, "a new master appeared: money. It took possession of the screen and the studios. Capital was frightened . . . of the lovers of freedom. The former disappeared, the latter no longer produce the rare apparitions in films."[66] Yet according to Desnos, when seen again fifteen years later, *Les Mystères de New York* still possessed the power to impassion the spectator despite its poor production values in comparison with those of contemporary films. Desnos noted the film's "naive" mise-en-scène, mediocre cinematography, and ingenuous script while praising the editing as preferable to that of feature films. Desnos found the film's découpage "marvelous" because while it "made use there, certainly, of a certain number of strings, they were better than the steel wire ropes of our current scenario writers."[67] Here, Desnos referred to the weak narrative thread, or "strings," that held the serial together, especially since *Les Mystères de New York* had been edited together from three different serials (albeit for commercial purposes), as opposed to the "steel wire ropes" of the psychologically motivated narratives of classical Hollywood cinema. This particular view followed the surrealists' general interest in serials as narratives strung together much like a filmic string of pearls (or, in the case of *Les Mystères*, a string of Pearls) in which one could easily break and then restring the narrative chain without disturbing its effect on the spectator.[68]

Moreover, Desnos and the surrealists did not merely admire Pearl White in print; they also attempted to transpose the "love and poetry" of her films into their own filmmaking practice.[69] In addition to Salvador Dalí's 1935 homage to *Les Mystères de New York* in his speculative scenario, drawings, and painting for the speculative film project "Les Mystères surrealistes de New York" (The surrealist mystery of New York [1935]), Desnos wrote the poem that became the basis for Man Ray's *L'Etoile de mer* (The star of the sea [1928]) and appeared in the film whose focus on the female body, disorienting images of starfish, and tenuous narrative thread suggests an affinity with a filmmaking style more in line with episodic serials than with classical Hollywood cinema.[70] In 1929 George Hugnet, surrealist poet and artist, and Henri d'Ursel (under the pseudonym Henri d'Arches), cinephile and fellow traveler of the surrealists, collaborated on *La Perle* (The pearl [1929]), a film that similarly aspired "to respect a realism that borders on the poetry of the dream" and "to locate poetry in the cinema" rather than achieve the "qualification of poetry."[71] Steven Kovács has argued that the impact of female serial film stars, especially Musidora, influenced Hugnet to feature "a group of similarly clad women" as well as a pearl necklace in *La Perle*, further suggesting a direct link between avant-garde film criticism and avant-garde film practice.[72]

La Perle does not so much tell a story as recount the narrative of a dream, both figuratively and literally. The film opens with scenes of a pearl diver retrieving a pearl and then quickly cuts to a young woman in a garden who "exemplifies the loveliness and graciousness of the classic fiancée of peasant novels."[73] The next cut is to a young man traveling to the city, alternately paddling a canoe, riding a tricycle, and striding purposefully until he finally reaches his destination, a jewelry shop, where he examines a pearl necklace. However, the necklace he wishes to purchase suddenly disappears from the display case and then reappears in the stocking of one of the saleswomen, who is discharged for her scandalous theft after it is discovered. The saleswoman and the young man next reunite on a country road just before the necklace's string breaks, scattering the pearls in all directions. The largest and most perfect of the pearls rolls by the saleswoman's foot and she cannot resist it, lodging it in her stocking once again. Due to her theft, the young man spends the rest of the day searching for the lost pearl, finally falling asleep on the ground. He dreams that he finds the saleswoman, chases her through the country, and then strangles her—his hands encircling her neck like the necklace—and then discovers that the missing pearl is not in her stocking but now in her mouth. In the next shot, he washes the dirt off the pearls, only to realize that the dirt is not dirt at all, but blood. When the young man awakens, he is relieved to find no blood on his hands and then heads back to town to purchase another pearl to complete the necklace. Only instead of returning to the jewelry shop, he enters a hotel and takes a room. Inside, he discovers, after looking out the window, that the rest of the pearls have disappeared from the nightstand where he left them only moments ago.

The young man's subsequent search for the pearls takes him into the hotel's hallway, where he examines every corner and doorway, all the while not noticing the movements of the "hotel mice" (several women who are dressed in identical gray silk body suits like Musidora in *Les Vampires*), who rob the place blind and then engage in their own unique forms of recreation—gambling in bathtubs, playing leapfrog—while one restrings the pearl necklace. Finally, the young man catches one of the women, who holds the repaired necklace in her hand. According to Hugnet's scenario for the film, the woman's "resemblance to the hunted saleswoman appears all the more striking" in a subsequent close-up.[74] Instead of strangling her, though, the young man and woman kiss; he then places the necklace around her neck, and they both return to his room for the night. The next morning we see the woman in bed, now wearing only the pearl necklace.

However, when the young man walks out on the balcony to smoke a cigarette, he notices another woman sleepwalking, holding the pearl necklace that just appeared around the other woman's neck. The young man follows the sleepwalker and the film then cuts to the fiancée waiting on a bench and then to the young man writing a letter breaking with her, informing her that he has given the necklace to someone else and that she should "sleep and forget." Then the photograph of her that has just now appeared on the desk in his hotel room (and that shows her in the garden) comes alive within the frame the moment before the sleepwalker inexplicably appears in the garden and places the necklace on the fiancée's neck, causing her to awaken. The

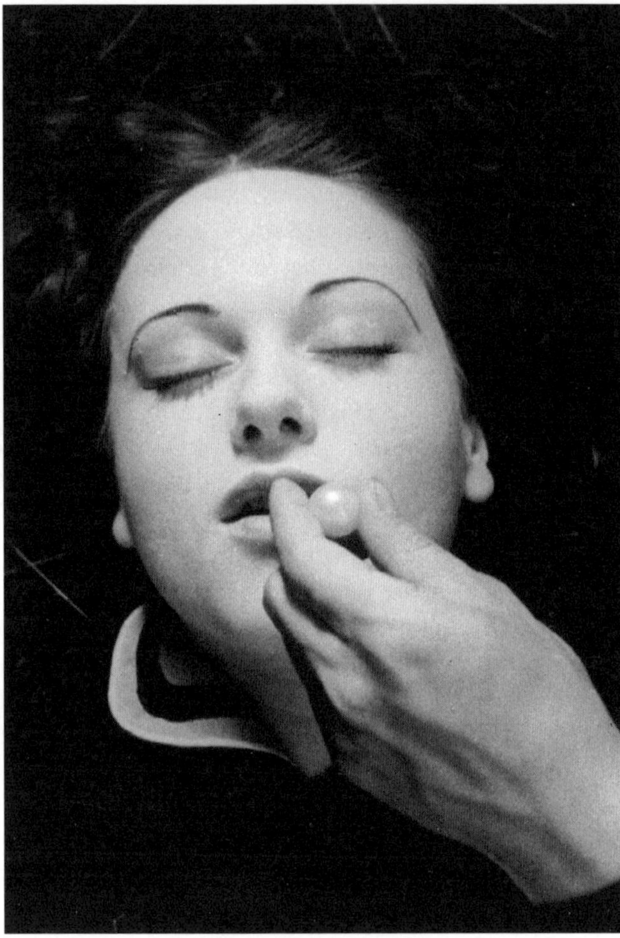

The pearl appears in her mouth, still from *La Perle* (1929).
Courtesy of Olivier d'Ursel and the Belgian Royal Film Archive.

young man arrives and gives his fiancée the letter he has just written, which she reads and which causes her to faint. He then leaves and returns to where he originally lost the pearl and hangs the necklace on a nearby tree branch. During his search, the "hotel mouse" appears and steals the necklace, fleeing to where the saleswoman died earlier in the young man's dream. When she reaches the exact spot, she falls and transforms from a gray silk-clad Musidora image into the saleswoman with the silk stockings. The young man again inspects her pantyhose and there finds the missing pearl, which seems to signal that he finally realizes her true identity. He kisses her, but she is truly dead this time,

One of the costumed women holding the necklace, still from *La Perle* (1929). Courtesy of Olivier d'Ursel and the Belgian Royal Film Archive.

and this moves him to contemplate the pearl and then crush it (much like he crushed the life out of his beloved) before he finally begins to cry.[75]

From this plot summary, one gets a sense of both the initial seeming incomprehensibility and the oneiric qualities of *La Perle*, demonstrating that although Hugnet had not yet officially joined the movement, he was already very much working within the surrealist mode.[76] In addition, the tenuous narrative construction of *La Perle* suggests that the influence of Pearl White and serial queen melodramas extended beyond its title. The plot of the film bears some similarities to the Pathé serial *The Seven Pearls* (1917), starring Mollie King (often considered White's successor) and directed by serial specialist Louis J. Gasnier. In *The Seven Pearls*, which followed King's serial debut in *The Mystery of the Double Cross* (1917), a pearl necklace entrusted to a friend by the sultan of Turkey is mistakenly stolen by Ilma's (King's) love interest, Harry Drake. After the theft is discovered, the sultan demands that Ilma recover the necklace within six months or join his harem. By this time, the pearls have been scattered all over the world, and the balance of the serial is spent recovering them.[77] In addition, the narrative organization of the film as well as its characters were designed not only to be disorienting like a dream, but also like film serials themselves, which Singer notes "became highly convoluted as they progressed over the weeks."[78] As one review described *The Seven Pearls*, "there are so many conflicting parties, and so many pearls in this latest serial of Pathé's that there are times when the observer is completely mystified as to who is who, which is which, and what is what."[79] As a surrealist text, *La Perle* translated this mystification into other formal aspects, including creating spatial discontinuities by alternately deploying and subverting the conventions of continuity editing. In particular, when the young man enters the jewelry shop at the beginning of the film, it is situated in the heart of the city. However, when he exits, the shop appears to be located in the country, causing the spectator to question the applicability of other rules of classical continuity to such a film.

Another group of avant-garde filmmakers took an even more radical approach to the adaptation of the serial form in a cultural milieu oriented toward bolstering a new political praxis. In "On Cinema" (1919), the Russian formalist Viktor Shklovsky valorized serials for repudiating the psychologically motivated narratives found in other art forms, such as novels and theater. He called for Soviet filmmakers to employ the serial's alternative form for Communist ends.[80] Yuri Tsivian has further excavated the importance of White and her films to the Soviet cinema of the 1920s. According to Tsivian, serial queen melodramas starring Cleo Madison, Kathlyn Williams, and Pearl

White formed the basis for what the Soviet filmmakers considered "American cinema" during that period: "When, after an interruption in film traffic caused by the Civil War, 'serial queen' melodramas reappeared on Russian (now Soviet) screens in 1922, we find future filmmakers Sergei Eisenstein, Grigori Kozintsev, Leonid Trauberg, and Sergei Yutkevich amongst their most devoted enthusiasts figuring out perhaps, how these films worked."[81] Due to their lowbrow status and freedom from older art forms and conventions, Tsivian argues that Soviet filmmakers considered serials the "future" of cinema, since "robust and dynamic, sensation serials seemed to emanate directly from within the film medium as such."[82]

For his part, Eisenstein traced his own antirealist filmmaking to an early love of serials and the world that they presented, which at once differed from reality and yet also, as they did for Desnos, suggested the revolutionary potential of the cinema. In "Dickens, Griffith, and the Film Today" (1944), he included the Pearl White serial *The House of Hate* (1918) among a series of American films that piqued the interest of Soviet cinephiles and budding filmmakers:

> There was the role of another film-factor that appeared, dashing along in such films as *The Gray Shadow*, *The House of Hate*, *The Mark of Zorro*. There was in these films a world, stirring and incomprehensible, but neither repulsive nor alien. On the contrary it was captivating and attractive, in its own way engaging the attention of young and future film-makers, exactly as the young and future engineers of the time were attracted by the specimens of engineering techniques unknown to us, sent from the same unknown, distant land across the ocean. What enthralled us was not only these films, it was also their possibilities. Just as it was the possibilities in a tractor to make collective cultivation of the fields a reality, it was the boundless temperament and tempo of these amazing (and amazingly useless!) works from an unknown company that led us to muse on the possibilities of a profound, intelligent, class-directed use of this wonderful tool.[83]

In this passage, one can sense Eisenstein's enthusiasm to engineer a new cinema for the new Soviet state based on American models rather than solely in opposition to them. What drew him and other Soviet filmmakers to serials such as *The House of Hate* was their sense, much like Delluc and Desnos, that here was a new form that could be broken down into its essential components (much as it had been originally conceptualized) and then reconstituted, like other constructivist works, to serve socialism rather than capital.

Their own films bear this out: Tsivian notes that Kozintsev and Trauberg's *Pokhozhdenia Oktyabriny* (The adventures of Oktiabrina [1924]) was "initially conceived . . . as an episode in a serial," signaled not only by its title, which borrowed from White's most famous serials, *The Perils of Pauline* and *The Exploits of Elaine*, "but also in the costume Oktiabrina wears below her red army hat and 'young pioneer' tie. A white blouse, dark skirt and leather boots make her look a bit like Helen Holmes in *The Hazards of Helen*." In addition, Tsivian identifies the outfits worn by Sofya Zhozeffi in Ivan Perestiani's *Krasnye Diavoliata* (Little red devils [1923]) and by Natalia Glan in Boris Barnet's Soviet serial *Miss Mend* (1926) as evocative of Pearl White serials.[84] In this way, *La Perle*'s use of costuming to signal its cinematic influences as well as its repudiation of classical notions of narrative causality can be linked to a larger group of avant-garde films. For like Hugnet and the surrealists, Eisenstein and the Soviets loved the nonclassical nature of serials as an alternate filmmaking style onto which they could graft their own agenda. Tsivian even traces the influence of American serials to Eisenstein's theory of the montage of film attractions, since as "strange as it may seem to us today, in order to substantiate his plotless 'principle of film attractions' Eisenstein would take recourse in Ruth Roland serials arguing that, rather than linking events into causal chains, these films piled up [narrative situations] without regard for those preceding them, thus reviving in film the 'Ben-Jonson tradition within the Elizabethan drama which put the impact on the perceiver before everything else.'"[85]

The Final Pearl

From this reconsideration of Pearl White's star image as detached from both the American and the mainstream European reception context, we gain a sense of White's unexpectedly widespread influence on the European avant-garde of the 1910s and 1920s. In many ways, White was the "figurative mother" not only of the thirty-year-old men in Desnos's Paris revival theater, but also of Delluc's concept of *photogénie*, the surrealists' notion of the marvelous and their particular brands of moviegoing and moviemaking, and even Eisenstein's theory of the montage of attractions. While Epstein decried the interchangeable nature of serial episodes, the surrealists seized on this feature as a mark of serials' ability to represent the unconscious and oneiric at the same time that Eisenstein viewed individual serial installments as building blocks for a new type of cinema that would direct "a brilliantly calculated blow of the billiard cue at the audience's cerebral hemisphere."[86] In this sense, White (and, by extension, her oeuvre) served as an integral ingredient of the unconscious of the first avant-garde, as an emblem of modernity, America, and the American cinema on the commercial screen and in avant-garde theory and practice.

While the avant-garde critics often lauded male stars like Chaplin, Keaton, and Hayakawa for their revelatory screen performances, Pearl White's embodiment of the revolutionary potential of cinema for such a variety of writers and filmmakers outside of the mainstream suggests that female stars were more important to the first avant-garde than previously considered.[87] The underlying socialism that Delluc and Desnos detected in White's films may seem at odds with White's image as one of the highest-paid female stars of the 1910s, yet there appears to be something about Pearl White's star image that defied the overlying capitalist thrust of commercial cinema. Delluc prized her youthful body for making physical culture accessible to the masses, and Desnos saw her films as emblems of sensuality in the face of the everyday violence of modern life. Perhaps most striking of all is White's own timelessness all the while her films were rooted in a specific historical moment. Two years after *Les Mystères de New York* premiered in Paris, Delluc evoked White as a paragon of contemporary life as she successfully navigated the perils of the modern era. Writing in 1921, Epstein considered White and her ilk best left in the past yet still conceded her continued popularity and importance even after the twilight of the serial craze. Finally, Desnos's conjuring of White's image over a decade after her heyday in order to describe an alternate future for cinema (one in which the images flickering on the screen obeyed the will of love rather than capital) suggests that her image both typified and transcended the "popular, foolish, novelettish, blood-and-thunderish" melodramas that she helped to establish. Through this retracing of White's reception by the European avant-garde, then, we can gain a sense of how her influence was felt across continents and movements, shaping avant-garde film theory and practice both in concert and in reaction to mainstream commercial film. While Pearl White may have been "the most assassinated woman in the world" in her own films, she also outlived her initial cultural moment to be resurrected in places one would least expect.

NOTES

1. Paul Morand, "La Glace à trois faces" (1925), in *Nouvelles complètes*, ed. Michel Collomb (Paris: Gallimard, 1992), 314. Translations are mine unless otherwise attributed.

2. For more on the avant-garde's futurism and antitraditionalist stance, see Renato Poggioli, *The Theory of the Avant Garde* (New York: Icon, 1968), 30, 68–74.

3. Jennifer M. Bean, "Technologies of Early Stardom and the Extraordinary Body," *Camera Obscura* 16, no. 3 (2001): 39–40; Ben Singer, *Melodrama and Modernity: Early Sensation Cinema and Its Contexts* (New York: Columbia University Press, 2001), 95–96.

4. Louis Delluc, "Pearl White," in *Ecrits Cinématographiques II: Cinéma et Cie*, ed. Pierre Lherminier (Paris: Cinémathèque Française, 1986), 78.

5. Ibid.

6. Singer, *Melodrama and Modernity*, 65.

7. Ben Singer, "Modernity, Hyperstimulus, and the Rise of Popular Sensationalism," in *Cinema and the Invention of Modern Life*, ed. Leo Charney and Vanessa R. Schwartz (Berkeley: University of California Press, 1995), 72, 93.

8. Delluc, "Pearl White," 78.

9. Bean explores the innervating experience of watching serials for those alienated from their own bodies according to Walter Benjamin's concept of mimesis. For Bean, "mimesis turns the relation between identification and desire on its head: identification emerges not as the result of the subject's unconscious desire for a loved object, but rather as an imitation by one 'self' of an 'other' that to all intents and purposes is indistinguishable from a primordial identification in which the organism first *acts* like, and only later desires, the outside or other." "Technologies of Early Stardom," 45.

10. Ibid., 79.

11. Ibid., 14.

12. Louis Delluc, "Masked Faces," in *Ecrits Cinématographiques II*, 227–28.

13. Ibid., 228.

14. Ibid.

15. Ibid., 230, emphasis added.

16. Louis Delluc, "Photogénie," in *Ecrits Cinématographiques II*, 273.

17. Ibid., 274.

18. Ibid.

19. Ibid.

20. Jean Epstein, "The Senses I (b)," trans. Tom Milne, in *French Film Theory and Criticism: A History/Anthology, 1907–1939*, vol. 1, *1907–1929*, ed. Richard Abel (Princeton, N.J.: Princeton University Press, 1988), 241.

21. Ibid.

22. Singer, *Melodrama and Modernity*, 281; Shelley Stamp, *Movie-Struck Girls: Women and Motion Picture Culture after the Nickelodeon* (Princeton, N.J.: Princeton University Press, 2000), 110–25.

23. Richard Abel, "Exploring the Discursive Field of the Surrealist Scenario Text," in *Dada and Surrealist Film*, ed. Rudolf E. Kuenzli (New York: Willis Locker and Owens, 1987), 60; Epstein, "The Senses I (b)," 246n1. Re-editing and repackaging foreign films for domestic markets was a common practice during the 1910s and 1920s. Yuri Tsivian has noted the practice of removing the happy endings from American films before their release to Russian theaters and has traced the impetus for Lev Kuleshov's editing experiments to his early days as "re-editor." Yuri Tsivian, "The Wise and Wicked

Game: Re-Editing and Soviet Film Culture of the 1920s," *Film History* 8, no. 3 (1996): 327–43. For further discussions of American serials and tie-ins at the French market, see Rudmer Canjels's contribution to this volume.

24. Abel notes that Georges Dureau was also worried about the confusion that might arise from such a mixture in "Genre nouveau," *Ciné-Journal* 323 (October 22, 1915): 15, 18, cited in *French Film Theory and Criticism*, vol. 1, 117n12.

25. Epstein, "The Senses I (b)," 242.

26. Ibid.

27. Ibid.

28. Ibid., 243.

29. Ibid. Epstein famously described Hayakawa's back as "as tense as an obdurate face. His shoulders refuse, reject, renounce." Chaplin's back is equally expressive when "on his shoulders is a bundle which probably contains nothing but a brick as a defense against unwelcome encounters."

30. Jean Epstein, "On Some Characteristics of *Photogénie*," trans. Tom Milne, in *French Film Theory and Criticism*, vol. 1, 314.

31. Ibid., 315.

32. Ibid., 318.

33. Cf. Germaine Dulac, "Aesthetics, Obstacles, Integral *Cinégraphie*," trans. Stuart Liebman, in *French Film Theory and Criticism*, vol. 1, 389–97, and Hans Richter, "Demonstration of the Universal Language," trans. Harald Stadler, in *Hans Richter: Activism, Modernism, and the Avant-Garde*, ed. Stephen C. Foster (Cambridge, Mass.: MIT Press, 1998). Epstein explicitly stated that "the film itself is a melody for which the accompaniment is written on the filmstock, but written in such a way that the melody cannot fail but be amplified within each spectator." "Fragments of Sky," trans. Richard Abel, in *French Film Theory and Criticism*, 422.

34. Epstein, "On Some Characteristics of *Photogénie*," 317.

35. Ben Singer, "Fiction Tie-Ins and Narrative Intelligibility 1911–18," in *Film History* 5, no. 4 (Winter 1993): 494.

36. Epstein, "On Some Characteristics of *Photogénie*," 318.

37. Louis Aragon, "On Decor," trans. Paul Hammond, in *French Film Theory and Criticism*, vol. 1, 167.

38. Bean, "Technologies of Early Stardom," 11; Walter Benjamin, "Experience and Poverty," in *Selected Writings*, vol. 2, *1927–1934*, ed. Michael W. Jennings, Howard Eiland, and Gary Smith, trans. Rodney Livingstone et al. (Cambridge, Mass.: Harvard University Press, 2001), 732.

39. Robert Desnos, "*Fantômas, Les Vampires, Les Mystères de New York*," trans. Richard Abel, in *French Film Theory and Criticism*, vol. 1, 399.

40. For more on the feature and its differences from the serial, see Eileen Bowser, *The Transformation of Cinema: 1907–1915* (Berkeley: University of California Press, 1990), 191–215.

41. Ado Kyrou, "The Marvelous is Popular," trans. Paul Hammond, in *The Shadow and*

Its Shadow: Surrealist Writings on the Cinema, 3rd ed., ed. and trans. Paul Hammond (San Francisco: City Lights Books, 2000), 68. "The marvelous is not the same in every period of history: it partakes in some obscure way of a sort of general revelation only the fragments of which come down to us: they are romantic *ruins*, the modern *mannequin*, or any other symbol capable of affecting the human sensibility for a period of time." André Breton, "Manifesto of Surrealism," in *Manifestoes of Surrealism*, trans. Richard Seaver and Helen R. Lane (Ann Arbor: University of Michigan Press, 1969), 16.

42. Robert Desnos, "*Les Mystères de New York*," in *Les Surréalistes et le cinema*, ed. Alain Virmaux and Odette Virmaux (Paris: Seghers, 1976), 130.

43. Steven Kovács, *From Enchantment to Rage: The Story of Surrealist Cinema* (Rutherford, N.J.: Farleigh Dickinson University Press, 1980), 16.

44. Ibid., 21. For André Breton and Aragon in their play *Le Trésor des Jesuits*, Pearl White's serials resonated with *both* the present and the future: "That which finds a marvelous echo in life. . . . Wait, since you are interested in the cinema, I will have you witness the apotheosis of a forgotten genre regenerated by everyday events. One will soon understand that there was nothing more realistic and more poetic at the same time than movie serials, which only recently used to create joy in those strong of spirit. It is in *Les Mystères de New York*, it is in *Les Vampires* that it will be necessary to seek the grand reality of the century." Ibid., 16.

45. Philippe Soupault, "Cinema U.S.A.," trans. Paul Hammond, in *The Shadow and Its Shadow*, 55–56.

46. Singer, *Melodrama and Modernity*, 242; Soupault, "Cinema U.S.A.," 56.

47. Soupault, "Le Vogue des films policiers—*La Maison de la flêche*," *L'Europe Nouvelle*, January 31, 1931, quoted in Kovács, *From Enchantment to Rage*, 17–18.

48. André Breton, "As in a Wood," trans. Paul Hammond, in *The Shadow and Its Shadow*, 73.

49. Ibid.

50. Ibid. In the American context, Stamp has traced the disorienting qualities of serial queen melodramas to their "unfinished" and open nature as opposed to the fixed and closed narratives of later features. Drawing on print sources, she notes that individual episodes that could be watched independently of the others became the most successful in any given serial, as they particularly epitomized serials' general ability to foster "a particular kind of viewing pleasure, built precisely around the suspension and deferral of narrative pleasure" (*Movie-Struck Girls*, 112–14). In addition, Stamp contends that, due to film serials' intertextual nature, the "*sequence* in which fans consumed print and celluloid renditions of [serials] was less significant than the *simultaneous* availability of varied, mutually supportive forms of the story" (ibid., 116). Due to the economic and social factors involved in serial film distribution, Stamp argues that one could easily have seen several serial episodes out of sequence in an urban metropolis like Chicago, depending on which neighborhood one frequented or traveled to see them as well as the fact that not all theater owners strictly respected the newspaper-to-film format of "read it here now, then see it all in the motion pictures"

(ibid., 117–18). Much like Pathé's repackaging of three different Pearl White serials into the single *Les Mystères de New York*, American theater owners were known to re-edit serial installments into a smaller number of episodes as well, highlighting their interchangeability and perhaps producing another site of narrative incoherence due to their interest in maximizing profits. Ibid., 119.

51. Michel Beaujour, "The Surrealist Map of Love," *Yale French Studies*, no. 32 (1964): 124.

52. Louis Aragon, *Anicet ou Le Panorama* (Paris: Gallimard, 1921), 117.

53. Ibid., 118. Here Aragon doubles the sentiments expressed in *Le Trésor de Jesuits*: "It is in *Les Mystères de New York*, it is in *Les Vampires* that it will be necessary to seek the grand reality of the century."

54. Ibid.

55. "The mind of the man who dreams is fully satisfied by what happens to him. The agonizing question of possibility is no longer pertinent. Kill, fly faster, love to your heart's content. And if you should die, are you not certain of reawaking among the dead? Let yourself be carried along, events will not tolerate your interference. You are nameless. The ease of everything is priceless." Breton, "Manifesto of Surrealism," 13.

56. Ibid., 14.

57. Desnos, "*Fantômas, Les Vampires, Les Mystères de New York*," 398.

58. Ibid., 398–99.

59. Ibid., 399.

60. Peter Bürger, *The Theory of the Avant-Garde*, trans. Michael Shaw (Minneapolis: University of Minnesota Press, 1984), 49. Desnos, "*Fantômas, Les Vampires, Les Mystères de New York*," 399.

61. Desnos, "*Fantômas, Les Vampires, Les Mystères de New York*," 399.

62. Desnos, "*Les Mystères de New York*," 129.

63. Ibid., 130.

64. Ibid., 131.

65. Ibid.

66. Ibid.

67. Ibid., 131–32.

68. Singer describes the cliffhanger structure of serial queen melodramas as similarly repetitive, since the same narrative arc was not only traced in each episode, but also in the narrative overlap built into each episode "wherein the 'next' episode briefly retraced (usually with cop-out modifications) the immediate situation leading up to the cliffhanger" (*Melodrama and Modernity*, 210–11). I am indebted to Jim Lastra for use of the term *string of pearls* here to describe the surrealists' narrative enjoyment of serials.

69. In addition to Pearl White and her films' influence on avant-garde poetry, Abel argues that film racontés like Decourcelle's *Les Mystères de New York* heavily influenced the avant-garde's decision to publish actual film scenarios in the late 1910s, beginning with Delluc's call for their publication in his "Notes pour moi" editorial

column in *Le Film*, as well as ciné-romans such as Jules Romains's *Donogoo-Tonka ou les miracles de la science* (1919) (Richard Abel, "American Film and the French Literary Avant-Garde [1914–1924]," *Contemporary Literature* 17, no. 1 [Winter 1976]: 92). Delluc called for such film scenarios to eschew the inclusion of illustrations, relegating the visual primarily to the film screen so as to not have any overlap between the two media. See Abel, "Exploring the Discursive Field," 60. In turn, such film-text practices became a style resource for the production of unfilmable scenarios by the surrealists in the late 1920s. As opposed to the film raconté's tendency to "subdue and stabilize the film's sequence of images and close off its meaning," ciné-romans attempted to return to the openness of French and American serials as well as Mack Sennett and Chaplin comedies and even earlier trick films (ibid., 63–64). In addition, since these scenarios were quickly sidelined in terms of realization, Abel argues that they became "a new textual form of *play*" with the cinematic image that surrealists such as Desnos, Benjamin Fondane, and Georges Neveux drew on in their conceptualizations of the dream image in cinema (Abel, "American Film and the French Literary Avant-Garde," 84–109).

70. For more on Dalí's attempts to reconcile both his experience of 1930s New York and his expectations based on the Pearl White serial as well as American gangster films of the early 1930s, see Matthew Gale, "Les Mystères surrealists de New York," in *Dalí and Film* (exhibition catalog), ed. Matthew Gale (New York: Museum of Modern Art, 2007), 132–39.

71. Georges Hugnet, "Scenario du Film," in *Pleins et déliés; souvenirs et témoignages, 1926–1972*, ed. Guy Authier (La Chapelle-sur-Loire, France: G. Authier, 1972), repr. in *Les surréalistes et le cinéma*, 191.

72. Kovács, *From Enchantment to Rage*, 18–19.

73. Hugnet, "Scenario du Film," 192.

74. Ibid., 198.

75. My summary of *La Perle* is based on both Hugnet's original scenario and the 35mm print of the film available at the Celeste Bartos International Film Study Center at the Museum of Modern Art, New York.

76. For his part, Kovács argues that the film cannot be considered a surrealism text since it was not made by a recognized member of the group and since it "was never even mentioned by [Hugnet's] Surrealist colleagues" (Kovács, *From Enchantment to Rage*, 10). However, as we know that *La Perle* was shown in 1929 at the Studio des Ursulines in the same program as Man Ray's *Le Mystère de château de Dé* (1929) and Luis Buñuel and Salvador Dali's *Un Chien Andalou* (1929), this seems to discount at least one of Kovács's objections. Indeed, François Buot considers this screening to be Hugnet's "consecration" to surrealism, even though he did not officially join its ranks until 1932, since it first grouped him publicly with other surrealist artists. François Buot, "Georges Hugnet: Une Vie en Toute Liberté," in *Georges Hugnet: Collages*, ed. Timothy Baum, François Buot, and Sam Stourdzé (Paris: Editions Léo Scheer, 2003), 181.

77. Kalton C. Lahue, *Continued Next Week: A History of the Moving Picture Serial* (Norman: University of Oklahoma Press, 1964), 51.

78. Singer, *Melodrama and Modernity*, 209.

79. Peter Milne, "The Seven Pearls," *Motion Picture News*, November 3, 1917, 31–32, quoted in Singer, *Melodrama and Modernity*, 209.

80. Victor Shklovski, "O kinematografe," *Iskusstvo Kommuny* 12 (February 23, 1919): 1, quoted in Yuri Tsivian, "Between the Old and the New: Soviet Film Culture in 1918–1924," *Griffithiana* 55–56 (1996): 41–43.

81. Tsivian, "Between the Old and the New," 39–41. Tsivian notes that the first American serial shown in Soviet Russia was *The Grey Ghost* (1917) in 1922. Also distributed were Pearl White's *The House of Hate* (1918) in six episodes and *The Exploits of Elaine*, under the title *Mysteries of New York*, in four episodes in 1924. Ibid., 61n31.

82. Ibid., 41.

83. Sergei Eisenstein, "Dickens, Griffith, and the Film Today," in *Film Form: Essays in Film Theory*, ed. and trans. Jay Leyda (New York: Harcourt, Brace and World, 1977), 203–4.

84. Tsivian, "Between the Old and the New," 43.

85. Ibid.

86. Sergei Eisenstein, "An Unexpected Juncture," *Selected Works*, vol. 1, *Writings, 1922–34*, ed. and trans. Richard Taylor (Indianapolis: Indiana University Press, 1988), 119.

87. For more on the influence of female stars (particularly Delluc's relationship with Belgian-born actress Ève Francis) on the European avant-garde of the early twentieth century, see Elizabeth Hutton Turner, "*La Jeune Fille Américaine* and the Dadaist Impulse," in *Women in Dada: Essays on Sex, Gender, and Identity*, ed. Naomi Sawelson-Gorse (Cambridge, Mass.: MIT Press, 1998), 4–21, and Paula Amad, "'Objects Became Witnesses': Ève Francis and the Emergence of French Cinephilia and Film Criticism," *Framework* 46, no. 1 (2005): 56–73.

CHAPTER 5

Fascinations for the Nation

American Serial Film, Czechoslovakia, and the Afterlives of Pearl White

KEVIN B. JOHNSON

A close study of the reception of Pearl White in Czechoslovakia uncovers an intricate tapestry woven from various threads of discourse and patterns of perception. White's story is inextricably entangled within the context of a more general craze for American action serials in the early 1920s. The varied written sources from the period comprise a landscape in which multiple, often contradictory discourses work to describe, promote, and create meaning from the new American imports. Strands of discourse related to Americanism, modernity, aesthetics, gender, performance, mental and physical health, nationalism, anti-Germanism, and cultural fantasies combine in intricate and often unexpected ways to create a diverse and complex picture. The Czech audience's relationship to Pearl White is intertwined with a unique historical moment in the nation's history and is therefore indelibly bound by a distinctive frame of reception.[1] Although Pearl White was one among many in the flood of new American stars, evidence shows that she in particular was a tremendous source of fascination for Czech (male) intellectuals as well as for the general public. The most curious inflection of Pearl White's fame in Czechoslovak society plays out in the literary works of a particularly fervent admirer, Felix de la Cámara, who styled himself as "Pearl White's author" and wrote her into a series of action novels. This author's work represents a

Pearl White on the title page of a leading Czech film weekly, published in mid-1921, a full year after her action serials hit. Prague. *Divadlo budoucnosti* 2, no. 27 (1921): 1.

uniquely Czech offshoot of the star phenomenon that was Pearl White. The following pages explore this and other "further adventures" of Pearl White in Czechoslovakia in order to illustrate how the blond star fueled the fantasies of a newly awakened Czech populace and to illuminate the subtle ways that this fascinating female persona was appropriated and re-imagined in the service of various discourses that spoke for the mental and physical well-being of the nation.

Although the record indicates that only a very few Pearl White serials were screened in post–World War I Czechoslovakia, the consistent recurrence of her name in Czech sources into the 1930s and beyond suggests that the acrobatic actress left a strong imprint in the minds of viewers during her short period of filmic success in the region. The span of time during which Pearl White's films were actively screened in Czechoslovakia was relatively brief, indeed a matter of only a few years, from January 1920 to early 1924. In this period a total of about ten of her films were seen by Czech audiences, half of which were dramas and comedies made with the Fox Film Corporation in the early 1920s. Yet the image of Pearl White as it appeared in the action serials (especially *The House of Hate*, 1918 [U.S. release]) remained a notable presence in Czechoslovak writing on cinema into the 1930s and beyond.[2] In fact, more than any other genre of the period, it is the American action serial that left the most pronounced imprint on the collective film memory in the first years of the Czechoslovak Republic. While it is perhaps not entirely correct to label White as the most successful of the "serial queens" among Czech audiences, she nevertheless occupies a conspicuous space in the history of Czech film culture and offers interesting perspectives on the Czech public's reception of American action serials.[3] The present essay focuses on the Czech career of Pearl White as a case study that can shed light on larger issues related to spectatorship, film aesthetics, and the creation of star mythology. As my scope is generally broad, the essay can only accomplish the early steps in unraveling a few strands of the complex tapestry of Pearl White's curious Czechoslovakian afterlives, yet it hopes to expose compelling threads for further investigation.

The Postwar American Film Invasion

By 1917 the astounding reach of Pearl White's fame beyond the borders of the United States was widely touted in American film trade journals.[4] Although her reputation had spread to many corners of the world market by this time, it would be another three years before Czech audiences would get the chance to swoon for the blond daredevil. Prior to 1920, White's films were completely unknown in Prague or Bohemia. Although American films were exhibited throughout Austria-Hungary, there is no evidence that any Pearl White films played in the provinces of Bohemia and Moravia prior to the outbreak of World War I in 1914. Generally speaking, until the end of the war, American productions were rarely seen in the region, which was dominated by French, German, or Danish films. Yet after the hostilities of battle ended, Pearl White was part of a massive onslaught of American stars that took the newly independent Czechoslovak state by storm. Czech audiences encountered most of these American performers for the first time in the latter part of 1919 and the beginning of 1920 as an entirely new array of stars suddenly lit the nascent nation's horizons.[5] In the span of just a few months, Pearl White, Dorothy Phillips, Marie Walcamp, Eddie Polo, Dustin Farnum, Constance and Norma Talmadge, Mary Pickford, and Ruth Roland all had their premiere appearances on Czech screens.[6] After the American film invasion of 1919–1920, only a small number of European actors maintained the star status they had cultivated during the war years, among them the Norwegian Gunnar Tolnaes, the Dane Valdemar Psilander, and the German Henny Porten.

To a certain extent, the sudden torrent of American films is testimony to the aggressive business strategies of American film producers racing to cash in on new markets in recently "liberated" Central Europe. Yet it is also evident that Czech audiences were eager customers, hungry for such entertainments, particularly the action serials. A perusal of the newspapers and film journals from the period reveals that the range of genres on the Czechoslovak market at the time were, in fact, quite diverse. In popular memory, however, the film culture during the first few years of the Czechoslovak Republic is most readily associated with American crime and action serials.[7] Although audiences saw comedies and family dramas with Mary Pickford and Olive Thomas as well as such grand works as D. W. Griffith's *The Birth of a Nation* (1915) and *Intolerance* (1916), it is the action serials (together with slapstick films) that stand out most prominently in later accounts of the period. American action serials are not only remembered more fondly than other U.S. films, but also more than works in that genre from other European countries. Although French serials had achieved a certain level of popular success, there was scant mention in the Czech press of the German serials that were also available, such as those featuring Stuart Webbs. What then can be said of the fact that it was above all American action serials that overwhelmingly captivated the Czech imagination? The question is twofold: why were Czech audiences so receptive to American films and what attracted them particularly to the action serial genre?

"America," Democracy, Modernity, and Optimism for the First Republic

In the case of Czechoslovakia, the analysis of social meaning associated with American serials must also take into account the unique political changes of the time. Ben Singer has illuminated the correlation between the rise of the genre of melodrama (which also includes action serials) and the disruptive uncertainties encountered by society as it enters a modern world no longer dominated by traditional morality and monarchical power structures.[8] The conditions he describes are also applicable to Czechoslovakia around 1920, as the nation was leaving the house of Habsburg to become a democracy for the first time. Yet the historical circumstances in this case demand that the Czechoslovak confrontation with the modern world be understood as convergent with the search for a new concept of statehood and national space. Throughout Central Europe, this was not only a time of emerging modernity and advanced capitalism, but also a time of a growing sense of nationhood and radical transition within the systems of cultural production and distribution. The fall of the Habsburg monarchy brought independence and a democratic system of government to the region in the form of the new state of Czechoslovakia. The fledgling nation, known in Czech history as the First Republic, was founded in October 1918 on the ideals of the French Revolution and took great inspiration from the United States. Together with the wave of enthusiasm for America that energized the country, anti-German sentiment intensified, rising ever more to the surface of public debate among the Slavic citizens.[9] After the hostilities of World War I had ended and films from former enemy countries finally burst onto the Czech market en masse in the early 1920s, Czech-speaking filmgoers and distributors actively sought out American and French films as a new alternative to the German, Austrian, and Scandinavian products that had dominated their market during the war years. In their eyes, Germanic films smacked of the old hegemonic structures from which the nascent Slavic state strove to distance itself. Conversely, the American films in particular offered insight into a world of new possibilities and fresh ways of thinking. This invigorating impulse was sensed most intensely in the slapstick and action genres. The American action serials fed Czech audiences' fantasies of geographical and social mobility, physical discipline, and an optimistic, liberating modernity. They opened up a sanguine perspective of the future for this new country arising from the ashes of old Europe after the Great War.

In the early years of the First Czechoslovak Republic, both among intellectuals and within society at large, America was a highly idealized model for a "new society" liberated from the bondage of European history.[10] Even before the founding of the new Czech state, liberal democratic intellectual Karel Čapek was praising the "innate optimism" and "chivalrous" vision of life he saw in American films.[11] For much of the Czech avant-garde, America not only exhibited the ideals of democracy but also encapsulated the truest expression of the cultural modernity that the avant-garde embraced. According to the 1923 diagnosis of Karel Teige, Czechoslovakia's most influential avant-garde artist and theoretician, "We are a people of an express-train mentality, with a stirred-up and enthralled sensibility whose elasticity enables all possibilities for development. Our world is a patented invention, with the dynamic beauty of speed, metallic and fiery, with the vibrant color of great hope. It is an environment of electrical exchanges, Americanism, news reports, and radiotelegraphy."[12] Czech intellectuals welcomed the modern worldview imported from America as the catalyst that would liberate Europe from the antiquated and repressive political systems that dominated the continent. According to Teige, "The Americanized Europe is becoming a single, chaotic, and cinematic metropolis, and the social transformations taking place there will render it, sooner or later, a harmonious international city."[13] As we can see in these citations, cinema played a prominent role in the profound blend of (often contradictory) meanings conveyed by the Czech idea of "America." A June 1919 trade press article by the film critic A. Ludvík titled "America on the Rise" ("Amerika na postupu") heralded the beginning of the postwar American film boom in post-Habsburg Central Europe.[14] Ludvík lamented that in previous years, Czech access to international cinema had been limited almost exclusively to German films and recounts how enthusiastic audiences greeted the first American productions with eager delight.[15] Ludvík neglected to mention, however, that in the years prior to the fascination that swept the country at fever pitch in 1919 and 1920, American films were already being championed by Czech intellectuals. The most notable early advocates of American cinema among Czechs were the Čapek brothers, two of the most prominent intellectuals of the period.[16] Writing in 1918, Josef Čapek opened his essay "Film" with the declaration that "American films are the best of all."[17] A year earlier, his brother Karel had dedicated an entire article in praise of the products imported to Prague by A.W.F.Co. (American World Film Company).[18] Published in late April 1917, a scant few weeks after the United States declared war on the Central Powers, this paean to American films reads as a subtle, subversive expression of opposition to the monarchical, German-speaking Austro-Hungarian hegemony over the Czech lands in favor of the ideals of equality promised by American-style democracy. In his praise for the optimism of American films, Josef Čapek declared that "the story should end with the victory of truth and goodness. Of course, such satisfying finales are not completely novel, but the American concept does not favor the artificialities of fate and chance; an especially virile and vital trait is visible everywhere, the ideal is strength, which takes aim at obstacles and errors on a path to correctness and goodness."[19] In his assessment of other national cinemas, Josef reserved some nice words for French and Italian films but judged "Danish and Norwegian films . . . rather boring and commonplace."[20] The harshest criticism, however, was leveled at German films, which "are fabricated without any emotion and taste; the story is usually nonsensical, bordering on stupidity; and frequently downright coarse or unbearably sentimental; the great majority are products that can satisfy only the basest demand. The worst of all are their farces, which are vulgar and spiritless, most often built upon an incredibly low and undignified concept of man and life, upon the downright shameful devaluation of all human emotions and qualities."[21] It seems fair to conclude that Čapek's criticisms here were informed as much by the Czech national aspirations of the time as they were by actual film aesthetics, if not more so.

Pearl White contra Caligari: The Avant-Garde, Aesthetics of Fitness, and Czech Nationalism

For most Czech intellectuals, American cinema came closest to realizing the potential of the still-developing medium. The avant-garde group Devětsil—which was coincidentally founded in 1920, just one year after American films began flooding into the country—was fascinated with the cinema and its implications for modern art.[22] The members of Devětsil (as well as the Čapek brothers) emphasized film's artistic sovereignty and the need for film to be liberated from theater and other archaic forms of art.[23] Taking his cue from the French theorist Louis Delluc, Teige emphasized in his 1922 published lecture on film aesthetics that cinema is an "art of spectacle" (*umění podívané*) rather than "narrative art" (*umění epické*).[24] He further added that film functions according to the "aesthetics of astonishment (*estetika údivu*), the aesthetics of surprise and the unexpected."[25] In Teige's words, film "should shut out elements that are foreign to it, carried over from the academic arts. It should mark out its own sovereign space, free of psychology and literature, and without 'Caligarism.' Yes, *The Cabinet of Dr. Caligari* [1920] is the best illustration of how the so-called 'art' film has gone astray. This unhealthy, hysterical film is not even a film at all; the hypersensibility of a madman is not modern art."[26] Given the importance of *Caligari* for defining a specifically German cinematic style, the anti-Teutonic impulse behind Teige's words is unmistakable.[27] From the perspective of Czech modernist thinking, it was precisely slapstick comedies and action serials from America that most successfully realized cinema's aesthetic potential, in contrast to the perceived sickly decadence of the German film industry, which dominated European production at that time. Against the unhealthy "hysteria" of the German aesthetic of "Caligarism," Teige prescribed a good dose of American films: "This optimism that keeps on smiling through the harsh stages of today, the dangers and eternal uncertainty of tomorrow, and the Yankee optimism of bluff is the most healthy exorbitance."[28] In these evocative reflections from the Czech avant-garde, we can imagine a sort of showdown in which virile American film heroes such as Pearl White are pitted against malignant (German) Caligaris that are infecting European cinema. The energy emanating from the physical spectacle of the female body stood for vitality and the future in stark opposition to the stagnant gloominess of those hysterical specters obsessed with the traumas of the past.

This merging of the discourse on cinema with the language of health, both physical and mental, is a common thread in Czech thought. As elsewhere in Europe, Czech writers were concerned with the implications of film on the human psyche. The positions of German theorists Georg Simmel, Siegfried Kracauer, and Walter Benjamin, who described film as an aesthetic consequence of human consciousness transformed by the shocks and hyperstimulus of modern (urban) experience, are well-known.[29] In striking contrast to this school of thought, Czech sociologist (and member of Devětsil) Bedřich Václavek saw cinema instead as healthy compensation for understimulation in modern life and thus describes the psychological importance of film in almost therapeutic terms: "As if on cue, film appeared at a time when human life was becoming more and more restricted and mechanized—and also less hazardous—as a sort of corrective measure to satisfy *mankind's instinct for adventure*, which through long decades had grown increasingly dormant."[30] For Václavek does not feature film as a symptom of a new mode of perception defined by the shocks and stress of stimuli associated with the shift to modernity, but rather as a necessary catharsis for a humankind trapped in an over-rationalized world that is incompatible with its animal nature: "Cinema contributes to man's liberation from the domination of the machine, resulting in his own metaphysical domination over the complex nature of world events. In experiencing the daring adventures of film heroes, a person discharges energy (formerly invested in war ventures) from a theoretically inexhaustible source and neutralizes it."[31] In this line of thinking, the higher the action level of a film, the greater its therapeutic effect on the viewer. It is, therefore, in accordance with society's healthy desires that "the auditorium remains empty during sentimental stories from the petit-bourgeois life, which are particularly abundant in German productions, while, on the other hand, American adventure stories and slapstick fill the seats."[32]

This predilection for cinematic thrills had been famously expressed one year earlier in the words of the modernist poet Stanislav Kostka Neumann in his 1923 poem "Film," where he proclaims, "yes, I too am fond of film, and

American first in line/ not a weepy novel, but a world that rushes."[33] The tendency to associate American films specifically with a sense of action goes back as far as 1908, when art and literature critic Václav Tille wrote praises to the dynamic nature of the "American style," which he associated with criminal intrigue and riveting car chases.[34] In his groundbreaking article "Kinéma," Tille described at length two action films that for him displayed elements of the "American" character. It is important to note, however, that neither film was made in the United States. Rather, the films were (most likely) French productions, namely *Brigandage moderne* (1905) and "Les Faux monnayeurs" (1908)—the third episode in the series *Nick Carter, le roi des detectives*.[35] Thus, already by 1908 the label "American" was being used in Czech lands to connote a certain (action) film aesthetic, independent of a film's actual land of origin. The term implied a cinematic predilection for suspense and visual thrills that transcended national borders. Due to a number of factors, however, the general public's fascination with American-style action cinema began to dwindle after the high tide of imports in the immediate postwar years. Writing as early as 1924, Václavek lamented the waning of such adventure films, which were gradually being displaced in Czech theaters by stories of bourgeois morality and weepy tragedy, much to the psychological detriment of the populace, he claimed. His diagnosis suggested a society in sickly decline as the result of waning stimulation from "healthy" films full of American-style cinematic excitements.

Other segments of the Czech discourse on health placed particular emphasis on the bodies of the action stars themselves and the intense physicality of their performance rather than on the psychological effects of the film's action in general. In some cases, on-screen physicality was promoted as a potential catalyst for social change in the new country. In anticipation of the premiere of the first Pearl White film to hit Czechoslovak screens, the film journal *Kino* presented in its December 19, 1919, issue an "introduction" to the American star and a detailed summary for each of the serial's twelve episodes. Yet rather than supplying elaborate biographical information about the actress, the introductory text, with the heading "Pearl White," expounded more broadly on the recent flood of American films into the country and the beneficial qualities they possessed over other (European) productions in their presentation of physical fitness. Since this source (like others that follow) is not readily available and has never been translated into English, it is worth quoting here at length:[36]

> From time to time, of course, one hears objections against these pictures, but these are simply dictated by spite and a lack of understanding. After

> all, the Americans are not trying to persuade anyone that these serials are works of art, at least not in the theatrical sense. On the contrary, they are concerned with educating the broad strata of the hypersensitive public to the valuable life lesson in the phrase "healthy in body, healthy in mind." Their pictures are a tribute to personal courage and physical prowess. They function like propaganda pictures, particularly in our country, where we are just now beginning to understand the great importance of physical education for our future.[37]

This reading of American serials suggests a link between the physical health of the cinema actor's body and the spiritual health of the viewing populace and thereby of the nation. The fact that this discussion appears within the context of Pearl White's introduction to Czech audiences is a testament to the serial queen's privileged status as an icon for Americanism in Czechoslovakia. Even more intriguing is the implied therapeutic effect of White's athletic prowess on the (mental and physical) well-being of the Czech nation.

The concept of cinema as beneficial to the national body was also promoted by the Czech patriotic organization Sokol (the falcon), whose aim was "the physical and in part also the moral education and improvement of all the nation, its nurturing for the enhancement of its strength, bravery, refinement, and defense."[38] Sokol (formed in 1862) was one of the most important institutions of the Czech national revival movement around the turn of the century and in the First Republic. The organization is particularly notable for the linkage of gymnastic training and nationalist/pan-Slavic ideology and for its massive investment in film theaters throughout the land. At one time, Sokol owned and operated as many as half of all cinemas in Czechoslovakia.[39] As elsewhere in Europe at that time (such as in Germany and the Soviet Union), we find in the Czechoslovak context a curious linkage between physical fitness, mass (nationalist) organizations, and cinema.

A connection between the performer's body and intellectual health is also suggested in the works of the Czech avant-garde, albeit without strong nationalist overtones. Karel Teige, for example, saw one of cinema's most important aesthetic qualities as the medium's ability to capture the energy of bodies in motion in order to create a "dramatic poem of movement."[40] In his first major work on the cinema, the 1922 treatise "Foto Kino Film," Teige included long lists of film actors notable for their mastery of bodily performance. Seeing their physical abilities as more in accordance with the true essence of cinema than the skills of classically trained theatrical actors, Teige placed the former in a position superior to the latter. His list was composed primarily of artists from vaudeville, cabaret, and the dance hall such as Loïe Fuller, Mistinguett, Harry Pilcer, Gaby Deslys, Vernon Castle, Stacia Napierkowska, Max Linder, Charlie Chaplin, and Fatty Arbuckle, but it also included Pearl White in its ranks.[41] At another point Teige more directly emphasized the athletic performances of action stars, where White also made an appearance:

> In the vast majority of cases, however, film finds its unique performers among the ranks of sportsmen, athletes, acrobats, and circus clowns. . . . Only sport of a very high level of perfection can provide film with such "smart" automobile drivers, equestrians, and cowboys as Rawlinson, Fairbanks, Marie Walcamp, Helen Holmes, Pearl White, Maciste, Harry Carey, W. [William S.] Hart, Ruth Roland, and others. Cinema as art is the crowning example of modern intellectual culture, which is nevertheless also a celebration of modern physical culture. It establishes a balance between the two, and therein lies its significant moral importance.[42]

Here again, we see the conspicuous alignment of physical health and moral strength, with both being delivered in equal doses by (American action) cinema. Although the leftist, avant-gardist Teige obviously envisions a different "moral" direction than the nationalist, traditionalist Sokol, both share a common fascination with cinema and its implications for the human and social body.

For his part, Teige understands the "ethical mission of cinema" to be firmly in alignment with the impulses of modern art and poetry, whose achievements are "the end results of a new, contemporary sensibility and mentality."[43] As he sees it, film's "daring spirit and intoxicating exoticism, together with its beautiful optimism, could have a most marvelous ethical influence."[44] In Teige's vision, the thrust of cinema's moral strength was oriented toward overturning tradition as part of society's evolutionary transition to modernity. Actors, specifically those who perform in a truly "cinematic" way, bringing forth astonishing spectacles of physicality and acrobatics, supplied much of the fuel for cinema's ethical engine.

The concept of film actors as conduits of moral energy is not unique to the Czechoslovak context. To some extent, it can be presumed that Czech writers such as Teige, who attributed ethical merit to athletic performance, took their cue from French film theory. Perhaps the biggest influence on Czech thought during this period was Louis Delluc, with whom Teige maintained a close relationship that included extensive written correspondence. Taking Pearl White as his example, Delluc discussed the "moral power" of cinema performers in terms of physical health: "Morally, the sight of Pearl White is a true cure. The spectacle of her exploits are [*sic*] better for the neurasthenic than the bitter genius of Charlot or even the sentimental and modest brilliance of Douglas Fairbanks. Pearl White is energy and brilliance, that's all . . . it is good health on pure impulse."[45] This alignment of extreme physical performance with discourses on health is reminiscent of many of the discussions from the Czech context cited above. One crucial difference in Delluc's assessment, however, is the attention to gender: here it is specifically the performance of the female body that is invested with therapeutic qualities in contrast to the more "bitter" and "modest" efforts of male actors.

In the text cited above, Teige equally populates his rosters of highly physical actors with both female and male performers, and he appraises their positive moral effects without any attention to gender difference. If anything, he implicitly favors the male actors, since the only performers he discusses at length are Chaplin, Fairbanks, and Hayakawa, while the females are relegated to brief appearances buried in his lists of names. Other Czech writers, however, expressed particular fascination with the physical performance of the serial queens and spoke to the distinction between these women and their male counterparts. For example, as the above-cited article about the Czech première of Pearl White's *The House of Hate* duly pointed out, "it is interesting that feats of balance and danger do not always rest in the hands of men and that very often it is *women* whose courage captivates us."[46] It is not the extreme physical stunts alone that this author found so fascinating, but the idea of women carrying them out. A month later, in January 1920, A. Ludvík wrote a series of columns in the newspaper *Právo lidu* about the recent deluge of American films, in which he explored the unique role of women performers more directly.[47] In the column focusing on actors, Ludvík praised "traditional" actors such as Mary Pickford, Ruth Clifford, and Dorothy Phillips but directed special attention to the "new" phenomenon of female action serial stars:

> The film serials have introduced an entirely new type of performer to our luminous theaters. The very nature of the serial film itself demands something extraordinary that enables it to consistently captivate the spectator and it is precisely the breathtaking performances of the main heroes that enrapture the audience with euphoria and panic simultaneously.[48] Let us simply recall the (today already) classic performances of *Mary* [*sic*] *Walcamp* in *The Red Ace* and *Liberty*, or the fabulous success of *Pearl White* in *The House of Hate* and *Ruth Roland* in the picture *Hands up!* These three female artists turn the fable of the "weaker sex" on its head, for their gymnastic accom-

plishments must surely inspire astonishment among even truly demanding sportsmen. There is, however, something else astonishing with these women. Anyone who sees, or rather who hears about, the breathtaking physical performances of these artists would presume that it would be to the detriment of the mimetic (i.e., the specifically internal) quality of their performance. Yet, this is not the case. With astonishment, we find that these athletes are also excellent mimetic actors. Thus, even in this respect they completely fulfill the requirements of the film.[49]

Ludvík's distinction between the theatrical performance style of "traditional" actors and the "breathtaking" physical style of action stars recalls Teige's observations on cinema acting. A key difference, however, is the recognition of gender difference in Ludvík's enthusiastic, almost giddy fascination with female performers. His description not only highlights the physical feats of these women, but it does so using terminology that emphasizes the physical effect on the viewers (for example, captivate, breathtaking, enrapture, euphoria, panic, and so on).

In the subsequent discussion, Ludvík only briefly mentioned male actors, almost as a side note. In stark contrast to the emphasis on the physicality of the female performers seen in the above quotation, his descriptions of leading men relied on formulations that highlight inner emotional character. For example, he pronounced Dustin Farnum "an actor of deep intelligence and profound emotion" and added, "his performance is executed in subdued tones and is never led astray by the desire for purely external effect."[50] In the same section, analogous vocabulary was used to characterize actor William Stowell. Whereas Ludvík placed the emphasis on the external, physical effects of female performance, his attention to male actors focused rather on internal or psychological aspects.[51] Furthermore, the discussion ascribed a somewhat hermaphroditic or hybrid nature to the female actors by highlighting their ability to execute dangerous "male" stunts. Indeed, what made these women so "astonishing" was that they were masters of both physical performance and emotional mimetic acting, which the author elsewhere in his article identified as a particularly male faculty.

In her discussion of Louis Delluc, Vicki Callahan describes how the "moral" impulse for action and energy championed by the theorist is better understood as a signifier for a sort of "countermorality" that demands a "fundamental upheaval of the old world and its lethargic pace of life."[52] In Delluc's writing, as in much French theory at the time, this new morality was frequently associated with the female body. In this way, the New Woman is not just emblematic of female emancipation but came to symbolize the whole population's liberation from the stagnation of the past and its antiquated social structures. In the French context, this transgressive (feminine) force tended to be narratively ascribed to "evil" women who—regardless of the potential for empowerment they represented—had to be sexually contained or resolutely dispatched in the end. The most iconic example is the black-suited criminal Irma Vep (performed by Musidora), from Louis Feuillade's serial *Les Vampires*. By contrast, Pearl White's blond, heroic incarnation of the New Woman is less threatening to male identity and consequently more palatable to male fantasies of social progress.[53] This more positive acceptance of feminine strength is not limited to Pearl White alone but also applies to American serial stars more generally. Given the shared desire for a fundamental overthrow of the old way of life, it is curious that Delluc's gender-specific praise for Pearl White as a sort of New Woman is not more overtly echoed in the writings of the Czech avant-garde, whether for White or for any other serial queen. Although Czech authors consistently sang praises to the revolutionary and therapeutic qualities of American action serials and the astonishing physical feats contained therein, they are more reticent when it comes to addressing the gender specificity of the leading actors in these serials. This suggests an underlying ambivalence toward the serial queens and the rearrangement of gender roles implied by their athletic prowess. Ludvík's comment that these female action heroes "enrapture the audience with euphoria and panic simultaneously" pointed to the mixed sense of fascination and fear their performance inspired in male Czech spectators. In general, the ambivalence expressed by these nongendered readings of Pearl White (and other serial queens) in Czechoslovakia appears to be more or less consistent with her reception in the United States as illuminated by recent scholarship.[54] However, a more pointed investigation into these matters is still needed in order to appropriately explore the particularities of Czechoslovak reception in terms of gender beyond the initial observations of the present essay.

Stardom Delayed: Pearl White's Czech Afterlives

Many of the American films that played in Czechoslovakia in the immediate postwar years experienced a sort of "second life," a popularity postponed several years after their initial theatrical runs. When large numbers of American films began to enter the market late in the summer of 1919, Czech companies were unable to afford the newest productions due to the poor economic circumstances in Czechoslovakia and the weakness of their newly introduced currency, the Crown. Consequently, distributors had access only to older American films made during the war years and for which there was decreased demand among the audiences of the Allied powers.[55] Thus, late 1919 and early 1920 saw the Czech premieres of many "old" serials like *The Red Ace* (1917) and *Liberty* (1916), as well as the Pearl White serials *The House of Hate* (1918), *The Fatal Ring* (1917), and *The Perils of Pauline* (the nine-episode European release from 1916).[56] In addition, the Griffith works *Birth of a Nation* (1915) and *Intolerance* (1916) both premiered in Prague four years after their original U.S. release (1919 and 1920, respectively). This situation had more or less abated by 1921, when Czech companies began to import "current releases." Eddie Polo's *King of the Circus* (1920), which played in Prague in May 1921, only about six months after its U.S. premiere, was one of the first examples of a "new" American film to play in Prague.

In the case of many American performers such as Pearl White, the Czechoslovak case presents a temporal oddity whereby their "Czech stardom" began only in 1919, often after they had been famous for many years in the United States and elsewhere across the globe. When her films first started playing to Prague audiences in early 1920, Pearl White was promoted as a "*new* American star" (emphasis added).[57] Of course, in this context she was only really new to Czechoslovakia. White had started acting nearly a decade earlier and had already achieved huge international fame by the mid-1910s, a good five years prior to her Czech debut.[58] Her first serial to play in Czechoslovakia, *The House of Hate*, began playing in the United States in March 1918 yet did not reach Prague until nearly two years later, premiering sometime around January 9, 1920.[59] This was the most heavily promoted of White's serials in Prague and consequently remained the most prominent of her films in Czech memory. On the occasion of the Prague premiere, the trade journal *Kino* ran an advertisement for *The House of Hate* on its cover and printed a plot summary for each of the serial's episodes over several pages. Hot on the heels of her debut, the serials *Lightning Raider* (*Činské tajemství* aka *Par amour* [1918]) and *The Fatal Ring* (*Ukradený diamant* aka *Dolarová princezna se nudí* [1917]) played in January and February.[60] Then, in May of that same year, the nine-episode European version of *The Perils of Pauline* (*Devět dobrodružství Pearl White* aka *Romantická nevěsta* [1914, this version from 1916]) had its run.[61] Evidence appears to indicate that these are the only four of White's action serials to play in Prague.[62] In late 1923 and early 1924, a number of the comedies and dramas she made with Fox were shown in Prague but were not nearly as successful

Cover of a Prague trade journal several weeks prior to the release of Pearl White's first serial, *House of Hate*, featuring a locally drawn promotional illustration for the film. *Kino* 1, no. 34 (December 19, 1919): 1.

as her earlier serials.[63] Even though their production was in decline by that time, it was the American action serials that continued to most successfully captivate the Czech imagination.[64]

Ironically, the rise of White's star persona in Czechoslovakia directly coincided with her decline in popularity in the United States and the effective end of her work in action serials, the genre that had defined her career. Although she was admittedly an enduring international star presence in 1920, the days of her best-known serials, such as *The Perils of Pauline* (1914), *The Exploits of Elaine* (1914), and *Pearl of the Army* (1916), were long gone. Of the more than two hundred films in which she appeared, only fourteen were made after 1918.[65] While many of these old films played in Czechoslovakia during the height of the serial craze in 1920, it was not until 1923 that some of White's more contemporary films were shown. Yet these films also had a delayed arrival in Prague, some being released as long as three years after their U.S. premieres. Thus, in a sense, White's star career was "twice delayed" in Czechoslovakia, coming in two main waves, 1919–1920 and 1923. Jennifer Bean has argued that "inasmuch as White figured as transnational icon and embodied a heroic new personhood freed from the laws of physics, she may be seen as the apotheosis of the metaphor of stardom."[66] As seen here in the case of Czechoslovakia, the light of international stardom does not strike equally in all places at once and sometimes did not even reach some nations until after the star itself had dimmed. As the following section demonstrates, when shone though different cultural prisms on a local level, this light often got refracted in intriguing ways.

The Con Man and Miss Pearl Whittingtonová

The American action serial and star phenomenon not only captivated audiences and inspired the avant-garde but also found a unique expression in Czech pulp fiction. Although essentially unknown today, Felix Achilles de la Cámara was a well-known author of adventure novels in the 1920s. At that time the Czech author was apparently living in Paris, where he worked as a correspondent for the Prague film trade journal *Divadlo Budoucnosti*, often contributing reports on Pearl White's visit to France.[67] In his writing, Cámara repeatedly expressed his adoration for White and even claimed that he had established an intimate friendship with her over the course of his time in Paris. He also wrote fictionalized versions of White into a series of adventure novels and further claimed that some of his stories were to serve as scripts for new films for the serial queen. The stories about his personal relationship with White cannot be taken at face value, as Cámara is far from a reliable source—indeed, he was notorious as a con man. Nevertheless, his writings represent a creative and uniquely Czech response to the American serial films in general and to Pearl White in particular. Although these examples of imaginative fiction might at first seem little more than curious oddities, they also represent a noteworthy contribution to the mythology of Pearl White in the

Czechoslovak context, a contribution that is remarkably consistent with the discourses of modernity, physical and mental health, fantasies of adventure, and femininity outlined above.

Cámara is an enigmatic and elusive figure whose life was shrouded in a fog of myth.[68] Little is known about his life, and those facts that are documented must be viewed with skepticism. Perhaps the most significant key to understanding Cámara is his fascination with the famous French imposter Count Cagliostro, after whom Cámara patterned the self-stylization of his own public image. Just as "Alessandro Cagliostro" was a pseudonym for Guiseppe Balsamo, "Felix Achilles de la Cámara" was merely an adopted name for this latter-day man of mystery, who was born Felix Emil Josef Karel Cammra in the town of Kutná Hora near Prague.[69] In spite of his Slavic origins, Cámara claimed lineage to a certain Spanish count, Cámara del Campo—just one gesture in the cultivation of his own public myth.[70] The mythology surrounding the forger and occultist Cagliostro also had a profound influence on Cámara's writing, which was wrought with stories of mystery and intrigue. Many novels even employed excerpts from a (fictional) study on Cagliostro as a primary narrative device.[71] Much like his German contemporary Hanns Heinz Ewers (author of *Der Student von Prag* [The student of Prague] and *Alraune*), Cámara's brand of popular fiction is heavily informed by legends, mythology, and the occult.[72] His stories contain elements derived from Egyptology, European mythology, and Hindu and other Eastern religions, as well as the rituals of secret societies such as the Freemasons. Thus, at least on a superficial level, his novels share inherent affinity to adventure films in terms of subject matter.[73] In addition, Cámara's narrative structures employ stylistic elements gleaned from action serials, such as criminal masterminded plots, simultaneous action in multiple exotic locales, communication via telegrams, and so on. Furthermore, the publication of a series of novels with an overarching storyline can be understood as an emulation of the serial film format itself. The imaginary world of the film adventure serial was thus a conspicuous source of inspiration and major narrative model for his novels, as well as for his own mythically stylized life.

Three of Cámara's first novels, *Černý Mág* (The black wizard; Kutná hora, Czechoslovakia: Nakladatelstyi Karla Šolce, 1920), *Jeho tajemství* (His secret; Kutná hora, Czechoslovakia: Nakladatelstyi Karla Šolce, 1921), and *Velekněžka magie* (Magic, the high priestess; Kutná hora, Czechoslovakia: Nakladatelstyi Karla Šolce, 1923), published between 1920 and 1923, form a trilogy that clearly shows a preoccupation with the style of action serial films, and with Pearl White specifically.[74] The leading heroine in all three books, a character to whom Cámara assigns the suggestively obvious name "Pearl Whittingtonová," is (of course) an American film actress—indeed "the queen of all American film stars," as one character calls her.[75] This character is not only a world famous action film star but is also entangled in the "real life" intrigues around which the trilogy of novels is constructed. When Whittingtonová is not busy on the film set, she can be found traversing the globe on dangerous adventures that mirror the cliff-hanger narratives of film serials.[76] Yet Cámara's creation of alternative, fanciful lives for his idol was not limited to this trilogy of novels. According to advertisements, White's fictional alter ego also appears in the following works: *Španělské markýzy* (Spanish marquises [1921]), *Filmová hvězda* (Film star [1922]), and *Fantomy* (Phantoms [1922]).[77] In addition, many of Cámara's books open with lyrical paeans to the real Pearl White, often including photographs of the actress. He also published an allegedly biographical account of White's life in *Perla filmu: Přběh života populární umělkyně Pearl White* (Pearl of the cinema: the life story of popular artist Pearl White), which also featured a picture of her autographed in dedication to Cámara, indicating his personal connection to her.[78] Assuming a myriad of forms, muse and artistic object alike, Pearl White was the preeminent shining star that illuminated Cámara's literary path and provided a fixed navigational point for his adventures.

Beyond his public expressions of admiration for the actress and the inclusion of the fictional Whittingtonová in his novels, Cámara publicly claimed to have an "intimate friendship" with the real Pearl White.[79] Indeed, one report went so far as to dub White and Cámara a "team" that worked closely and often together.[80] There were also recurrent references to Cámara as "Pearl White's author," a term that emerged in 1920 when one of his novels was allegedly accepted as source material for a new Pearl White action serial. A dispatch from Paris printed in *Divadlo budoucnosti* reported on the plans for this film: "Pearl White, the famous American beauty and film artist, will travel to Berlin for filming. There she will meet with Mr. De la Cámera, author of the novel *Černý mág*. This recently published Czech adventure novel is now being reworked for filming by a large American company. The novel is dedicated to Miss White, who according to reports, will play the main role in the film."[81] There are, however, no reports outside this trade journal (for which Cámara worked) that document plans to realize a film version of *Černý Mág*, raising the suspicion that this is simply a planted rumor—yet another facet of Cámara's self-styled public myth.[82] Undoubtedly, the information cited in the report stemmed from none other than Cámara, and it may be that he actually wrote

An intimate dedication in the opening pages of de la Cámara's "biography" of Pearl White. The Czech caption, which translates the autograph on the photograph, reads "To Felix de la Cámara my good author—Pearl White" and indicates "Paris 1921." Felix de la Cámara, *Perla filmu: Příběh života populární umělkyně Pearl White* (Pearl of the cinema: The life story of popular artist Pearl White) (Kutná hora, Czechoslovakia: Nakladatelství Karla Šolce [1923]), 15.

the piece himself. Curiously, this same journal, *Divadlo budoucnosti*, was by far the most consistent in printing enthusiastic reports on Pearl White even after 1921, when coverage of her had effectively disappeared from other journals. It is clear that Cámara was a prime motivator behind the publication of such reports, and in this he can be seen as a sort of self-appointed "promoter" of her image in the Czechoslovak press. In the end, the author's fortune in his homeland was closely entwined with White's, as he relied on her star status to promote his novels and thereby his own celebrity. In fact, Cámara also wrote (clearly recognizable) fictionalized versions of himself into his novels—for example, the character Don Alexandre Félix José de la Cartaya in the trilogy mentioned above—in an obvious attempt to amplify his "real life" connection to Pearl White by extending his relationship with her into his fictional world.

The nature of Cámara's cult of Pearl White was thus twofold. In the first place, he sought to promote his own celebrity by touting a relationship with the real-life actress; yet more significantly, he made concrete and significant contributions to White's star mythos by creating fictional afterlives for her. In a sense, Cámara's novels can be seen as independent offshoots of the hype-generating machine manufactured by the film studios and maintained by the film trade press. The inclusion of a character named Pearl in his novels is analogous to the early film convention whereby characters in the narrative had the same or similar names to the stars playing them (for example, *Pearl of the Army*). Without a doubt, many readers read the character of Pearl Whittingtonová as synonymous with the actual actress herself (which was, of course, the author's clear intention).[83] Although his works were not serialized in newspapers or magazines, they nevertheless mirrored the style of the action serial and functioned similarly to the print media tie-ins commonly used to promote stars and their films.[84] In a sense, these Czech adventure novels can be thought of as inverted tie-ins, or something akin to a spin-off. Rather than hyping White's films with his books, Cámara sought to bolster his own fame by hitching his wagon to her star.[85] In the act of promoting the real-life Pearl White, he also promoted his own fictionalized characterizations of her (and ultimately of his own mythical public image). Cámara's literary approach is not a far cry from the practices, employed by the trade press and film studios in the cultivation of star images, that sought to blur the lines between star and film character, a process that Bean describes as the "eclipse of the character by star . . . the semantic slip between the 'she' of the character and the 'she' of the star."[86] In much the same way, the aura of mystery and sensation surrounding Cámara's writing was amplified by his own public myth creation, by the blurring of the lines between truth and rumor, between real-life figures and the world of fiction. Ultimately, his works not only borrow narrative structures and characters from the action serials but also operate within the massive (international) synergy of hype that fuels the film star phenomenon itself.

Despite the aura of dubiousness surrounding him, Felix Achilles de la Cámara remains a key thread for conceptualizing the Czechoslovak reception of Pearl White in the late 1910s and the 1920s. In the first place, the simple existence of these multiple books based on Pearl White's life and screen persona served as demonstration of the cultural capital of her star image among the Czech public. At the same time, Cámara's series of adventure novels contributed to the cultivation of Pearl White's mythos in Czechoslovakia and became a significant factor in shaping the popular reception and memory of Pearl White. Finally, these adventure novels represented a curious manifestation of the fantasies of modernity, physical fitness, and mental health that Pearl White and American action serials fueled in the Czechoslovak imagination.

The works of Cámara brought the fantasy world of the American serials closer to the everyday experience of the average Czechoslovak citizen.[87] His novels offered a mode for audience identification with the fantasy world of American adventure serials by placing their narrative partially in Prague and through the inclusion of Czech characters and (often fictional) local lore. For example, parts of *Černý mág* purported to be taken from a manuscript by the Czech doctor Jan Pavel Frinta, in which he documents the existence of a mysterious "phantom of the Lesser Town" (*malostranský fantom*) that haunts the neighborhood beneath the Prague castle. In the early 1920s, the Czech film industry was not developed enough to support the production of its own "local" serials in the American mode, which would incorporate elements particularly adapted to a Czech audience by incorporating familiar images of Prague and Czech society. Whereas the films of Louis Feuillade thrilled French spectators and the Stuart Webbs serials brought American-style action closer to home for German audiences, the Czech reception of adventure serials always involved a fanciful encounter with an outside culture. For as much as Czech intellectuals and artists sought to transplant the spirit of the American serials to their nation, these films remained "foreign." Cámara's novels endeavored to bridge this cultural divide by providing, at least in printed form, a particularly Czech variation on the action serial theme. The prime mediator in his project was the star persona of Pearl White. It is therefore no coincidence that Cámara's engagement with the action serial genre lasted only as long as White herself was still a viable cultural icon in the country. The first of his serial novels was released during White's heyday in Czechoslovakia in 1920, and the last book with Pearl Whittingtonová appeared in 1923 at roughly the same time as the last film of "the queen of the serials" was playing at Prague theaters. During this time, however, Cámara was able to utilize the Pearl White alter ego and the adventure serial format to tap into Czech fantasies of geographical mobility and cosmopolitan, urban culture. The action of *Černý mág* alone transports the reader from Prague to Berlin, Hamburg, Paris, and London, while the later installments of the trilogy trace the plot to Seville, Chicago, Bayside (New York City), Salt Lake City, Manitowoc (Wisconsin), and beyond. In Cámara's fictional world, we can see echoes of the Americanized, chaotic, cinematic metropolis envisioned by Teige in the theoretical text cited earlier. The appropriation of the adventure serial predilection for shifting the action among numerous exotic locations created the effect of a "harmonious international city" (to borrow Teige's words), in which Prague performed an essential function on the same level as Berlin, Paris, Chicago, and other urban centers.[88]

The most noteworthy aspect of Cámara's appropriation of Pearl White's star persona with regard to the issues at hand, however, lies in his characterization of the fictional Whittingtonová. Much as Ludvík emphasized the physical attributes of female serial stars, Cámara was preoccupied with Whittingtonová's outward appearance and her athletic prowess. *Jeho tajemství*, the second installment of the aforementioned adventure trilogy, opens with a summary of the previous novel, *Černý mág*. In an otherwise concise recap of major plot points, devoid of detailed character description, Cámara dedicated a full page to a highly eroticized introduction to the figure of Whittingtonová: "The youthful artist of graceful movements and eurhythmic gait was clothed with exceptional elegance. Above her delicate, brown-powdered face, which possessed such fine, tiny lips as to make any redness from a lipstick redundant, sat a small, dark beret-cap, an adorable model with a small, green feather that charmingly extended her figure. She wore a dark dress and polished stilettos adorned her delicate feet. When she gracefully removed her exquisite fur coat, she revealed shoulders of Grecian beauty, playfully exposed by the sleeves that ended above her elbows."[89] This sexually charged image of the actress was reinforced throughout the trilogy by suggestive photographs of the real Pearl White (often at the beginning of the books) and graphic illustrations of Whittingtonová that largely conformed to this verbal description. Yet this fictional actress was not merely a beautiful object to behold; she was also an amazingly skilled athlete. For her work in the cinema, she had to learn how to "swim, ride a horse, as well as drive automobiles, motorcycles, airplanes, locomotives, motor boats etc. In addition, she had to learn the rules and how to play tennis, golf, and hundreds of other games."[90] Whittingtonová further

Illustration from de la Cámara's *Velekněžka magie*, depicting the semifictional heroine Miss Pearl Whittingtonová (with chapter title "V jejích stopách" [following in her footsteps]). Felix de la Cámara, *Velekněžka magie* (Magic, the high priestess) (Kutná hora, Czechoslovakia: Nakladatelství Karla Šolce [1923]): 9.

admitted that she had brushed with death hundreds of times while performing stunts for her films but always prevailed on account of her remarkable agility. In other words, the actress was every bit as physically elegant and athletically skilled as the characters she played on screen.

Beyond her physical attributes, though, the fictional Whittingtonová also possesses a healthiness of mind that stands in direct opposition to the evil, occult powers that menace the protagonists of the adventure trilogy. At the beginning of *Černý mág*, four respectable gentlemen from Prague attend a séance in the notorious Golden Lane within the walls of the Prague castle during which they become accidentally entangled in the activities of the mysterious sect of the Broken Cross, which worships the satanic figure of Baphomet. In the ensuing encounters with the forces of black magic, one of the men dies, another one mysteriously disappears, and a third is stricken with a mortal illness as a direct result of his experiences. Upon traveling from Prague to Berlin to convalesce, this sick man meets Pearl Whittingtonová, with whom he immediately falls in love. The relationship with the American actress has a remarkable therapeutic effect on him. He "forgot about everything, even about the phantom of the Lesser Town, dedicating his thoughts instead to the blond artist," whereby his affliction suddenly abates.[91] When the remaining Czech protagonists tell of their encounters with black magic, Whittingtonová, being an "American woman of practical mind and modern upbringing," rejects their stories as mere superstition, refusing to recognize the power of such occult forces.[92] In this way the novels construct an image of Europe, still plagued by shadowy, supernatural elements from its medieval past, which is confronted with the virility of the modern, practical mode of being as embodied by the beautifully robust American film star.

At the end of *Černý mág*, this female emblem of American vigor herself defeats the evil forces that have proved such a difficult match for the Czech protagonists. In true action serial style, Whittingtonová miraculously appears at the novel's climax to rescue the two main male characters just as they are about to die at the hands of the mysterious satanic cult. Having secretly followed the men from Paris to London, Pearl arrives in the nick of time to shoot down the high priest of Baphomet and dispose of the black wizard before any harm comes to the male protagonists. This confrontation between the oppressive, sickly elements of European culture and a physically and mentally robust American film star is profoundly reminiscent of the showdown that Teige imagined between the "unhealthy hysteria" of Caligarism and the "Yankee optimism" of American cinema. In fact Cámara's self-serving instrumentalization of Pearl White can be thought of as a uniquely profound illustration of the more general patterns of American serial film reception by the population as a whole. The *mise en abyme* that the author fashioned in Miss Pearl Whittingtonová was itself a reflection of the complex web of discourses circulating at various levels of Czech society as it strove to create meaning from these thrilling cinematic entertainments and to accommodate them to the needs and concerns of the still-nascent national body. As we have seen, the American serial film, and the female stars in particular, were a profound source of inspiration for intellectuals and average citizens alike. Indeed, at the time he was writing, Cámara could hardly have chosen a more fascinating figure than the blond action star Pearl White to capture the imagination and excite the male fantasies of Czech audiences at the moment when they had thrown off the constraints of the Old World and were turning optimistically toward the future.

NOTES

1. The record shows that Pearl White's films also played in cinemas that catered to Czechoslovakia's sizeable German-speaking population. It appears as if the very same films discussed here in the context of Czech-speaking spectatorship were also seen at around the same time by German audiences in the country. These were marketed under German translations of the English titles and presumably contained German intertitles. The current essay, however, is concerned exclusively with the reception of Pearl White among the country's Czech-speaking majority.

2. Both Karel Smrž writing in the 1930s and Zdeněk Štábla in the 1980s specifically name only *The House of Hate* from among Pearl White's films. Karel Smrž, "Morální a nemorální," *Svět ve filmu* 1, no. 54 (1932): 7; Zdeněk Štábla, *Data a fakta z dejin čs. kinematografie 1896–1945*, vol. 2 (Prague: Čs. filmový ústav, 1988), 116–17.

3. Other serial queens, such as Ruth Roland and Helen Holmes, had successful careers in Czechoslovakia that actually outlasted White's period of fame. Yet for at least a few months in 1920, White was the undisputed champion among audiences. An often-cited survey printed in *Národní listy*, one of Prague's leading newspapers, in January 1920 listed Pearl White as the most popular female actress in the country. In terms of all actors, she was ranked second only to the male favorite, Eddie Polo. In the same survey, White's serial *The House of Hate* ranked high on the list of most beloved films. See, for example, the summary of the survey in *Československý film* 2, no. 3 (February 15, 1920): 3–5, which also highlighted the tremendous popularity of American films in general.

4. See, for example, the *Photoplay* article from 1917 cited in Jennifer M. Bean, "Technologies of Early Stardom and the Extraordinary Body," *Camera Obscura* 16, no. 3 (2001): 11.

5. During the war years, the marketing strategies of the local film industry and trade press promoted a star system centered on German and Scandinavian actors. After the war, many new American performers were first introduced to Czech audiences by means of comparison to these established stars. Mary Pickford was originally labeled "the American Henny Porten," the German actress who until the end of World War I was the biggest female star in the Czech lands, as well as in most of Central Europe. See, for example, the newspaper reports on *Daddy-Long-Legs* (*Táta Dlouhán*):

Unsigned, "Biografy," *Národní listy* 59, no. 268 (November 15, 1919): 3, and Unsigned, "Biografy," *Národní listy* 59, no. 273 (November 21, 1919): 4. Likewise, when debuted in Czechoslovakia, Dustin Farnum was dubbed the "American Psilander" after the famous Danish actor Valdemar Psilander.

6. Before Pearl White was known in Prague, Czech audiences had already become acquainted with the likes of Marie Walcamp, Mary Pickford, Ruth Clifford, Eddie Polo, and Dustin Farnum. The Czech public's first introduction to the American action serial altogether was Walcamp's *The Red Ace* (*Červené eso* [1917], also with Eddie Polo), which played in Prague from July 18 to August 7, 1919 (according to Štábla, *Data a fakta z dejin čs. kinematografie*, 116–17). That October saw the premieres of Walcamp's *Liberty* (1917) and Dustin Farnum's *The Light of the Western Stars* (*V září hvezd Kalifornie*, 1917).

7. See, for example, Smrž, "Morální a nemorální," 7; Štábla, *Data a fakta z dejin čs. kinematografie*, 116–17; and Luboš Bartošek, *Náš film: kapitoly z dějin (1896–1945)* (Prague: Mladá fronta, 1985), 59.

8. Ben Singer, *Melodrama and Modernity: Early Sensational Cinema and Its Contexts* (New York: Columbia University Press, 2001), 131–39.

9. For in-depth analysis of the complex issues of nationality and modernity in Czechoslovak society, see Derek Sayer, *The Coasts of Bohemia: A Czech History* (Princeton, N.J.: Princeton University Press, 1998).

10. Evidence for the inspiration provided by the American democratic model can also be seen in the renaming of public spaces in Czechoslovakia. In a prominent example, during the First Republic the name of Prague's main railway hub was changed from Emperor Franz Joseph station to Wilson station (Wilsonovo nádraží) in honor of the U.S. president.

11. Karel Čapek, "A.W.F. Co.," *Národ* 1, no. 4 (May 24, 1917): 73–75, English quotation in *Cinema All the Time: An Anthology of Czech Film Theory and Criticism, 1908–1939*, ed. Jaroslav Anděl and Petr Szczepanik (Prague: National Film Archive, 2008), 112.

12. Karel Teige, "Estetika filmu a kinografie," *Host* 3, nos. 6–7 (April 1924): 143–52, English quotation in "The Aesthetics of Film and *Cinégraphie*," in *Cinema All the Time*, 145–46. Teige was co-founder of the avant-garde group Devětsil, a leader of the poetist movement, and later a key member of the Czechoslovak surrealists. Although the depth and importance of his work places him on par with his contemporaries in France and Germany, he is generally, and tragically, unknown outside of the Czech Republic. For the most extensive writings on his life and work to be published in English, see Eric Dluhosch and Rostislav Švácha, eds., *Karel Teige/1900–1951: L'enfant terrible of the Czech modernist avant-garde* (Cambridge, Mass.: MIT Press, 1999).

13. Teige, "Aesthetics of Film," in *Cinema All the Time*, 146.

14. A. V. Ludvík, "Amerika na postupu," *Kino* 1, no. 13 (June 20, 1919): 2–6.

15. Specific film titles mentioned by Ludvík are *A Modern Othello*, aka *The Mad Lover* (*Moderní Othello* [1917]), *Bread* (*Chleb* [1918]), and *Žena rukojmi* (Woman hostage [n.d.]).

16. Karel Čapek was primarily a dramatist and writer of fiction, but he also published numerous nonfiction works, including a series of conversations with T. G.

Masaryk, the founder and first president of Czechoslovakia, with whom he was a close friend. His brother Josef was also a writer of prose and criticism, but he is best remembered as the leading Czech representative of cubist painting. Both brothers were fascinated with film and published numerous works on the subject.

17. Josef Čapek, "Film," *Cesta* 1, no. 18 (October 4, 1918): 477–78, English quotation in "Film," in *Cinema All the Time*, 116.

18. Despite the general ban on products from the United States during World War I, the American World Film Company managed to export a number of productions from the United States into Austria-Hungary. According to Štábla, the first of these was the Clara Kimball-Young picture, *Hearts in Exile* (1915), which played in Prague in late September 1916. The exact ways these films made it into Austria-Hungary are not known. Štábla suggests a scenario whereby they were "smuggled" in through neutral Switzerland under the pretense of being Swiss films. However, Štábla fails to indicate his sources for these claims, so his speculations remain to be independently confirmed. Regardless of how they ended up in Prague, the Czech public clearly perceived them as American films. Films discussed by Karel Čapek in "A. W. F. Co." include *The Boss* (1915), *A Butterfly on the Wheel* (1915), and *Camille* (1915). The article also expresses his admiration for the actors Holbrook Blinn and Alice Brady.

19. Josef Čapek, "Film," 116.

20. Ibid., 117.

21. Ibid., 117. Josef Čapek went on to assert that American film photography "has an incomparably more beautiful tone than that in German films," a fact that he attributed to a higher degree of perfection within the photographic materials themselves. The implication is that the United States is superior to Germany not only aesthetically, but also in terms of scientific innovation (see his discussion on p. 119). A. Ludvík also specifically praised the photographic quality of American films, which he claimed superseded that of Italian and Scandinavian productions (hitherto considered at the pinnacles of achievement in this field). See A. V. Ludvík "Amerika na postupu" (America rising), *Kino* 1, no. 13 (June 20, 1919): 3.

22. The loosely organized Devětsil was the most salient association of modern poets, artists, architects, actors, musicians, and theoreticians in Czechoslovakia. At one point or another, its ranks included Karel Teige, Bedřich Václavek, Vitěslav Nezval, Jaroslav Seifert, Vladislav Vančura, and a host of other important figures, many of whom became involved in film production in the 1930s. In a further demonstration of their cinematic tastes, the group claimed both Charlie Chaplin and Douglas Fairbanks as honorary members. For a brief summary of Devětsil, see Sayer, *Coasts of Bohemia*, 209–10.

23. In addition to the works quoted in this essay from *Cinema All the Time*, see also in the same volume: Karel and Josef Čapek, "The Cinema," 104–6 (originally as "Biograf," *Stopa* 1, no. 19 [November 4, 1910]: 595–96); Karel Čapek, "The Style of the Cinematograph," 107–10 (originally as "Styl kinematografu," *Styl* 5, no. 5 [June 1913]: 146–48); Vítězslav Nezval, "Photogénie," in *Cinema All the Time*, 165–69 (originally as

"Fotogenie," *Český filmový svět* 3, no. 9 [June 1925]: 5–6); and Vítězslav Nezval, "Film," in *Cinema All the Time*, 170–73 (originally as "Film," *Český filmový svět* 3, nos. 10–11 [September 1925]: 6–7). Most of these works, together with texts by other Czech authors, were published in English for the first time in this anthology.

24. Teige, "Aesthetics of Film," in *Cinema All the Time*, 152. Teige was, in fact, friends with Delluc, and the two exchanged letters. The writings of Delluc and his fellow French theorists Jean Epstein and Léon Moussinac were widely known in Czech intellectual circles of the early 1920s and were a profound source of inspiration for Teige and the other members of Devětsil, especially Vitěslav Nezval and Jíří Voskovec. Most texts by these French theorists likely circulated only in their original language, although some of Delluc's "cinematic dramas" were translated into Czech. Of particular importance for the Czech poetists were the French concepts of cinégraphie and photogénie, which featured prominently in the film theory of Teige, Nezval, and Voskovec (in the transliterated forms kinografie and fotogenie). Later, in the 1930s, Epstein's writings would play an influential role in the theoretical filmic thought of Jan Mukařovský and Roman Jakobson, the primary representatives of the Prague Linguistic Circle. See *Cinema All the Time*, 37–39, 129, 145, 161, 165, 254–56, 273.

25. *Cinema All the Time*, 148.

26. Ibid., 152. Although such terminology resonates with the "degenerate art" argument that German Nazism leveled against expressionism, Teige's modernist program was decidedly distinct from the mystical, neoclassic aesthetic championed by the Nazis.

27. For a brief summary of *Caligari*'s role in establishing a recognizable German style of cinema on the international market, see Sabine Hake, *German National Cinema* (New York: Routledge, 2002), 28–30.

28. Teige, "Aesthetics of Film," in *Cinema All the Time*, 154.

29. For a detailed analysis of the theories of Simmel, Kracauer, and Benjamin, see Singer, *Melodrama and Modernity*, 101–30, and Ben Singer, "Modernity, Hyperstimulus, and the Rise of Popular Sensationalism," in *Cinema and the Invention of Modern Life*, ed. Leo Charney and Vanessa R. Schwartz (Berkeley: University of California Press, 1995), 72–99.

30. Bedřich Václavek, "K sociologii filmu," *Pásmo* 1, nos. 5–6 (1924): 4, English quotation in "On the Sociology of Film," in *Cinema All the Time*, 156.

31. Václavek, "On the Sociology of Film," in *Cinema All the Time*, 156–58.

32. Ibid., 159.

33. Stanislav Kostka Neumann, "Film," *Červen* 2, no. 19 (July 10, 1919): 170–71, English quotation in "Film," in *Cinema All the Time*, 10.

34. See Václav Tille, "Kinéma," in *Cinema All the Time*, 86–87. This originally appeared as the serialized article "Kinéma" in the following issues of *Novina*, vol. 1: no. 21 (October 6, 1908): 647–51; no. 22 (November 13, 1908): 689–93; and no. 23 (November 20, 1908): 716–20.

35. See *Cinema All the Time*, 86–87n17–18.

36. The same rationale holds true for all subsequent long quotations in this essay.

37. Unsigned, "Pearl White," *Kino* 1, no. 34 (December 19, 1919): 2.

38. Quoted in Sayer, *Coasts of Bohemia*, 106. See also Sayer's further discussion of Sokol for more background on its patriotic aspirations and national foundations.

39. According to Lubomír Linhart, "Proletarischer Filmkampf in der Tschechoslowakei," *Arbeiterbühne und Film* 2, no. 2 (1931): 28, repr. as "The Proletarian Film Struggle in Czechoslovakia," in *Cinema All the Time*, 187.

40. Teige, "Aesthetics of Film," in Cinema All the Time, 153.

41. See Karel Teige, "Foto kino film," in *Život: Sborník nové krásy*, ed. Jaromír Krejcar (Prague: Výtvarný odbor Umělecké besedy, 1922), 153–68, English quotation in "Photo Cinema Film," in *Cinema All the Time*, 138.

42. Teige, "Photo Cinema Film," *Cinema All the Time*, 141.

43. Teige, "Aesthetics of Film," in *Cinema All the Time*, 154, 145.

44. Ibid., 154.

45. Quoted in Vicki Callahan, *Zones of Anxiety: Movement, Musidora, and the Crime Serials of Louis Feuillade* (Detroit: Wayne State University Press, 2005): 101–2. The French text cited by Callahan comes from Jean Mitry, "Pearl White," *Anthologie du Cinéma*, vol. 5 (Paris: L'Avant-Scène, 1969), 11.

46. Unsigned, "Pearl White," *Kino* 1, no. 34 (December 19, 1919): 2.

47. The series was called, quite descriptively, "Americká záplava," or "American flood."

48. The author's choice of words in gender-sensitive Czech would imply that the heroes here are male (*hrdiny*) rather than female (*hrdinky*), or at least a mixture of genders, since the male plural also serves as default form. It is notable that Ludvík chooses to not use the specifically feminine plural form even though he addresses only female performers here. The later use of "artists" and "athletes" is also grammatically marked as male, even though the reference is clearly to females. In one instance, though, Ludvík does employ the feminine plural form of "artist" (*umělkyně*), which I have indicated with the inclusion of the modifier "female" in my translation. Ludvík's grammatical choices can perhaps be read as an expression of the gender ambivalence embodied by the serial queens as described by Bean, Singer, and Stamp (see note 54).

49. A. Ludvík, "Americká záplava III" (American flood III), *Právo lidu, Pražské pondělí* 2, no. 3 (January 19, 1920): 5.

50. Ibid.

51. It should also be noted here that the films of Douglas Fairbanks and Charlie Chaplin arrived in Prague only after this particular article was written. Perhaps the author would have offered a different take on the division between male and female performance had he been familiar with the intensely physical style of acting that made these actors famous. The impact of Fairbanks and Chaplin is clearly visible, for example, in the writings of modernists Nezval and Teige.

52. Callahan, *Zones of Anxiety*, 102.

53. For more on the variant receptions of Irma Vep/Musidora and Pearl White in

France, see ibid., 73–116, and Annette Förster, "Schwärmerei für einen Schatten: Musidora und das Nachleben von Irma Vep," *montage/av* 8, no. 2 (1999): 51–76.

54. See, for example, Bean, "Technologies"; Singer, *Melodrama and Modernity*, 221–62; Ben Singer, "Female Power in the Serial-Queen Melodrama: The Etiology of an Anomaly," *Silent Film*, ed. Richard Abel (New Brunswick, N.J.: Rutgers University Press, 1996), 163–93; and Shelly Stamp, *Movie-Struck Girls* (Princeton, N.J.: Princeton University Press, 2000), 102–53.

55. Writing in January 1920, Ludvík commented that Charlie Chaplin's best films had not yet played in Prague, as they were the most expensive products on the market and Prague companies simply could not afford them due to the weak purchasing power of the Czech Crown. Instead, distributors satisfied their customers with the films of Chaplin imitator Billy West. See A. Ludvík, "Americká záplava III," *Právo lidu, Pražské pondělí* 2, no. 3 (January 19, 1920): 5. Thus, the Czech audience's first contact with the Chaplin phenomenon was via imitation, through simulacra of "Chaplin." According to Štábla, the first authentic Chaplin films played in January 1920 (*Caught in the Cabaret*, 1914; *Mabel's Busy Day*, 1914; and *The Bank*, 1915). Štábla, *Data a fakta z dejin čs. kinematografie*, 140. Note that all three films were at least five years old by that time.

56. This phenomenon was by no means unique to American imports. The summer of 1920 also saw Prague premieres of a number of older French action serials directed by Louis Feuillade, including *Les Vampires* (1915), *Judex* (1916), *La Nouvelle mission de Judex* (1917), and *Tih Minh* (1918). Similarly, the world-famous Italian epic, *Cabiria* (1914), did not premiere in Prague until the summer of 1921.

57. See, for example, Unsigned, "Pearl White," *Kino* 1, no. 34 (December 19, 1919): 2.

58. Ibid.

59. U.S. release date as indicated on IMDb, the Internet Movie Database, at http://imdb.com/title/tt0009204/releaseinfo (accessed December 2, 2012).

60. It is interesting that the Czech distribution titles for these serials are not direct translations of the English titles. The translation of the Czech name for *Lightning Raider* is "The Chinese secret" (*Čínské tajemství*), while some sources identify this serial using the nontranslated French name, *Par amour*. The two Czech variations for *The Fatal Ring* translate to "The stolen diamond" (*Ukradený diamant*) and "The Boredom of a dollar-princess" (*Dolarová princeyna se nudí*).

61. The original 20-episode serial from 1914 was shortened to a 9-episode version when exported to Europe in 1916. The literal translation of the Czech title, "Nine adventures of Pearl White," makes it clear that this was indeed the later version of the serial. The alternate Czech title translates as "The romantic bride."

62. There are indications of plans to import White's serial *The Black Secret* (1919) by mid-1920, yet the film does not turn up in any reviews or cinema announcements from that period. See Julius Schmitt, "Co přinese podzim u Biografie," *Československý film* 2, no. 5 (March 15, 1920): 6.

63. The Czechoslovak distribution branch of Fox Film Corporation, which was established in Prague in 1923, brought five of Pearl White's films to the market: *Tygrovo*

mládě (*The Tiger's Cub* [1920]), *Nedostižitelná žena* (*Beyond Price* [1921]), *Znáte své muže?* (*Know Your Men!* [1921]), *Panenský raj* (*A Virgin Paradise* [1921]), and *Zlodej* (*The Thief* [1920]). After these five features, Fox no longer carried her films, and she disappeared from promotional advertisements highlighting the company's stars.

64. This resulted in widespread repeated runs of the most famous films. In 1923 at least one Prague cinema (with the fitting name "American") reprised several American action serials, including *The Fatal Ring* (*Ukradenený diamant*) and *The Perils of Pauline* (*Devět dobrodružství*), with Pearl White, and Ruth Roland's *Hands up!* (*Ruce vzhůru!*). See, for example, Unsigned, "Toulky po kinech," *Filmová Praha* 4, no. 19 (May 11, 1923): 150; Unsigned, "Toulky po kinech," *Filmová Praha* 4, no. 25 (June 22, 1923): 197; Unsigned, "Toulky po kinech," *Filmová Praha* 4, no. 30 (September 21, 1923): 238.

65. Note that this was not always so. In the case of Mary Pickford, for example, who was not introduced to Czechoslovakia until 1919, all of the films imported at that time were relatively recent productions.

66. Bean, "Technologies," 11.

67. The journal's title translates literally as "theater of the future." It began publication in 1920 and was renamed *Filmová Praha* (Film Prague) in 1923, the fourth and last year of its existence.

68. The most extensive account of Cámara's life is provided in Ivan Adamovič, *Slovník české literární fantastiky a science fiction* (Prague: R3, 1995), 61–62. This work also includes a list of Cámara's fantastic novels on pp. 276–77. For more on Cámara's elusive biography, including discussions of his alleged fascist and Nazi sympathies, see Vladimír Forst, ed., *Lexikon České literatury* (Prague: Academia, 1993), 1266–67; Milan Nekonečný, *Novodobý český hermetismus* (Prague: Vodnář, 1995): 214–19; Martin Valášek, Václav Petrbok, and Jakub Krč, eds., "Rozhovor s Jiřím Brabcem nejen o nacionalismu, fašismu, antisemitismu a literatuře," *Souvislost* 6, no. 4 (1995): 3–9, also at http://www.souvislosti.cz/archiv/brabec4-95.htm (accessed December 2, 2012); Anastasie Kopřivová, "Polozapomenuté přiběhy: Osudy ruských emigrantů spjatých s Národním divadlem," *Divadelní revue* 15, no. 1 (March 22, 2004): 45–62.

69. Other documented pseudonyms include Cámara del Campo, F. A. Fournier-Cámara, and J. Chernonval.

70. Otakar Štorch-Marien, *Tma a co bylo potom* (Prague: Aventinum, 1993), 230.

71. In fact, just one year later Cámara himself published a study of the infamous forger titled simply *Hrabě de Cagliostro* (Count de Cagliostro) (Kutná hora, Czechoslovakia: Nakladatelství Karla Šolce, 1922).

72. Like Cámara, Ewers also wrote fictionalized characters based upon himself into his novels and also like him became involved with the Nazi Party in the 1930s.

73. White's *The Lightning Raider*, for example, featured Egyptian mummies and a mysterious Chinese underground organization. Also, note that by 1921 Cagliostro's story had already been the subject of multiple films, including *Cagliostro, aventurier, chimiste et magicien* (dir. Camille de Morlhon and Gaston Velle, 1910) and *Der Graf von Cagliostro* (dir. Reinhold Schünzel, 1921), the latter of which is specifically mentioned

in the preface to Cámara's *Jeho tajemství* (Kutná hora, Czechoslovakia: Nakladatelství Karla Šolce, 1921).

74. It is also worth noting that the titles of the first two books in the trilogy appear to have been directly gleaned from the Pearl White serial, *The Black Secret* (1919).

75. Cámara, *Jeho tajemství*, 124. Note that the "-ová" ending is the common nominal designation for females in the Czech language (as well as in Slovak), being simply tagged onto the male version of a last name. Since the character in Cámara's books is American, the Czech feminine ending can be understood as a merely lexical addition for the Czech readership in compliance with Czech grammar (as is still common practice when writing foreign names in Czech). Thus, Whittingtonová is merely the female inflexion of Whittington. For the purposes of this essay, I maintain the Czech gender marking in the name of this fictionalization of White.

76. The novels also include direct references to other existing film personas. In *Jeho tajemství*, for example, the character Pearl Whittingtonová speaks about working on her next action film with actor William Clifford. Interestingly, the fictional Whittingtonová does not have too high an opinion of Clifford, mentioning in a brief aside that she would prefer as her acting partner one of the other characters in the novel (see Cámara, *Jeho tajemství*, 123). This encounter on the film set is, of course, also pure fantasy, since the "real life" White and Clifford never appeared on screen together.

77. The presence of Whittingtonová in these novels is indicated in the advertisements at the (nonpaginated) back of Felix de la Cámara, *Perla filmu: Příběh života populární umělkyně Pearl White* (Kutná hora, Czechoslovakia: Nakladatelství Karla Šolce, 1923).

78. Ibid., 15. According to announcements on the Czech release, this book is the Czech translation of *Miss Pearl White*, originally published by Cámara in French. The existence of a French version has not been independently confirmed. It is likely that the "French background" was merely a marketing ploy to increase the exotic appeal of the book to the Czech public.

79. Beyond his ostensible ties to White, Cámara was also purported to be close friends with Mary Pickford and Douglas Fairbanks (see, for example, the article "Mary Pickfordová," *Divadlo Budoucnosti* 2, no. 31 [1921]: 1, which also features an autographed photo of Pickford dedicated to de la Cámara).

80. "Pearl White—F. A. de la Cámara," *Filmová Praha* 4, no. 41 (December 14, 1923): 322. This article was published as part of the journal's hyping of Cámara's new book, *Perla filmu*. Supposedly, the article was translated into Czech from a French original written by "P. d'Hincourt."

81. Unsigned, "Novinky z týdne," *Divadlo Budoucnosti* 1, no. 10 (1920): 1.

82. Later in his career, though, Cámara did become active in the film industry, authoring the screenplays for seven Czech films from 1936 to 1940, the most famous being *Divka v modrém* (1940), with Lída Baarová and Oldřich Nový. He even served as co-director (with Svatopluk Innemann) for one film based on his own script (*Tvoje srdce incognito*, 1936).

83. Also note that *The Perils of Pauline* was marketed in Czechoslovakia as *Devět dobrodružství Pearl White* (Nine adventures of Pearl White), with the conflation of the actress with her screen role being evident in the title itself.

84. See Stamp, *Movie-Struck Girls*, 103–10.

85. Note that his novel, *Černý mág*, was originally marketed as the alleged source material for a new Pearl White film, although it is unlikely that there were actual plans to realize such a film. See discussion above.

86. Bean, "Technologies," 21. See also her analysis of how film companies promoted actors by manufacturing a life full of "stunts" to be presented to the public; in other words, inventing stunts that the actors had supposedly done in their real lives to intensify their star image. Ibid., 23–24.

87. The aesthetic of American films also left an indelible mark on the fictional works of the Czech avant-garde, albeit as part of a much different project: these artists took inspiration from American cinema for the creation of innovative poetic forms. Their fascination with cinematic themes from the United States, especially action serials and the films of Chaplin, is evident in the "photogenic poems" composed by members of Devětsil as an attempt to capture in literature the essence of the filmic medium. For a detailed analysis of these lyrical screenplays, see Viktoria Hradská, *Česká avantgarda a film* (Prague: ČS. filmový ústav, 1976).

88. Teige, "Aesthetics of Film," 146.

89. Cámara, *Jeho tajemství*, 16.

90. Ibid., 17.

91. Ibid.

92. Ibid., 18.

CHAPTER 6

Not Quite (Pearl) White

Fearless Nadia, Queen of the Stunts

ROSIE THOMAS

It was June 1935 on a dark, monsoon-lashed Bombay night and J. B. H. Wadia was taking one of the biggest gambles of his film production career. His new venture, *Hunterwali* (Woman with the whip; dir. Homi Wadia [1935]), was premiering at the Super Cinema in downtown Grant Road. The film had been an unprecedented six months in the making and cost more than eighty thousand rupees, but no distributor had come forward to buy it. Rumors in the industry suggested it was a turkey: the film starred a large, blonde-haired muscle woman with fearsome fighting skills who thrashed Indian men into the ground—on the face of it, an unlikely proposition for Indian audiences at the height of the nationalist movement. JBH and his partners had been reduced to pooling their own resources to secure a release. Extravagant pre-publicity had reeled in large crowds for the opening night. It was now up to their new star, Fearless Nadia, aka Mary Evans, in her role as a masked avenging angel, to deliver the goods. Billed as the "Indian Pearl White" and playing a swashbuckling princess in disguise, she roamed the countryside on horseback sporting hot pants, big bosom, and bare white thighs, and when she wasn't swinging from chandeliers, kicking or whipping men, she was righting wrongs with her bare fists and an imperious scowl. By the time Nadia hitched up her sari and cracked her whip in the third reel, declaring "*Aaj*

Fearless Nadia in *Lootaru Lalna* (Dacoit Damsel) (1938): publicity booklet cover. Used with permission of Wadia Movietone / Roy Wadia.

se main Hunterwali hoon" (From today I am [to be known as] the woman with the whip), the audience was cheering. Within days the Wadia brothers knew they were sitting on a gold mine; the film ran to packed houses for more than twenty-five weeks and became the major moneymaker of the year. Fearless Nadia became a sensation across the country, and unofficial merchandising followed. Fearless Nadia whips, belts, matchboxes, and playing cards appeared, and her famous yell, "*hey-y-y*," became a catchphrase. Nadia went on to secure a reputation as one of the biggest female film stars of the Indian screen in the 1930s and early 1940s.

Also in 1935, just outside Bombay in rural Malad, an urbane Brahmin beauty, Devika Rani, and her charismatic husband, producer Himansu Rai, were launching a visionary new studio enterprise, Bombay Talkies. Already the toast of London high society for her debut as a glamorous oriental princess in Rai's Anglo-Indian co-production, *Karma* (*Fate*; dir. J. L. Freer-Hunt [1933]), Devika quickly established her own and Bombay Talkies' reputation at home with the phenomenal box-office and critical success of *Achhut Kanya* (Untouchable girl; dir. Franz Osten [1936]). This premiere was a grand affair at Bombay's Roxy Cinema, boasting a glittering cosmopolitan audience that, legend has it, included Nehru. Devika's role as a doe-eyed, tragic heroine, an untouchable village belle trapped in a doomed romance, was seen as a social comment on caste iniquities, establishing her as a major icon of Indian cinema and the other top female star of the era.

The two women could scarcely have been more different: where Nadia was big, buxom, blonde, and blue eyed, a white-skinned former circus artiste who had been the darling of the soldiers in the North-West Frontier, Devika was a conventional Indian beauty. Petite, almost childlike, with long dark hair and large velvety brown eyes, she was upper class and upper caste, London-educated at South Hampstead High School and the Royal Academy of Dramatic Art (RADA), and widely known to be a grandniece of Tagore. While Nadia and her director (later to be her husband), Homi Wadia, moved in the world of Bombay clubs and horse racing and openly admired and adapted the popular comic book fare of Hollywood action serials and comedies, Devika and her husband and director, Himansu Rai, moved among the European cosmopolitan elite, learning their craft at Berlin's UFA studios and drawing their inspiration—and many of their technicians—from German cinema. Where Devika was the aristocrat who made her screen reputation through playing an outcaste, Nadia was the outcaste who played princess. The two star personae—neither of them the most likely of nationalist icons and both of them speaking poor Hindi—are in interesting ways inversions of each other. In examining the late colonial period, we might see the two as complementary exotic fictions, speaking to the project of defining Indianness while simultaneously exploding the idea of Indian cinema as isolated from the rest of the world.

Nadia, in her heyday, was the queen of the box office. It was, however, Devika who became the "First Lady" of Indian cinema, celebrated by the critics and fêted throughout Europe. Until recently, Devika dominated the histories of Indian film of this period as the embodiment of good, serious, and patriotic cinema, her movies seminal in establishing the genre of Indian film melodrama.[1] Nadia, despite her extraordinary popularity with mass audiences, both in India and throughout the diasporic distribution networks of Southeast Asia, the Middle East, the Caribbean, and Africa, was virtually unknown in Europe or America and had been largely erased from official Indian cinema histories until recent years.[2]

Focusing on the intriguing figure of Fearless Nadia, this essay explores the construction of one form of modern Indian femininity in the late colonial period, examining Nadia within the film production context of 1930s Bombay and, in passing, drawing comparisons with her shadow persona, Devika. I ask why Nadia was chosen by the Wadias and why she was so popular with her contemporary audiences. I explore how the Wadia brothers dealt with her whiteness/otherness and negotiated the points of tension in her image, especially in the context of the nationalist movement. Finally, I ask to what extent she simply copied Hollywood stunt stars such as Pearl White—and how these role models were Indianized. I conclude by suggesting that this was a form of colonial mimicry in reverse that provided potent currency in the nationalist era.

Wadia Brothers

It has been well documented that in the early decades of the twentieth century, the world of Indian cinema boasted very real exchanges of personnel between Bombay and the cinemas of both Hollywood and Europe.[3] Indian audiences had been exposed to Hollywood from the earliest years: the stunt and action films and serials of stars such as Pearl White, Ruth Roland, Charlie Chaplin, Eddie Polo, and Douglas Fairbanks ran to full houses throughout the 1910s and 1920s, when four out of five films screened were foreign and Douglas Fairbanks's *Thief of Bagdad* (dir. Raoul Walsh [1924]) was the decade's most popular film. *The Perils of Pauline* hit Bombay in mid-1915 along with a massive marketing campaign: the *Bombay Chronicle* ran a forty-part, full-page serialization of the stories over three months, alongside ads claiming, inter alia, that "The Vivacious and Charming MISS PEARL WHITE" was now "THE SOLE TOPIC OF CONVERSATION IN THE CITY OF BOMBAY."[4]

Like many young men growing up in the early decades of the twentieth century, the Wadias were avid movie fans, eagerly consuming the Hollywood westerns, comedies, stunt films, and serials that ran to packed houses across the subcontinent.[5] In 1926 Jamshed (widely known as JBH), aged twenty-five, scandalized his respectable Parsi family, master shipbuilders to the East India Company, by giving up a promising career in law and banking to become a freelance writer and director for the silent movies. Homi, ten years his junior, soon joined him, working first as his assistant at the Devare Film Laboratory at Kohinoor studios, then as his "trusted lieutenant" and partner in Wadia Brothers' Productions, perfecting his camera and editing skills and soon directing his first silent film, *Diler Daku* (aka *Thunderbolt*; dir. Homi Wadia [1931]).[6] Between them the Wadia brothers showed remarkable populist flair, and a run of successful silent films, all written by JBH, proved that big money could be made in the movies. Their final silent film, *Dilruba Daku*, (aka *The Amazon*; dir. A. H. Essa [1933]), introduced a swashbuckling female lead for the studio's "beautiful and doll-like" Bengali star, Padma, resplendent in mask and sword—a prototype for the *Hunterwali* persona two years later.

The release of *Alam Ara* (Beauty of the world; dir. Ardeshir Irani [1931]), India's first sound film, caused some panic among other Bombay producers, but JBH soon linked up with Parsi entrepreneurs and industrialists—M. B. Bilimoria and the Tata brothers—who offered to set him up with his own studios and a distribution office for both Indian and foreign films. Wadia Movietone was launched in 1933.

Its first sound film, *Lal-e-Yaman* (Jewel of Yemen; dir. J. B. H. Wadia [1933]) was a melodramatic Arabian fantasy, a musical that drew its storyline and visual style from Parsi theater: JBH had shrewdly invested in the talent of Joseph David, the acclaimed theater director who had written *Alam Ara*. The film was a major hit, and on the proceeds of this and other early successes, Wadia Movietone was soon able to build impressive studios in the well-heeled Parel area of Bombay, within the grounds of the Wadias' ancestral home, Lovji Castle. This became a major business enterprise, run along factory lines, which by the mid-1930s had around six hundred people on the payroll, ranging from carpenters and cleaners to its top stars. Homi, reminiscing, described the discipline as "like a school": when the ten o'clock bell rang, stars clocked in along with everyone else and a register was called to check for absences. Those not needed on set would rehearse; go home; or, in the case of the stunt artistes, work out in the studio gym. Studio production specialized in comedy, stunt, and action films along with orientalist fantasies.

When Nadia arrived in Bombay in 1934, the studio was buzzing. Foreign dignitaries were welcome guests, and JBH openly acknowledged the influence of Hollywood filmmakers such as Douglas Fairbanks. But the studio also prided itself on its homegrown talent: local musicians, theater writers, and self-taught film technicians. The ambience fitted well with Nadia's own culturally heterogeneous background.

Nadia, born Mary Evans in Perth in 1908 to a Greek mother and British father, arrived in India in 1911 with her father's army unit.[7] Following his death on the French battlefields in 1915, Mary's mother, a onetime belly dancer, decided to settle in Bombay, where her daughter became a weekly boarder at Claire Road convent school. In 1922 they joined an uncle, an army veterinarian in Peshawar, and Mary spent an idyllic adolescence learning dancing, horseback riding, and other outdoor skills from her army friends. She was also an enthusiastic movie fan: "My favourite films were the weekly serials of Ruth Roland, Pearl White, and others. They were very entertaining and full of amazing dare-devilry that I used to like. In the *Perils of Pauline* I remember one sequence where Pearl drives a race-car to save a hero from some spies. It was wonderful to see a woman driving such a fast car . . . it really inspired me to try it. . . . In time, when I could afford it, I purchased as many cars as I liked. And I always remembered Pearl White."[8] Back in Bombay in 1926 with a baby son, Bobby, politely referred to as her "brother," she needed work. Finding shop life at the Army and Navy stores too dull and law office work stultifying, she decided to take up her hobby, dancing, professionally. She toured the country first with Madame Astrova's Russian ballet troupe, making her name as an acrobat, singer, and dancer. After a brief stint with Isako's circus, she became a vaudeville singer and dancer touring army and civilian clubs and cinemas, where she might sing playback to silent stars or perform risqué songs in Hindustani. After flirting with a number of names, including the highly inappropriate Carmen Miranda—"quite ridiculous, I didn't look at all Spanish"—she became Nadia, a name suggested by an Armenian fortune-teller who promised it would bring her fame and fortune. Mary was pleased because "Nadia . . . was accepted as being both Indian and foreign enough."[9] In 1934 her screen potential was spotted by a Mr. Kanga, the manager of Regal Theatres in Lahore, who offered to introduce her to his old friend, J. B. H. Wadia.

The meeting was a success. The Wadia brothers were clearly captivated by her sense of fun, charming lack of deference, and plucky "can-do" attitude, as well as her obvious stage talents: singing; dancing; gymnastics; and a wonderful, curvaceous body that she displayed with little inhibition. She was hired at 150 rupees per month on condition that she pass a screen test.

JBH definitely had qualms about introducing a buxom, blue-eyed, blonde as an Indian heroine. Nadia herself noted that he seemed surprised when she arrived: "I don't think he expected me to be quite so large or fair." The screen test seven days later was apparently disastrous, her Hindi diction laughable.

She was told she would have to work hard with a voice coach on her Hindi, to change her name, and to wear a wig or dye her hair, "otherwise people will think you are a *buddhi* [old person]." She claimed to have tried an auburn tint, but it went lighter than before, so she decided to let it be. But she also flatly refused a black wig with long plaits: "Look here Mr. Wadia, I am a white woman and I'll look foolish with long black hair." She also refused to change her name to the Hinduized Nanda Devi: "That's not part of my contract. Nadia rhymes with Wadia and besides, I'm no *devi* [goddess]."

JBH decided to try her out with a tiny role in his *Desh Deepak/Josh-e-Watan* (Light of the homeland; dir. J. B. H. Wadia [1935]), an orientalist costume melodrama being shot at the studios with Joseph David. Although she had only three minutes of screen time, Nadia's sequence—as a skimpily clad slave girl and nationalist supporter—hit the cinemas in full color. Wadia had organized hand coloring on twenty-five prints, emphasizing her golden curls, bright blue eyes, and ample flesh spilling out of a tight *choli* and diaphanous golden sarong. As a slave market auctioneer details Nadia's considerable physical charms, the camera obliges us with cutaway close-ups on her teeth, her mouth, her eyes. JBH had already decided on the two features that, together, would sell Nadia to Indian audiences: a voluptuous white body and populist nationalism. Audiences went wild, and fan mail started pouring in, especially from the northwestern provinces where she already had a reputation as a stage performer.

With her additional success as Princess Parizad in the musical melodrama *Noor-e-Yaman* (Light of Yemen; dir. J. B. H. Wadia [1935]), in a small role in which she had to speak, sing, dance, and cry, J. B. H. Wadia felt confident enough to let her take the lead in his remake of *Dilruba Daku/The Amazon*. Openly inspired by both *Mark of Zorro* and *The Perils of Pauline*, the script was *Hunterwali*. Twenty-four-year-old Homi Wadia was chosen to direct the film, only his second "talkie." Shooting began as soon as a gap appeared in the studio schedules, and carried away by enthusiastic reports from the floor and impressive rushes, JBH extended the production period from six weeks to six months as songs and a romantic subplot (starring another actress) were added. However, when the film was finished, his business partner, Bilimoria, got cold feet about Nadia, considering her feisty persona too risky in the Indian context: "An Indian woman doing all that fighting—the public may not like it—we must sell the picture." Fortunately for the Wadias, there were no serious takers, and they were forced to release the picture themselves, thereby retaining for Wadia Movietone one of the biggest box-office hits of the decade.

Over the next few years a run of stunt and action films—with and without Nadia—enriched Wadia Movietone, which produced around six films a year. Nationalism and the Freedom Movement were a constant subtext of the early Wadia films, including *Hunterwali*. Like many in the film industry, the Wadias were early Congress supporters, and the brothers' beliefs underpinned their films. Although strict British censorship forbade overt references to the Freedom Movement, filmmakers of the 1930s and 1940s would slip casual references to Congress songs and symbols into the soundtrack or screen. A princess rescuing an oppressed kingdom from a wicked foreign tyrant would have obvious resonances in 1930s India.[10] Nadia saw her role—on screen and off—as supporting the nationalist movement, and she stated explicitly, "In all the pictures there was a propaganda message, something to fight for, for example for people to educate themselves or to become a strong nation."[11]

Socially responsible themes were becoming de rigueur at this time for producers who wanted critical status. The 1936 success of Devika Rani's *Achhut Kanya* had upped the stakes and, while Wadia Movietone's reputation for "cheap" films for the "masses" was unchallengeable, Bombay Talkies—and other studios making socials, such as Prabhat—were considered more "respectable."[12] JBH responded to *Achhut Kanya* (aka *Untouchable Girl*) with a jokey twist on the caste theme in *Hurricane Hansa* (dir. R. N. Vaidya [1937]), in which Nadia played a *harijan*[13] [untouchable] girl who, in a wordplay, changes her name from "harijan Hansa" to "Hurricane Hansa," dons her trademark mask, and takes revenge on a villain who destroyed her family.

Inspired by the ideas of the radical Bengali Marxist and humanist, M. N. Roy, JBH left the Congress Party and in 1938 became a founding member of Roy's Radical Democratic Party.[14] As his political commitment grew, JBH became increasingly frustrated with his own filmmaking. While he wanted to follow his peers and make socials, his business partners had no intention of killing the golden goose—theirs was the most profitable studio of the day. Reluctantly, they allowed JBH one nonstunt film a year. His formal experiment, *Naujawan* (Youth; dir. Aspi Irani [1937]), billed as the first Indian sound film without songs, had been a flop. He now focused on infusing his stunt films with social issues. For example, Nadia starred in *Lootaru Lalna* (Dacoit Damsel; dir. Homi Wadia [1938]), taking on the explosive issue of Hindu-Muslim unity, and in *Punjab Mail* (dir. Homi Wadia [1939]), attacking the class system and championing women's rights.[15] The influence of M. N. Roy's humanist ideas became increasingly visible, culminating in *Diamond Queen* (dir. Homi Wadia [1940]), which dealt with women's emancipation and

Fearless Nadia in *Hurricane Hansa* (1937): publicity booklet cover.
Used with permission of Wadia Movietone / Roy Wadia.

presented the tough and capable Nadia for the first time without her whip and mask. This film hit the jackpot of combining box-office glory with the critical acclaim JBH so desired, prompting even the usually acerbic *filmindia* to praise "a thought-provoking film that enlightens as it entertains."[16]

However, a crisis was brewing at Wadia Movietone. While JBH wanted to pursue the now-fashionable social melodramas, Bilimoria and JBH's brother, Homi, wanted to go aggressively for box-office hits. In autumn 1942 the company was split. With the box-office failure just months later of their new venture, Basant Pictures' first film, *Mauj* (Wave; dir. Homi Wadia [1943]), a social drama in which the Wadias experimented with Nadia playing a vampish femme fatale, JBH suggested cancelling the stunt stars' contracts. At this point the brothers fell out, their differences apparently irresolvable.

Homi, ever loyal to Nadia, who was by now also his long-term lover and unofficial partner, decided to concentrate on making the most of his assets: the stunt star contracts. He decided to follow a hunch that what a sizeable section of the audience really wanted was the old, whip-cracking Nadia. He suspected that if produced cheaply enough, the films could make money. Produced on a shoestring, *Hunterwali ki Beti* (Daughter of Hunterwali; dir. Homi Wadia [1943]) was an immediate success, and Homi had found his formula. Cheap, quickly made action, stunt, and jungle films followed, and Basant went from strength to strength with such films as *Flying Prince* (dir. Homi Wadia [1946]), *Tigress* (dir. K. Talpade [1948]), *11 O'clock* (dir. Homi Wadia [1948]), *Baghdad ka Jadoo* (The magic of Baghdad; dir. John Cawas [1956]), and *Circus Queen* (dir. Nosir Engineer [1956]).

Meanwhile, JBH's fortunes at Wadia Movietone dwindled, and by 1946 he had to sell his studio buildings to his old rival, V. Shantaram. The Wadia brothers teamed up again and, following the 1947 success of *Ram Bhakt Hanuman*, discovered a lucrative market niche in quality mythologicals that sustained Basant for many years, while Homi continued to knock out cheap action films for Nadia until she retired in 1959.

The split between the Wadia brothers is invariably characterized as the clash of two visions: Homi, the shy, conservative, technical genius and astute business brain who left school at sixteen, unashamedly loved lowbrow entertainment and despised intellectual pretensions; J. B. H. Wadia, MA, LLB, the self-assured, cultured, radical humanist, a teacher and writer who craved critical acclaim and international recognition. The situation was, in fact, more complex, as JBH was himself torn between the high ideals of his political and intellectual passions and his own love of Hollywood entertainment and brilliant understanding of the popular Indian imagination.

At stake were two different visions of the nationalist project—and two different relationships to modernity and the West. "India is most truly national when it is international," Nehru famously wrote, but the tug between national self-definition and global modernity could be articulated in different ways. JBH straddled the two. Like the European-educated Congress intellectuals of the 1930s, he saw the nation-building project as comprising humanist social reform at home and proud display of modern India's classical heritage abroad. Modernity meant a national self-definition that drew on the roots of a "pure" tradition, setting these within "modern" European social values: a humanistic and scientific worldview. This worthy vision valued "realist" melodramas on social issues and orientalized classical dance films for European audiences.

However, JBH also understood market forces and saw that popular passions would be the seed for new modernities that could not be neatly controlled from the center. He valued aspects of the West that the intellectuals dismissed as Hollywood "trash," as well as popular Indian entertainment forms. It appears that he brilliantly understood hybridity and recognized that national identities would be forged through playful negotiation rather than simply imposed from above. This vision of modern India drew comfortably on global popular culture but looked to its home markets, rather than the international stage, for its validation.

While wholeheartedly celebrating the remarkable achievements of Indian filmmakers, JBH unashamedly paid homage to Hollywood pioneers of technical skills and storytelling conventions, naming, among others, Charlie Chaplin, Douglas Fairbanks, Harold Lloyd, and D. W. Griffith.[17] He also openly acknowledged the influences of character and storyline; as we have seen, Nadia was billed as "India's Pearl White," her co-star John Cawas as "India's Eddie Polo."[18] Moreover, JBH spoke uninhibitedly about adapting, not simply copying, such films as *Mark of Zorro* and the Tarzan series for Indian audiences. This might be seen as an example of the mimicry we associate with sites of anticolonial struggle, but it was also sharp marketing: these were huge brand names, and the Wadias understood their value. At the same time, they knew how to "Indianize"—in both subject matter and form. Their films were, at their core, sites of negotiation of a new Indian modernity; alongside Hollywood they drew on Urdu Parsi theater (via Joseph David), Indian myth and legend, and contemporary political debate.

While both visions of the nationalist project acknowledged the transnational, the first was largely premised on an essentialized Indian cultural tradition, while the second better recognized the hybridity and fluidity within the porous borders of this modern "India." The former tended toward melodrama as a film form, the latter toward action, comedy, and masquerade. As Vijay Mishra has noted, stunt films are "the only form [in Indian cinema history] that arguably escapes from [melodramatic] staging."[19] The Wadias' films embodied an ongoing tension between these two forms and the two visions of the transnational arena. Fearless Nadia—"Indian Pearl White"—was constructed within the framework of this dual vision.

Nadia Persona

Nadia was undoubtedly the Wadias' most brilliant discovery and creation. If they were looking for an Indian heroine, she was not an obvious choice, and at first sight perhaps the strangest aspect of the Nadia phenomenon was that, despite her indisputable "whiteness," she was so easily accepted as an Indian heroine in films that were read by many audiences as anti-British allegories.

From the very first, her ethnicity was an issue for the Wadias, and Indianizing her was a conscious project: hair color, name, Hindi diction were all areas they sought to control. Interestingly, while JBH's original concern had been that Nadia might appear too European for Indian audiences, on *Hunterwali*'s release Bilimoria was worried that audiences might reject her for behavior inappropriate to an *Indian* woman. A number of strategies were used to "fix" her identity as Indian. Taking no chances, *Hunterwali*'s promotional booklet introduced her as a "brave Indian girl who sacrificed royal luxuries to the cause of her people and her country." As the films went on, she was increasingly referred to as "Bombaiwali" (the woman from Bombay), connoting cosmopolitan sophistication and modernity, thereby justifying her apparent transgressions of traditional Indian female dress codes and mores while retaining her identity as an all-Indian heroine. A certain fluidity accompanied her physical appearance in posters and on screen: although she was adamant about not wearing a wig, in posters her hair was sometimes hand-colored light brown and, in black and white films, shadows could render her coloring ambiguous. The mask itself helped weaken the visual impact of her ethnic identity. In fact, however, in the context of the nationalist movement, Nadia's heroism and support of the underdog was almost enough in itself to place her on the Indian side. Girish Karnad recalled that "the single most memorable sound of my childhood is the clarion call of Hey-y-y as Fearless Nadia, regal upon her horse, her hand raised defiantly in the air, rode down upon the bad guys. To us school kids of the mid-forties Fearless Nadia meant courage, strength, idealism."[20] However, her Western looks were undeniably part of her exotic appeal and, in choosing her, the Wadias were involved in a careful calculation. Billing her as India's Pearl White, they could imbue their films with all the glamour of the Pearl White brand and the exoticism of the "white mem" while simultaneously constructing an all-Indian Nadia. Played cleverly, they could have it both ways, conflating two traditions: the Hollywood stunt queen (and by implication the whole Hollywood stunt genre—her persona referred as much to Fairbanks as to White) and the legendary Indian warrior woman. Through these a cosmopolitan modern femininity could be forged.

The Wadias did not invent the masked fighting woman. She was a well-established convention of the silent cinema, and Wadia's 1933 silent film, *Dilruba Daku* (aka *Amazon*), *Hunterwali*'s immediate predecessor, was part of a contemporary vogue for warrior women, known as *viranganas*. Kathryn Hansen, in her study of Nautanki theater, describes how historical and legendary figures from various eras and different parts of India (from Razia Sultana to Lakshmibai, queen of Jhansi) fed the imagery and stories of a significant body of work within popular theater and early cinema, as well as folk songs, comic books, and calendar art.[21] The *virangana* prototype portrays a good queen who takes over the throne when a male kinsman dies, leads her people into battle dressed as a man, displays astonishing military skills, and dies defending her kingdom against invaders. The key image—a turbaned woman on horseback brandishing a sword above her head—has been enthusiastically exploited by female politicians over the years, notably Indira Gandhi.

British government censorship of overt references to the nationalist movement fueled the popularity of *virangana* stories in all forms of mass entertainment between 1910 and 1940, as figures such as the queen of Jhansi had become a focus for nationalist activism. Thus, fictionalized biographies of historical and legendary female warriors, as well as fictional warrior queens, princesses, and female outlaws, became popular staples of early cinema.[22] Four aspects of this counterparadigm to the long-suffering, traditional *sati savitri* woman are relevant to Nadia.

The first concerns the body. Hansen writes that "the *virangana* ideal commends physical training and active deployment of the body in combat."[23] Nadia's proud display of a muscular and athletic body, her fighting skills, and championing of exercise and gym sessions are pure *virangana*. Like her American counterparts, Pearl White and Douglas Fairbanks, she was always admired for doing all her own stunts[24] and was, from the first, identified with her body and its power in a way that heroines such as Devika Rani (who frequently suffered and died) were not.

Secondly, the *virangana* shows moral strength. "The *virangana* arrives not simply when force is required but when moral order needs to be restored."[25] Nadia always occupies the position of moral strength within her films—she rights wrongs and restores order and justice, being introduced from her first *Hunterwali* appearance as a "protector of the poor and punisher of evildoers."

Thirdly, the *virangana* has unprecedented sexual freedom: "Because her virtue is not reducible to the sexual transactions of the female body, physical relations cannot impugn her truth."[26] In the *virangana* tradition, sexuality is irrelevant—women can have lovers without being defined by their sexual

The "voluptuous but prim" Fearless Nadia in *Hunterwali* (1935): film still. Used with permission of Wadia Movietone / Roy Wadia.

transgressions. While her sexuality was not explicitly marked within the films' diegeses, Nadia's on-screen sexual and erotic appeal was enormous—she could carry off an (almost) nude bathing scene in *Hunterwali* and still be seen by fans as "voluptuous but prim."

Finally, the *virangana* cross-dresses. "The *virangana* . . . in these dramas claims male positions for the female body; she rides on horseback, wears male dress, wields weapons ordinarily carried by men."[27] Nadia regularly wore masculinized clothing, especially in confrontations with the villains. This ranged from riding breeches and hacking jackets to sailor suits or Fairbanks-style cloaks and swords. However, Nadia invariably played a split persona, characterized by either a double life (*Hunterwali*) or the complex Bombaiwali construction (*Diamond Queen*), so she also regularly wore a sari—the ultimate signifier of Indian femininity.[28]

Even the Wadias underestimated the extent to which the *virangana* ideal underpinned and legitimized Nadia's persona, discovering at their expense how limited a range of roles she could play. While she could champion the cause of the oppressed on almost any issue—from caste to class, from anticommunalism to women's issues—she was never allowed to show weakness. "Nadia cannot cry," one distributor exclaimed, insisting that an emotional scene in *Mauj* be cut from the final film. Moreover, while she could wear clothes that revealed more female flesh than any other Indian actress of her day, and while her image was undeniably erotically charged, her appearance as a "vamp," smoking, drinking, and flirting as part of a double role in *Muqabla* (Competition; dir. Batuk Bhatt and Babubhai Mistry [1942]), was not a box-office success. She had to be emphatically coded as the "good girl"—albeit within the conventions of *virangana* morality. A telling anecdote describes how, in later years, a churlish Homi responded to his brother's request that he direct a mythological for him with the retort, "only if Nadia plays Sita"—a calculatedly provocative suggestion as the Ramayana heroine, Sita, is the embodiment of dutiful femininity, becoming a *sati* by walking into fire to prove her chastity.

In an earlier essay examining the contradictions within the star persona of Nadia, I proposed two answers to the question of her popularity as an icon within a nationalist context despite her whiteness.[29] First, as a white woman her status was liminal—the threat of her physical prowess could be contained and her sexuality could be vicariously enjoyed. Her whiteness, simultaneously recognized and disavowed, undoubtedly underpinned the ambivalent frisson of her erotic appeal, the classic colonial miscegenation fantasy. Second, her identity was fixed within the films' diegeses through identifying her not with whiteness but with the cosmopolitanism and modernity of the Bombaiwali. What the Wadias spotted was the potential to build Nadia as a *virangana* for a modern world. The Wadia films are importantly a reverie of potency within modernity, and Nadia was, throughout the films, associated with a gamut of signifiers of Western technology: cars; planes; and, importantly, trains.

While Devika Rani's modernity constructed her as both a cipher for humanist values and fount of purity within an orientalized "tradition," Nadia's was firmly situated within the (male, Western) world of technological progress, where she was unambiguously in control, whether driving a car or riding the roof of a hurtling train. Fearless Nadia was frequently shown running triumphantly along the tops of trains, fistfighting her male tormentors, parading burly men high above her shoulders before chucking them to their deaths on the tracks below. While Devika's attempts to challenge traditional orthodoxies in *Achhut Kanya* left her crushed under the wheels of an oncoming train, the tragically wronged woman, a victim of social ills, Nadia championed the oppressed and effected change in the world from the giddy heights of the train roof, empowered rather than crushed by technology.

The significance of both stars as key icons of the era emerges through Qurratulain Hyder's autobiographical *Memories of an Indian Childhood* (1965). Devika Rani is remembered for her family background, *Achhut Kanya* being one of the few films Hyder's parents allowed her to watch on the grounds that "India had at last entered the era of cultural revolution because Gurudev's [Tagore's] own niece had become a cinema actress."[30] Meanwhile,

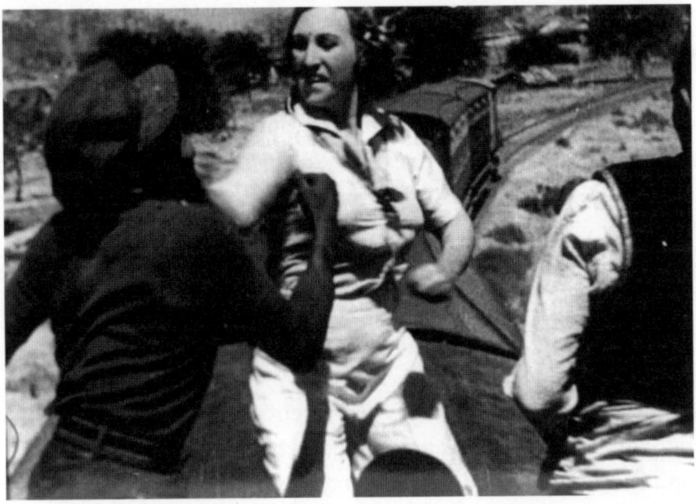

Fearless Nadia "unambiguously in control" in *Miss Frontier Mail* (1936): film still. Used with permission of Wadia Movietone / Roy Wadia.

"Miss Nadia of *Hunterwali* fame" was a cultural reference point against which children compared the skills of a local circus Well [*sic*] of Death motorbike queen. In what appears as a dichotomy between substance and performance, Devika's significance stemmed from her social status as an upper-middle-class Brahmin, or *who she was*, while Nadia's importance came from her body and its skills, or *what she could do*.

Diamond Queen

Diamond Queen, sometimes celebrated as the Wadias' best film and probably the most seamless fusion of the brothers' two visions, offers fascinating insights into the balancing act that was the Nadia persona. It was the seventh in the Diamond Thriller series that began with Homi's first sound film, *Veer Bharat* (Indian warrior; dir. Homi Wadia [1934]). *Hunterwali* was the second, and audiences were by now fond of its cast of side characters: the faithful horse, Punjab ka Beta (Son of the Punjab); a baby Austin car christened Rolls Royce ki Beti (Daughter of Rolls Royce); and Moti, the plucky dog.

In *Diamond Queen*, Nadia plays Madhurika, a modern cosmopolitan girl who returns to her small town, Diamond Town, after five years of education in Bombay. She finds the people terrorized by the villain Kedarnath and his gang, who have taken over the kingdom during the ten years that the good prince has been abroad. Their corrupt and decadent regime sabotages local literacy campaigns, steals taxes from the poor, and threatens the chastity of local women. Madhurika links up with Diler, a bandit with a heart of gold and his own reasons for seeking revenge, to expose Kedarnath's corruption and restore order. With the help of her friends, including Miss Radha, the pretty school teacher, Radha's father Sevakram, a respected elder of the community, and Prince Ranjiit Singh, who has disguised himself as a Westernized bumbling fool in order to find out the truth about Kedarnath's rule, Madhurika defeats the villains and allows the good prince to return and rule benignly. In the process she espouses the causes of women's independence, education, and physical exercise programs.

Madhurika is undoubtedly the film's central pivot. Although Diler's life story bookends the film—his boyhood and his marriage—Madhurika is the Diamond Queen of the film's title and focus of the villain's wrath. "I fear bandit Diler less than the free and fearless Madhurika—her poisonous thinking will spread through Diamond Town unless we get rid of her,"[31] Kedarnath snarls from his palatial den. Madhurika motivates the action, and it is she who ultimately kills Kedarnath.

Madhurika is visually constructed within *virangana* codes. We first meet her through a sequence of eroticized body parts emphasizing her physical strength: a close-up of a white fist, swiftly followed by a muscular arm that lands a sharp punch in the face of the lascivious brute who is threatening to abduct Miss Radha. The camera moves to Madhurika's feet as she crushes a male hand attempting to grab a fallen knife, then pans slowly up her body—wide black trousers, taut across her large hips, tight white blouse and big bosom, natty neck scarf and brooch—eventually revealing a regal blonde dominatrix, high cheekbones, aquiline Greek nose, tight blonde curls. After she has disposed of the villains—kicked, thrown, and spectacularly detrousered—she responds to her father's and friends' astonishment at the way she has changed in Bombay with a smile and a casual throwaway: "I've been training in a women's gym."[32]

Madhurika unequivocally upholds the moral order. She punishes villainy and protects and rescues the vulnerable good: virtuous young women who epitomize Indian traditional arts and culture (Miss Radha), tortured animals (her horse, Punjab ka Beta), benevolent wise old men (Sevakram), and the community itself that has been cheated for years by its corrupt rulers. While Diler enthusiastically supports Madhurika, seeing her as a potential partner in his own lone campaign to rid Diamond Town of its corrupt rulers and seeing her as a future lover and wife, she primly rejects his criminal methods.

Fearless Nadia with romantic interest, John Cawas, in *Diamond Queen* (1940): film still. Used with permission of Wadia Movietone / Roy Wadia.

Demurely draped in a white embroidered sari and sporting a halo of backlit blonde curls, she entreats him to give himself up to the law. "A criminal cannot arrest a criminal," she gently cajoles. Only when he has paid his dues in jail will she consider marrying him. Throughout the final assault on the villains, Madhurika is at the helm: she organizes her gang, draws up the plans, is in the driver's seat throughout the car chase, and finally wrestles Kedarnath to his death on top of a hurtling *tonga*, Diler looking on admiringly.

Comparison with Nadia's Hollywood counterparts, notably the Pearl White character in *The Perils of Pauline* serials, is relevant here. Although Nadia was always accompanied by a male hero, usually John Cawas, for romantic interest, we see here that Nadia was primarily a fighter and rather more than Pearl White's plucky daredevil stunt woman. Nadia was always the primary agent of the villains' demise and as likely to rescue her hero as to be rescued. Invariably, a second heroine, in this case Miss Radha, provided the focus for romance, emotion, and song and dance in Nadia's films.

Two narrative threads run through *Diamond Queen*, and only Madhurika has the physical and moral power to resolve both threads. Madhurika sets out her terms of engagement in her first scene. The disgruntled boor she has just crushed complains of the insult to his virility: "*main mard hoon, mard*" (I'm a man, a [real] man), but Madhurika retorts with what, within the 1940s context, appears an astonishing, "Hey mister, don't think today's women are so weak they'll submit to the brutality of men.... If India is to be free, women must be given their freedom.... If you try and stop them you'll face the consequences."

Thread one, the fight between good and evil, is told through action scenes that push the narrative forward, where Madhurika, in her most masculinized outfits, challenges the tyranny of the villains. These include the scenes of greatest tension: fights, car chases, and choreographed swashbuckling, building excitement through skillful editing and intercutting storylines. Madhurika wears eroticized, Westernized clothes: trousers and blouse in two key scenes and riding breeches and hacking jacket in a third, while for the only other major showdown with the villains, she wears the knee-length black dress in which she kills Kedarnath. In these revealing costumes, she performs all her most physically demanding feats while simultaneously commanding the moral authority of the film: Douglas Fairbanks meets the *virangana* queen.

Thread two, which challenges outdated tradition, notably women's traditionally subservient roles, unfolds predominantly through spectacular excess—songs, love scenes, slapstick—a combination of melodrama and comedy. A mostly sari-clad Madhurika challenges, negotiates with, and supports a range of ineffectually "modern" Indians: her father, Diler, Miss Radha, Sevakram, and Prince Ranjiit—all in varying degrees sympathetic to radical reform but unable to make it happen without Bombaiwali, Madhurika. The success of the film's ideological project depends, to some extent, on how skillfully this thread is integrated into the body of the film and resolved within the moral order.

Two of the film's four songs openly deliver nationalist, reformist messages promoting education and exercise and are barely contained within the diegesis. At a literacy campaign concert, the lovely schoolteacher, Miss Radha, performs a classical Indian dance to a song exhorting townspeople to "forge ahead a path of reading and writing ... for ... the pen is mightier than the sword," while her father, a socially enlightened community leader, lectures his audience: "education is the first step to freedom ... [it is] vital to solve the country's problems ... knowledge is power." Later, in Miss Radha's school playground, quasi-militaristic rows of children stretch, bend, and march to patriotic music, a final Busby Berkeley–style overhead shot revealing a swastika formation.[33] The song's words proclaim, "Thank the Lord for exercise, all hail god Hanuman—to exercise is to live in bliss, always be courageous, banish weakness, be brave and strong ... let strength be your weapon—the pride of the nation is the power of its people." Two romantic subplots also contribute to this thread. In her one love scene with Diler, a glamorous Madhurika in dramatic black sari and *bindi*, her tight, dark-looking curls profiled against a

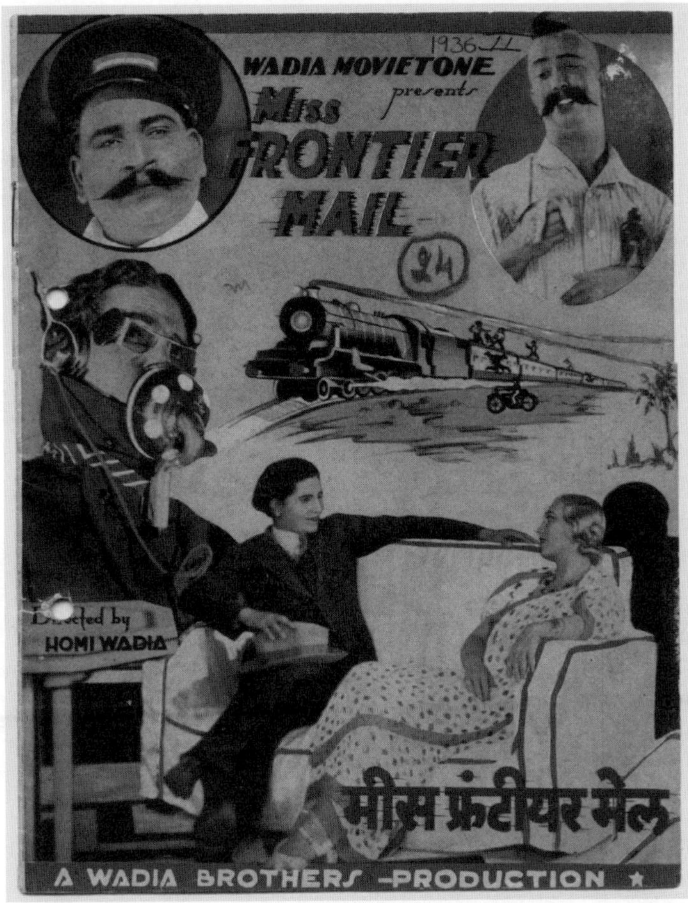

"Bombaiwali" Fearless Nadia in *Miss Frontier Mail* (1936): publicity booklet cover. Used with permission of Wadia Movietone / Roy Wadia.

spectacular waterfall, shows modern Indian woman in control as she leans to kiss Diler—before the camera quickly pans away across the rocky landscape to find her father, anxious for a showdown with her, asking, "Is this how you use your education?" On the other hand, Miss Radha and Prince Ranjiit's romance is played more conventionally, through misunderstandings and a melancholic love song, but it is no less an exploration of the boundaries of modern relationships between the sexes.

Ultimately, the two threads work together to contain the radical ideas within a traditional moral order—barely. Madhurika's apparent transgressions of traditional values are justified by a greater moral and political vision than her father's. Despite her rebelliousness, she ultimately saves the community and gets married, although the farcically schematic nature of this coupling—Madhurika seated in white sari and *bindi* beside a miraculously transformed bandit Diler, who now wears a Western suit and tie, with Miss Radha and Prince Ranjiit in traditional Hindu wedding clothes beside them—is underlined by two comic couples larking about on a tree behind them, a gentle parody of the main action.

However, it is the tag "Bombaiwali" that does most to legitimize and redeem Madhurika's rebelliousness and fix a revised model of contemporary Indian feminine identity. She may be as "foreign" as Pearl White and Douglas Fairbanks and as "traditional" as India's warrior women, but she is ultimately Bombaiwali, the epitome of Indian cosmopolitan sophistication and modernity, and a fiery nationalist to boot. The excessive potency—and ambivalence—of her image warrants further exploration.

Mimicry

Parama Roy, drawing on the work of Homi Bhabha and others on colonial mimicry, argues that, if we are to understand the formation of Indian national identities, we need to examine not just Anglicization but the variety of forms of impersonation and mimicry which exist alongside that. She aims to "open up the field of identity formation and nation formation to a more heterogeneous model than that of Anglicization" and suggests that "[impersonation] is . . . central to the ways in which nationalism imagines itself: hence the production of the nation is almost invariably mediated . . . through such practices as Gandhi's impersonation of femininity, an Irishwoman's assumption of Hindu feminine celibacy, or a Muslim actress's emulation of a Hindu/Indian mother goddess."[34] The Wadias were, at one level, brilliant Anglicizing mimic men. Hollywood was their acknowledged role model and JBH, on at least one occasion, produced orientalist fare for European approval.[35] However, their films were also rich vehicles for far wider forms of mimicry and impersonation. Fearless Nadia directly reverses (and broadly challenges) the mimicry of Anglicization: white woman mimics Indian woman. But her persona is also a conflation of other impersonations: white woman mimics white man (Douglas Fairbanks), white woman (Pearl White), Indian woman (Jhansi ki Rani—the *virangana*), and Indian man (masked heroine disguised as a man).

In hiring Nadia, JBH had demonstrated an astute, if unstated, understanding of the potential fluidity offered by Nadia's whiteness. White memsahibs had been a popular exotic feature of Urdu Parsi theater since the early years of the century, and in the context of the nationalist movement of the day, his decision was not inherently risky. Many nationalist men had white European wives or followers—both of M. N. Roy's wives were white Westerners, while Vivekananda's most loyal disciple, Nivedita, was an Irish woman. Parama Roy, in tracing the relationship between Vivekananda and Nivedita, describes how he recruited her in London in 1897 as "a real lioness, to work for the Indians, women especially," firmly believing no man or Indian woman could do the job: a Western woman had to "become" a Hindu woman in order to educate Hindu women.[36] She argues that

> of all the figures in the Colonial scene—western man, Indian man, western woman and Indian woman—it seems that it is only the western woman whose identity is available—for the Indian man—as relatively open, mobile, malleable. She is distinct from the Indian woman, whose identity has to be, in the nationalist context, fixed quite as much as the Indian male's is. What we have here is the familiar process of (colonial) mimicry performed in reverse, and for the Indian nationalist male; (Hindu) nationalism demands at this point its mimic woman.[37]

The parallels with the Nadia persona are interesting: Nadia was a white woman impersonating an Indian (invariably coded as Hindu) woman, whose mission was to educate and "save" Indian women (and oppressed men). She was white but not white—and white but not (Pearl) White. But also, as Roy says of Nivedita, she was not quite/not white (or even not quite not quite/not white). While, Roy contends, Nivedita partially substitutes for Indian woman, her racial difference is crucial, for this "guarantees . . . the Indian male's . . . Indianness and masculinity"—a white woman impersonating an Indian (Hindu) heroine allows the Indian male to constitute himself at the center of the project of nationalism.[38] Did the Wadias want their mimic woman in order to construct themselves as Indian nationalists?

Nadia's persona is complex since, although she was white, she was known to have grown up in India. There was considerable fluidity around "Indianness" at that time, and visual markers were (and still are) often ambiguous. Nadia described struggles over her own identity when growing up: "[At school] I was always considered to be English. However Mummy was Greek and spoke English with a heavy Greek accent. Many of my friends would tease me about this and I felt very embarrassed. . . . I guess you could say that I was never too sure as to where I belonged, though I never thought of myself as un-Indian. Many people used to call me Anglo-Indian, even though I was not born in India."[39] When she first arrived at Wadia Movietone, workers expressed anxiety about how to address her: "you see she was a white mem and we at the studio were not sure how to react," although they soon relaxed when her unpretentious ways made her one of the gang. It was only later, especially after 1945, "without the machinery of the studio to protect her," that we get reports that she was singled out for malicious gossip on account of her skin color—equated with loose morals—and her status as an unmarried mother.[40] Wadia Movietone had been a particularly comfortable environment for Nadia. Owned by Westernized Parsis, workers included a generous representation of Parsi, Muslim, and other non-Hindu communities. JBH, discussing his films' feminist themes, admitted that, at least in his early days, "I was . . . out of tune . . . with the overall Indian way of life. . . . As an insular [Westernized] Parsee I had not taken any interest in the pattern of family conventions of Hindus or Muslims . . . for the world of me I could not understand . . . why or how women subscribed to the male chauvinist ideology which infested the so-called social film."[41] While the reality of India was—and still is—a hybrid society, a key imperative of the nationalist project was to negotiate the boundaries of the imagined community that was to become the homogeneous "nation."

Films and their stars provide a terrain for such negotiation—within the broader arena of "public culture." The melodramatic "realist" social offers one model of negotiating national identity, tending to resolve and disavow ambivalence, hiding the exclusions necessary to define an essentialized tradition. With a more inclusive and hybrid model of Indian modernity, the focus changes. The Nadia persona—in all its complexity—is a figure at play within a liminal zone of fluid racial, ethnic, gender, and religious categories, where multiplicity and heterogeneity are celebrated. In the Wadias' stunt films, the key players explore new identities through mimicry and impersonation, "fixed" only temporarily to help disguise the inherent instabilities of the border and the anxieties about what, within mainstream nationalism, is being repressed.

There were undoubtedly many reasons for the Wadias' failure to find respectability through their films, not least sheer snobbery: their primary audiences were proletarian and the films were unabashed commercial entertainment. However, the Wadia films and their characters would have represented sources of profound anxiety for the nationalist project, and some of their popular appeal may have derived from precisely the frisson that this engendered. Where Bombay Talkies was headed by Hindu aristocrats who could place themselves firmly at the center of the nationalist project, Wadia Movietone represented all that was peripheral: Parsis, Muslims, Christians, and "white trash." As JBH's attempts to fix his films within the nationalist mainstream grew ever more hysterical ("right on," or "politically correct," themes; high-minded lectures; films without songs; and films with classical music and dance), he lost his audience. One can only speculate how much it was because Homi pulled the films back from social melodrama to playful mimicry that explored and reveled in the gamut of modern Indian identities that the films once again succeeded with their subaltern audiences, especially the proletarian and Muslim masses.

Within the Wadia oeuvre, the Nadia films represented a small but significant stream, at their best the most satisfactory resolution of the brothers' competing visions of cinema and nationalist identity. While JBH would have hated being immortalized by his 1986 obituary headline, "King of the Stunt Film Dead," the importance of Nadia's stunt films is now undeniable. In comparison with Devika Rani, the liberal, modern, cosmopolitan beauty, Nadia was—for better or for worse—a thoroughly postmodern hybrid woman/man. While Devika ends up under the train, dead on the tracks, Nadia remains on its roof, an ebullient *virangana* in a modern world. While Devika is now more or less lost to time, Fearless Nadia—whip held aloft, thigh-high boots dug into the flanks of her trusty steed, Punjab ka Beta—looks set to ride the global media once again, this time as a Hollywood biopic star,[42] returning to Hollywood a version of its earlier self that is not quite Pearl White, ready to do new work within the cultural flows of a postcolonial late capitalist world.

NOTES

This is a substantially condensed version of an article originally published in *Bollyworld: Popular Indian Cinema through a Transnational Lens*, ed. Raminder Kaur and Ajay Sinha (New Delhi: Sage, 2005).

1. See, for example, Vijay Mishra, *Bollywood Cinema: Temples of Desire* (New York: Routledge, 2002).

2. Erik Barnouw and S. Krishnaswamy, authors of what was for many years the key authoritative work on Indian cinema, made no reference to Nadia at all, despite a brief mention of *Hunterwali*. Erik Barnouw and S. Krishnaswamy, *Indian Film* (New York: Oxford University Press, 1980), 110. Vijay Mishra and his co-authors also fail to mention Nadia in their list of Indian imitators of Hollywood stunt stars and then proceed to claim, somewhat contentiously, that the imitations of Hollywood "never really produced a star as text." Vijay Mishra, Peter Jeffery, and Brian Shoesmith, "The Actor as Parallel Text in Bombay Cinema," *Quarterly Review of Film and Video* 11, no. 3 (1989): 52.

3. Indian Cinematograph Committee, *The Report of the Indian Cinematograph Committee, 1927–8* (Calcutta: Government of India Central Publication Branch, 1928), and Indian Cinematograph Committee, *Indian Cinematograph Committee 1927–8, Evidence,*

4 vols. (Calcutta: Government of India Central Publication Branch, 1928), offer a rich flavor of this era.

4. *Bombay Chronicle*, October 1, October 8, 1915.

5. The information on the early days of the Wadias draws on the author's 1986 interview with Homi Wadia; the documentary *Fearless: The Hunterwali Story* (dir. Riyad Vinci Wadia [1993]); and Riyad Wadia's unpublished 1994 research dossier, together with other Wadia Movietone papers he kindly provided. Also J. B. H. Wadia's own writings: *Looking Back on My Romance with Films* (Bombay: Jayant Art Printer, 1955); "Those Were the Days," *Cinema Vision India* 1, no. 1 (1980): 91–99; and "JBH in Talkieland," *Cinema Vision India* 1, no. 2 (1980): 82–83.

6. "Aka" because at this time, almost all silent films had both Hindi and English titles.

7. Previous articles, including my own, have invariably set her birth date as 1910—a fiction Nadia herself promoted. Information on Nadia's life story is drawn primarily from Nadia herself through conversations and an interview with the author and Behroze Gandhy in February 1986. Additional material is drawn from Girish Karnad, "This One Is for Nadia," *Cinema Vision India* 1, no. 2 (1980): 84–91, and Riyad Vinci Wadia, "Unmasked: The Life and Times of Fearless Nadia," unpublished research notes, courtesy of Wadia Movietone Private Ltd., received by the author in 1994.

8. Riyad Wadia, *Unmasked*, 12.

9. Karnad, "This One Is for Nadia," 86.

10. In 1984, J. B. H. Wadia openly admitted that "a revolt against a tyrannical king or a minister for Azadi (freedom) was nothing if not against the British Raj, although indirectly." Quoted in Prem Chowdhry, *Colonial India and the Making of Empire Cinema: Image, Ideology, and Identity* (Manchester, UK: Manchester University Press, 2000), 97.

11. Behroze Gandhy and Rosie Thomas, "Three Indian Film Stars," in *Stardom: Industry of Desire*, ed. Christine Gledhill (London: Routledge, 1991), 107–16.

12. In Indian cinema, the term "socials" is used to describe films that are set in contemporary times and are crafted within broadly "realist" conventions. They are distinguished from other genres such as "historicals," "fantasies," "mythologicals," and "stunt" films.

13. Child of god—Gandhi's name for untouchables.

14. Roy was a charismatic activist and political intellectual who had traveled widely throughout Europe, the Soviet Union, and the Americas. At one time a leading figure in the international Communist movement and a confidante of Lenin, he became disillusioned equally by Communist and Congress Party politics and attempted to forge a new democratic humanism.

15. In "Those Were the Days," J. B. H. Wadia wrote, "When I became a filmmaker I tried to equate [*sic*] my conscience by weaving the screenplays of some of my early Talkies around the problem of emancipation of Indian womanhood," referring to the Nadia films as "the genre which was much maligned and least understood by many 'all-knowing' film critics and producers of 'social' films" (94).

16. Baburao Patel in *filmindia* (editorial), August 1940.

17. J. B. H. Wadia wrote, "Wadia Movietone's 'Diamond Thrillers,' as they were called, were frankly inspired by American films like those of Douglas Fairbanks, Harry Carey, and Tom Mix and serials of Francis Ford, Pearl White, Marie Walcamp, Eddie Polo, and others. Be it recorded here that JBH has never hesitated to acknowledge his debt to the American film." In "How *Toofani Tarzan* Came to Be Produced," unpublished memoirs, Wadia Movietone archive, Mumbai.

18. According to J. B. H. Wadia, "In the early years of the Indian cinema it had become a fashion to enhance the box-office value of our stars by comparing them indiscriminately with Hollywood celebrities. We had our Indian Douglas Fairbanks and Mary Pickford, Pearl White, Ruth Roland and Marie Walcamp, Eddie Polo, Francis Ford and Richard Talmadge et al." "Those Were the Days," 94.

19. Mishra, *Bollywood Cinema*, 36.

20. Karnad, "This One Is for Nadia," 86.

21. Kathryn Hansen, *Grounds for Play: The Nautanki Theatre of North India* (Berkeley: University of California Press, 1992), 188–98.

22. For more on the active heroines of India's silent cinema, see Rosie Thomas, "Miss Frontier Mail: The Film that Mistook Its Star for a Train," in *Sarai Reader 07: Frontiers*, ed. Monica Narula et al. (Delhi: Centre for the Study of Developing Societies, 2007), 301–3.

23. Hansen, *Grounds for Play*, 189.

24. In all cases this was largely studio marketing: stunt doubles were regularly used. See Arthur Wise and D. Ware, *Stunting in the Cinema* (London: Constable, 1973), 215–19. However, anecdotal accounts confirm that Nadia, as a former vaudeville artiste, did do most of her own stunts, especially in her early years.

25. Hansen, *Grounds for Play*, 192.

26. Ibid., 189.

27. Ibid., 192.

28. However, this was frequently the Maharashtrian sari—nine meters long and with much greater freedom of movement—which also refers to the *virangana* tradition of Maharashtrian horsewomen.

29. Gandhy and Thomas, "Three Indian Film Stars," 110–16.

30. Qurratulain Hyder, "Memories of an Indian Childhood" (1965), in *The Picador Book of Modern Indian Literature*, ed. Amit Chaudhuri (London: Picador, 2001), 213.

31. Dialogue translations are from Channel Four UK's 2002 transmission of *Diamond Queen*.

32. Implicit here are references to other films in which Nadia is seen working out in her gym—which apparently stimulated a keep-fit craze at the time.

33. The swastika here refers to the Indian peace symbol, not Nazi Germany.

34. Parama Roy, *Indian Traffic: Identities in Question in Colonial and Postcolonial India* (Berkeley: University of California Press, 1998), 4.

35. *Raj Natarki* (*Court Dancer*; dir. Madhu Bose [1941]).

36. Parama Roy, *Indian Traffic*, 121.

37. Ibid., 123.

38. Ibid., 122.

39. Riyad Wadia, *Unmasked*, 11–12.

40. Ibid., 61.

41. J. B. H. Wadia, "Those Were the Days," 93.

42. In the middle of the twenty-first century's first decade, at least two biopics were in development, including a Cate Blanchett Hollywood project with Shekhar Kapoor.

CHAPTER 7

From Pearl White to White Rose Woo

Tracing the Vernacular Body of *Nüxia* in Chinese Silent Cinema, 1927–1931

WEIHONG BAO

In 1921 a prominently placed picture of Pearl White appeared in the first issue of one of the earliest Chinese film journals, *Yingxi zazhi* (The shadow play magazine), following an opening feature on Charlie Chaplin. White's picture was framed by festive lanterns celebrating the inauguration of the journal, and the accompanying caption told of her popularity:

> Among the serial detective films [*zhentan changpian*] imported from America, Baolian's [Pearl White's] films comprise the greatest number. Films such as *The Perils of Pauline*, *The Black Hooded Thief*, *The Circle of Trouble*, and *The Great Secret of Germany* are all well known by everyone, including the women and the children. Among many of those who do not understand English, whenever they see a female star in a shadow play, they always call her "Baolian," as if the word "Baolian" has become a common noun. One can imagine her fame in China.[1]

This brief passage, in which Pearl White's popularity is gauged by the transformation of her proper name into a common noun, is not atypical of what happened in the international market of the 1920s to the hegemony of classical Hollywood cinema as the first "global vernacular."[2] How an American product was transformed through its global circulation is a story of inevitable

Pearl White Portrait. *Yingxi zazhi* 1, no. 1, 1921.

tensions and contradictions. This is evidenced symptomatically in the simultaneous elevation and displacement of White's name and the recognition and misrecognition of her image. The tensions in this local-global transplantation are further complicated by the Chinese translations of the very name Pearl White. Her first name, "Baolian," was in fact transliterated from her character name, Pauline, in *The Perils of Pauline* (*Baolian yuxianji*). The name Baolian, meaning "precious lotus," also resonated in popular memory when *Baolian deng* (The precious lotus lantern) was revived in the 1910s on the Reformed

Beijing Opera stage (*gailiang jingxi*). Spectacular stage sets, modern costumes, martial arts stunts, and a mechanized stage apparatus gave the so-called traditional opera—and mainstay of *The Precious Lotus Lantern* repertoire—a face-lift. On other occasions, when the rendition of her full name "Bai Baolian" was provided, the literal translation of her last name as "Bai," which signifies whiteness, gave Baolian (Precious Lotus) a distinctive skin color. At the same time, the Chinese phrase "Bailian," or "White Lotus," invokes connotations ranging from purity to the riotous religious Sect of White Lotus (Bailian jiao), which further removed the actress's proper name from its original.

A historical inquiry into the global impact of Hollywood cinema—here embodied in a robust female figure associated with a "low" genre, the serial queen thrillers—does not exempt us from questioning the power context of our own discursive adventure. If the distribution and exhibition of Hollywood cinema worldwide necessarily involves a cultural translation practice such as the public recognition and misrecognition of Pearl White, we also have to clarify the position from which we are approaching the practice of translation. Rather than reinforcing the hierarchy of the original over the secondary, the source over the target, the authentic over the copy and thus risk reproducing yet another round of Hollywood hegemony, we need to shift our vantage point from the original to the local site of reception and search for a model of cultural encounter beyond the polar positioning of domination and resistance.[3] For this purpose, Lydia Liu's notions of "guest" and "host" languages, replacing the model of original and translating languages, can help locate Chinese agency in the process of cultural translation. By considering translation as a site "where the guest language is forced to encounter the host language . . . until new words and meanings emerge in the host language itself," our inquiry into the global impact of Hollywood cinema necessarily shifts to an investigation of the coining of a local cinematic idiom.[4]

On the other hand, a locally centered approach to the genesis of a cultural practice, regardless of its compulsory encounter with the Western presence, can be equally misleading. The recent revival of the martial arts films in various transnational productions—*Crouching Tiger, Hidden Dragon* (dir. Ang Lee, Taiwan/Hong Kong/U.S./China [2000]), *Hero* (dir. Zhang Yimou, Hong Kong/China [2002]), *Kill Bill, Vol. 2* (dir. Quentin Tarentino, U.S. [2004])—has paralleled a perpetually retrospective gaze in Chinese film historiography that traces their global success all the way through the 1960s and 1970s Hong Kong movies and the 1920s Shanghai martial arts film craze back to the configurations of *xia* (knight errantry) in traditional Chinese fiction. The "Chinese" origin of the martial arts genre is paid proper tribute in Quentin

Tarantino's *Kill Bill, Vol. 2*. In the film (opening with a Shaw Brothers logo), the training of Uma Thurman by the white-browed Chinese Daoist martial arts master enables her "yellow-haired" embodiment of female knight errant, *nüxia*. However, this figure of *nüxia*, so prominent in the Shaw Brothers films and its 1920s Shanghai predecessors, conveniently eclipses Thurman's own heritage, the Pearl White figure. Historiographies and film practices like this force us to ponder upon the entwined practices between the global economy and politics of cultural difference.

This article pauses at the ever-shifting and problematic location of origin to explore the mediated cultural encounter between the American serial queen adventure and a subgenre of Chinese martial arts films—*nüxiapian*, or films featuring a female knight errant—which first appeared on the 1920s silent screen and had a lasting influence in Chinese cinema. In highlighting the neglected presence of American serial queen films in the Chinese entertainment world of the 1910s and 1920s, I question the cultural essentialist association of the martial arts films as a purely "Chinese" genre largely identified with persisting tradition and local culture. At the same time, I examine the local as the site of irreducible heterogeneity that enabled active and plural modes of cultural translation, resulting in the "vernacular" body of *nüxia*.

I evoke the notion of "vernacular" to revisit three strands of its theoretical and historical underpinnings. First, my use of the term "vernacular" is indebted to Miriam Hansen's discussion of classical Hollywood cinema as a form of vernacular modernism. The "vernacular" denotes a radically understood modernism informed by Walter Benjamin's aesthetic conception of the history of sense perception within "mass-produced, mass-mediated, and mass-consumed modernity." This modernism, with its reflexive relationship to modernity, is "vernacular" because of its association with idiomatic usage, local inflections, promiscuity, and the practice of the everyday.[5]

Second, the "vernacular" concerns the global impact of Hollywood cinema and relates directly to issues of translation. For Hansen, the currency of American film as "the first global vernacular" resides in both its own translatability and its subjection worldwide to local practices of translation. This raises a tension between the assumption that Hollywood cinema has an intrinsic appeal (the notion of translatability) and the local translation practices by which it is adapted. More importantly, this formulation brings out the linguistic and experiential dimensions of the "vernacular." Whereas the experiential "vernacular" is identified with "mass-produced, mass-consumed" everyday practice in which (Hollywood) cinema remains a privileged reflexive and mimetic modern medium, the linguistic sense of the "vernacular" registers the global-local dynamics in the notion's dual aspect of dialect on the one hand and universal language on the other. What remains to be explored is how the experiential is traversed with the linguistic and how the linguistic duality of the local-global traffic accounts for heterogeneous forces within the local beyond the West/non-West dichotomy.

The third dimension of the vernacular, particularly relevant within the context of modern China, is its close association with the May Fourth Vernacular Movement, initiated in 1919. Zhang Zhen has relocated this movement within the transformation of urban modernity beyond linguistic and literary domains, doing so by reassessing vernacular writing as the technological renovation of modern print culture in interaction with the "mass-mediated visual literacy, cinema."[6] This broadened horizon of the vernacular then further associates the cinematic vernacular with female embodiment. As Zhang illustrates in the case of early Chinese film actresses, their enactment and transformation as modern women on and off the screen realized the larger cultural ambition of the Vernacular Movement to renew the perception of the body and its means of expression.[7] The question, however, remains whether the female embodiment of the Vernacular Movement could stay autonomous and self-empowering without challenging the linguistic and cultural agenda of that movement.

What I would like to underscore is the dual promise of the May Fourth Vernacular Movement and its implication for Chinese cinema. As constitutive of the Enlightenment project that advocated the democratization and modernization of the Chinese language to approximate the oral, everyday language of the common people, the Vernacular Movement also involved systematic attempts at rationalization and standardization to construct a modern national language. Built on the basis of Beijing dialect at the expense of other Chinese dialects, this modern language, submitted to an occidentalization of syntax and vocabulary and a purification of pronunciation and idioms, was largely deprived of its colloquial aspect. The nationalization of the vernacular was thus a paradoxical gesture of inclusion and exclusion, liberation and normalization.[8] Further, the Vernacular Movement's disavowal of earlier (late Qing) vernacular innovations, its rewriting of Chinese literary history by rebuilding the Chinese canon from traditional vernacular literature, and its nationalist agenda betray the Vernacular Movement as a highly selective and constructive process, despite the grassroots image it thrived on.

Similarly, the vernacular nature of Chinese silent cinema as a concrete, "mass mediated visual literacy" of modern experience, which Zhang Zhen has convincingly illustrated, must also be counterbalanced with an understanding of its normative and hegemonic impulses in instituting a Chinese national cinema. Moreover, these normative impulses must be understood not as external persecuting agents outside Chinese cinema, but rather as intrinsic to its very formation. In the case of Chinese martial arts films, the homogenizing forces did not come about only with the Nationalist government's censorship in 1931 or the left-wing film movement in 1932. The very composite and conflicting nature of the vernacular is already registered in the female body of the *nüxia* and martial arts films as they emerged in the 1920s.

With these three dimensions of the vernacular in mind, the following inquiry traces the interaction between American serial queen films and the Chinese local entertainment world to examine the plural forces and conflicting agendas involved in the process of cultural translations. By naming such plural forces "vernacular" and locating them in the configuration of the female body of *nüxia*, I hope to highlight the ambiguities associated with the discursive and experiential dimensions of the "vernacular." In so doing, I hope to qualify the utopian association of the vernacular and nuance the democratic promise of female embodiment. In the end, my inquiry is not so much about the itinerary of the American serial queen in Chinese cultural scenes as the rise of a particular configuration of the female body on the Chinese silent screen.

My inquiry will take the route from "site" through "body" to "action." First, I will examine the initial site of this cultural encounter, the exhibition venue where American serial adventure films shared the same stage with the burgeoning modern Chinese popular drama (New Drama and Reformed Beijing Opera). This media cross-fertilization, as I will argue, contributed to the cinematic emphasis on the body, particularly a new image of the extraordinary female body with its action-oriented performance skills. Shifting from this popular domain, I will then turn to a less-discussed constituent of the popular culture of the period: the elitist discourse on Chinese martial arts films, in particular, their understanding of action. More specifically, I regard New Heroism as an occidentalist and high modernist appropriation of American adventure films that was combined with nationalist sentiment. This discourse intersects in important ways with the extraordinary female body in martial arts filmmaking. Finally, I will return to the silver screen with a case study of Huaju *nüxia* films starring Wu Suxin, which demonstrates how the female performance of gender ambiguity negotiated multiple forces and how the female heroic figure was submitted to two conflicting versions of the vernacular in Chinese film history.

Between Stage and Screen: An Inter-mediated Encounter

Although the subgenre of *nüxia* films did not emerge in China until 1927, the presence of the American serial queen adventure in early film exhibitions was clearly felt in other cultural realms and contributed to the formation of the *nüxia* subgenre.[9] The popularity of serial queen thrillers in China began at a transitional moment in the Chinese film market, with the decline of French film dominance in the wake of World War I and the simultaneous increase in American film exports and the sweeping success of the "low" genres such as slapstick comedy, Westerns, adventure serials, and detective films. The period between 1913 and 1927 is thus a particularly rich interval to examine for the cultural reception of the serial queen adventure.

Between 1913 and 1926, American film exports to China increased approximately seventeenfold, from 189,740 to 5,912,656 feet. By 1926 an average of 75 percent of the films shown in China were from America. According to C. J. North, "pictures of a particularly lurid nature which would never receive first-run showings in the United States" were distribution favorites in the early years and were received with enthusiasm by local audiences.[10] These "low" genres, especially the Wild West pictures, "immediately achieved startling popularity among Chinese theatergoers and at once stamped American life in their minds as an almost continuous medley of hard drinking and riding, interspersed with gun play and violent deaths for all but the favored few."[11] Adventure serials followed the success of Wild West pictures and incited "even greater excitement of the Chinese audience."[12]

The earliest serial queen adventures, including Pearl White films, appeared around 1916 and coincided with the rise of American power in Asia. In 1917 the twenty episodes of *The Iron Claw* (1916), starring Pearl White, were shown, as was another Pearl White serial, *The Clutching Hand* (aka *The Exploits of Elaine* [1914]).[13] Other films starring Pearl White included *Pearl of the Army* (1916), shown in China in 1921; *The Perils of Pauline* (1914), shown in China in 1916; *The Black Secret* (1919), released in China in 1920 as *The Great Secret of Germany*; and a few yet to be properly identified.[14] These films were tremendously popular.

Other stars, including Ruth Roland, Clara Kimball Young, Mabel Normand, Marguerite Courtot, and Eileen Percy, also sustained the presence of the serial queen in Shanghai movie theaters. The rhetoric of stardom for these female daredevils was similar. In an advertisement for *Ruth of the Rockies*, Roland was praised for her stunts, similar to those of Pearl White: "Riding

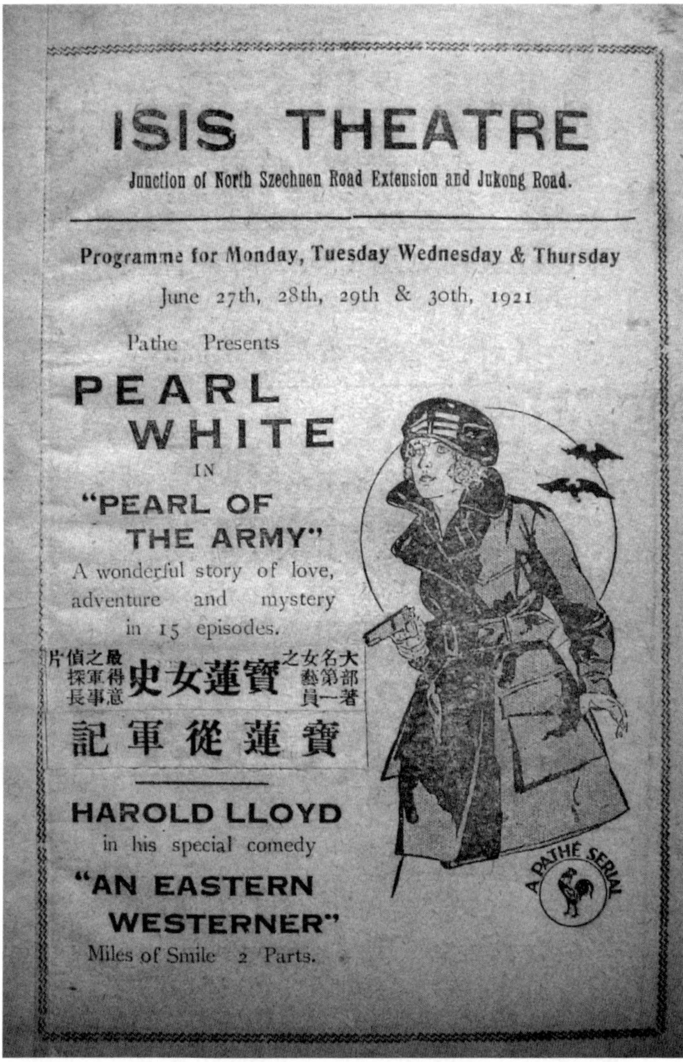

Pearl of the Army film program, 1921, private collection.

on a furious horse climbing the cliff as if walking on flat land, her talents are unsurpassable."[15] This verbal depiction was also rendered pictorially in an illustrated synopsis for the movie in the film journal *Yinngxi zazhi*. Renewing the iconography of female heroism with the visual portrayal of a sexualized Western woman conquering the craggy cliff while maintaining full control of the unbridled horse—a metonym of her own physical prowess and carnality—advertisements and illustrations like this created a new fantastic body whose physicality contrasted with the asexual body of *nüxia*, the female knight errant recurrent in Chinese folkloric imagination.

Because Chinese film journals did not emerge until 1921 (coinciding with the rise of the domestic film industry), the popular reception of these films is difficult to trace. However, the newspapers of the period reveal the impact of serial queen films on the local cultural scene, including live entertainment theatrical genres. Browsing through newspapers from 1911 to 1923 in Shanghai, one might be surprised to find that the chief form of popular entertainment was not cinema, but a hybrid dramatic form that was alternatively called Civilized Play (*wenmingxi*), New Drama (*xinju*), or Reformed New Drama (*gailiang xinxi*). These productions combined attributes of Beijing Opera, realist drama, and Japanese *shimpa geki* and featured mechanized spectacles on the stage.[16] At the same time, the Beijing Opera in Shanghai also updated itself by minimizing its singing sequences, adopting modern costumes, and addressing contemporary issues under the name Shanghai Style Beijing Opera (*haipai jingxi*).[17]

A closer look at the New Drama and the Reformed Beijing Opera reveals an increasing interaction between adventure film serials and these dramatic forms. Film and theater shared not only the same exhibition space and exhibition mode, but also similar narratives. On the New Drama stage, two episodes of a serialized play were shown each night, often along with two episodes of a detective serial film. In addition, many of the serialized plays were themselves detective adventures, including *Shijie diyi da zhentan Fu'er mosi* (The world's greatest detective, Holmes [1917]) and *Jiushi wo* (It's me [1916]). The two media converged most intimately in the practice of "linked plays" (*lianhuan ju*). Modeled after Japanese chain drama, these plays combined modern popular drama and film into a single entity by integrating filmed sequences into stage performances for exterior scenes and scenes of magical martial arts.[18] The linked plays effectively serialized each episode into an alternation between stage and screen and spoke most eloquently to the interpenetration of the two media.

The interaction between cinematic serial adventures, the New Drama, and the Reformed Beijing Opera precipitated an intense competition among various modes of realism. A parallel phenomenon can be found in America at the turn of the twentieth century. In Ben Singer's account, cinema was believed by American film and drama critics of the 1910s to be superior in its rendition of diegetic realism.[19] Yet as Singer points out, such a conception of realism was built more on an absorptive than apperceptive principle. It underestimated the realism of live interactions between audience and stage when the artificiality of devices, overt theatricality, heightened media awareness, and presentational style of performance were fully acknowledged and appreciated by spectators.[20]

In the Chinese context, sensational stage realism garnered higher praise than cinematic realism for both aesthetic and political reasons. Aesthetically, cinema seemed a pale rendition of the spectacular realism so flaunted on the Shanghai popular stage, with its use of footlights, raucous color, and sound effects in addition to real material objects placed in the representational space of the stage. The very thin line between the stage and the live audience was constantly traversed by the audience's loud calls, actors' gestural and vocal addresses to the audience, and the material "overflowing" of water, fire, and stage objects into the audience. Politically, this live interaction was often incorporated in many of the popular stage productions, which capitalized on recent events and stories. Improvised political speech and direct address perpetuated a shared public sensation of radical social change carried by the utopian promise of the Republican Revolution.

In contrast, the technological production of the cinematic real paradoxically distanced the material world and the audience. The anchoring of the real in cinema, then, had to be found elsewhere, and it was precisely the human body that provided this anchorage point through its ability to "give a name and a face to the spectacle, to humanize the machinery of production," as Jennifer Bean has said of the American serial queens.[21]

Extraordinary and Technological: The Female Body in Action as the Locus of the Real

The competition between cinema and popular modern drama over the articulation of reality provided a cultural context for the iconic emphasis on the extraordinary female bodies of the Western serial queens in Chinese film advertisements. Also, these images appeared at the moment when the female body entered public consciousness most prominently. Social discourses of medicine contrasted with a literary cult of sentimentality; the May Fourth celebration of free love and women's liberation endorsed the rise of the nuclear family yet clashed with ideas on singlehood, divorce, and cohabitation; a glamorous refashioning of the female body through consumer culture paralleled popular exhibitions of grotesque and monstrous female figures; the eroticism of anonymous encounters in the modern metropolis was rationalized by prostitution in the age of capitalism.[22] As the battleground among competing discourses concerning social reorganization of the body and as the eroticized embodiment of capitalist circulation, the female body provided the experience of modernity with a tangible image in early-twentieth-century China. Its visibility, enhanced by new means of mimetic technologies of reproduction such as lithography, copperplate printing, and photography, resonated with the rise of the female star on the Chinese silent screen.

As a result of the Qing imperial prohibition of actresses on stage, female actors had been almost absent from the most popular dramatic forms. Although the coexistence of male and female actors on the same stage was seen beginning around 1914 in smaller theaters (which, significantly, also served as venues for film exhibition), the most popular stars playing the female leads in the big productions of the New Drama and the Reformed Beijing Opera were still men. This perhaps explains the irony of a play such as *Hua Mulan* (Mulan joins the army [1914]), in which the triumphant female cross-dresser who becomes a heroic warrior was performed by the male star Wang Youyou.[23] One of the earliest Chinese narrative films, *Zhuangzi shiqi* (Zhuangzi tests his wife [1913]), still steeped in the New Drama conventions, cast the filmmaker, Lai Mingwei, as the heroine while Lai's wife (Yan Shanshan) played the servant, marking the first female presence in Chinese cinema.[24] The rise of female actresses on screen in the 1920s corresponded with the growing popularity of photographic media culture, constructing a referential continuity between their screen image and their naturalized gender difference.[25]

The ascendance of martial arts films and the subgenre of *nüxia* films coincided with a new generation of film actresses, including Hu Die and Ruan Lingyu, emerging in the mid- and late 1920s. Unlike the first generation during the early and mid-1920s, who were not fully trained and therefore established themselves with their physical appearance rather than their acting ability, the members of this new generation were required to refine their acting skills.[26] One of the new stars, Wu Suxing, whom I will discuss at length below, seems to have demonstrated such sought-after talent. In an essay titled "On Actions in Film," Cheng Yan reviewed favorably Wu's acting in the 1927 film *Bai furong* (The white lotus), an action-packed film reminiscent of Pearl White's adventure serials in terms of both the theme and the title. Most important, the reviewer, inspired by Wu Suxing's body in action, saw a significant transformation of female acting with the emergence of martial arts film as a major genre.[27] Ranking action films as the most demanding genre, the author observed that film genres such as romance and melodrama do not require "true competence" (*shili*) because an actor can learn how to fake any emotional expression, such as crying. On the other hand, "true competence," as Cheng argued, cannot be achieved by practice. A fight or a fall cannot be faked because a mere tinge of fakeness can spoil the real and exciting quality of film. The idea that the camera can fool the audience with substitute tears but not with action denies the authenticity of biological bodily functions, which are thought to be easily reproduced and reenacted. The aura of the real is instead attested by a singular extraordinariness of the (female) body, articulated in "true competence" and at the same time paradoxically realized by its demonstration of particular skills that conflate techniques, skills, and technology.

This confusion between aesthetic techniques, physical skills, and mechanical technology already appeared in the preface to the inaugural issue of *Yingxi zazhi* that featured Pearl White's picture. The editor, Gu Kenfu, obviously impressed by the adventure serials imported from the West, regarded film as composed of literature, science, and technology. By "technology," Gu does not mean film equipment, which he refers to as "science"; rather, Gu defines technology in terms of acting. He gives some examples of technology, including singing, martial arts, gesture, and movement in Beijing opera and oral delivery and transmission of emotions in New Drama. For film actors, technology means something unusually demanding: "We have seen many films imported to China from America and Europe, where they have to show their real technology in swimming, horse riding, boat rowing, operating an airplane, driving a car." Gu marvels at how the actors seem to master these presumably difficult tasks with ease.[28] His peculiar use of the term *jishu* (technology) should not be reduced to "technique," or "skill," as illustrated by his examples of action adventures. To Gu, the actor's body in action is at once technological and human/organic, often in synchrony with the cars and trains displayed on screen. The extraordinariness of the actor's body as the locus of the real is not so much a "cover-up" of technology's artificiality and inhumanity as a negotiation between the mechanical and the organic; the human "true competence" vis-à-vis mechanical technology does not so much naturalize a prosthetic body but offers itself as an equally demanding and coexisting technology. Precisely this struggle between the two technologies makes action films more exciting and hence more real than tears or laughter.

The body itself, then, is not sufficient as the locus of the real but has to be mobilized in full action. Similarly, the teary faces of the first generation of actresses on the silver screen that touched many hearts with "true feelings" were no longer moving and needed to be replaced by bodies in motion. This emphasis on action derived not only from within the machinery of film production but also from the broader social context. But before we examine the details of this context, a brief overview of the Chinese film industry and the rise of martial arts films seems in order.

Modernist Action: Toward an Aesthetics of New Heroism

As opposed to the aesthetics of live interaction found in the New Drama and the Reformed Beijing Opera, the cinematic image of the extraordinary female body and her action-packed performance skills anchored a rivaling source of authenticity and excitement. However, by the time of the rise of the martial arts films in 1927, the dynamic between cinema and theater was already much altered, as was the whole landscape of Chinese film exhibition and production. The two modern, popular dramatic forms had receded into the marginal entertainment venues of Shanghai. The domestic film industry, which emerged around 1922, had mushroomed to more than 100 film studios by 1926 and consolidated into 32 studios by 1927. The domestic exhibition space grew to approximately 150 movie theaters in 1927, which provided second-run opportunities for Chinese films. The tides of Chinese film genres had shifted from sentimental melodramas to social problem plays to romance to costume drama and provided a growing film audience with a constant supply of novel narratives, styles, and female film stars.

The rise of martial arts films is usually regarded as a popular commercial phenomenon mobilizing a modern folk culture that grew out of populist traditions. The canonical *History of the Development of Chinese Cinema* (1963) describes martial arts films as popular articulations of alternative justice and representations of struggle amid drastic social change, emerging when the nationalist war of the Northern Expedition, which ended years of factional warlordism, gave way to the Chiang Kai-shek-led GMD massacre of Communists in April 1927.[29] More recent scholarship has highlighted the internal logic of the film industry and its role in a wider scope of commercial culture.[30] According to film historians Li Suyuan and Hu Jubin, the end of the Northern Expedition brought about stable economic growth and improved transregional communication that further boosted the domestic film industry. Emulating the success of costume drama between 1925 and 1927, martial arts films as a rival genre thrived on the growing market of martial arts narratives in the burgeoning print culture and the ongoing storytelling tradition. For Li and Hu, the "superstitious" masses, entrenched in the popular cult of folkloric heroes, spirits, and ghosts, were susceptible to belief in the magical effects of martial arts films that were, ironically, the product of maturing film techniques and technologies in the Chinese film industry.

Zhang Zhen instead has suggested that this alloy of "magic and science" was a popular intervention of the teleological logic of modernization. For Zhang, the vast reservoir of folkloric imaginations, remobilized by a modern print culture and cinematic technology, created a mosaic space with "overlaid temporality."[31] The "anachronistic" conflation of folk culture with the anarchic energy of the technologically produced fantastic body posed a threat to the nationalization and modernization agendas upheld by cultural forces from both the Right and the Left. For this reason, as Zhang recounts it, martial arts films were eventually excised from the Chinese film industry by liberal critics and the Nationalist government (despite their initial enthusiasm) and were rejuvenated in Hong Kong, when the Shaw Brothers Studio's predecessor, Tianyi Studio, migrated from Shanghai to Hong Kong in 1937.[32]

This conception of martial arts films as popular commercial products that were antithetical to elitist and nationalist endorsements of unidirectional modernization, however, underestimates the internal connection between these polar forces that was to persist in later years of Chinese film history. Amid the plural discourses of modernization, nationalization, anarchism, and Marxism catalyzed by the Northern Expedition, martial arts films were indeed celebrated by various elite modernists among whom the advocates of New Heroism were most enthusiastic. Clustering around Lu Mengshu, the editor in chief of the highbrow film journal *Yinxing* (The silver star), a group of literary scholars, art historians, literary writers, and screenplay writers recognized in martial arts films a refreshing film aesthetic that they identified as New Heroism. Vaguely defined and often used together with neo-romanticism, New Heroism was a composite modernist discourse interwoven with a class-conscious social critique and a nationalist emphasis on Chinese cinema.

As a modernist aesthetic, New Heroism identified itself with neo-romanticism, a May Fourth umbrella term for fin-de-siècle literary movements, particularly aestheticism, symbolism, and decadent literature. Considered as a new milestone in Western literary history, neo-romanticism was the ideal combination of scientific objectivism and subjective power overcoming the limitations of previous aesthetics such as romanticism and naturalism.[33] The New Heroist critics saw neo-romanticism as best embodied in film, the newest form of art. By advocating a radical cinema, the critics simultaneously elevated Chinese cinema as the latest addition to a naturalized and universalized Western aesthetic teleology.[34]

This neo-romanticist cinema was in contrast with costume drama by virtue of its distinct aesthetics. While costume drama was seen as representing "benign" beauty that was, however, "artificial, passive, and languid," neo-romanticist cinema unearthed an aesthetic of the ugly as the most desired beauty. As the screenplay writer Chen Zhiqing put it, "Why don't we nakedly expose all the ugly and painful matters of life in the films so that the audience will be shocked heart and soul, and feel a cathartic release? The representation of such ugly and painful matters is mobile, vigorous, and dynamic, or we can say it is beauty closer to evil; it is genuine beauty. What we need in the New Heroist cinema is precisely such a mobile, robust, active spirit, and the articulation of all that is ugly and painful: it is beauty that approximates evil."[35] By championing the neo-romanticist ugliness and associating it with the motion, force, and action of cinema, Chen taps into two significant social impulses. His emphasis on the "ugly and painful matters in life," which harbored a symbolist penchant for "the hidden beauty beyond the exterior," first called for a New Heroist social exposure. This was in line with the ascendant Proletarian Literature movement, which addressed the inhuman condition of metropolitan life and recognized that scientific progress and materialist improvement was only exacerbating the exploitation of the proletariat.[36] Second, upholding the ugly as the vehicle of force and mobility was part of a nationalist self-critique focused on a flawed "national character"—the lack of "life force"—observed in the images of frailty in Chinese costume drama.[37]

The call for life force rested on the symbolic capital of Western philosophy, specifically a Japanese-mediated understanding of Bergsonian vitality.[38] By identifying its absence in Chinese national character, the New Heroists mapped a colonial lack in a gendered global order. As Chen Zhiqing put it, the lack of life force produced gender inadequacies in Chinese men and women. He deplored the "fragile scholar" as an inferior Confucian standard of male beauty, comparing it unfavorably to the Euro-American triumph of physical strength (*li*). As for Chinese women, Chen considered them mere "shadows," whose efforts to preserve feminine fragility, tenderness, and propriety were eclipsed by foreign women with their fully developed and fleshy bodies and lively and charming spirits. Worse still, Chinese men and women were considered to be introverted in spirit that "does not radiate from inside to the outside, but contracts from outside to inside" and hence were deemed unsuitable for the "extroverted spirit of cinema." Chen concluded that the predominant representation of so-called Oriental Culture in Chinese cinema, especially in the costume drama, would only be ridiculed by foreigners.[39] Instead, one should change the national character so as to produce successful Chinese films.

A qualitative difference between Western and Chinese cinema was likewise described by Lu Mengshu, who attributed to Western films "vigorous motion and passionate love" while calling Chinese films "gray," with static and regressive qualities.[40] Again and again the New Heroism discourse reiterated the East-West binary of national character, the East (China) being mysterious and spiritual as opposed to the West's being "naked, fleshly, macho, competitive and bloody." Boiled down to one point, the Chinese "character" was seen as static (*jing*) while Westerners were perceived as being dynamic (*dong*).[41] This dynamism was also unambiguously identified with American national character as it was manifest in American music (jazz), dance (the Charleston), and drama (the musical). The American character of mobility became a worldwide Zeitgeist through the dissemination of American action films that emphasized bodily movement over facial expressions and favored speed, agility, and intense action.[42]

These binary oppositions of national character, which had been previously articulated in the traditionalist discourse with a reversed hierarchy, came to justify a new cinema with a distinct look and energy just as the widely popular costume drama was waning. The new nationalist sentiment was emphatically occidentalist in upholding the Western national character as the universal cultural and aesthetic standard, as it was derived from American serial queen and male action films. More specifically, Chen's embrace of the "extroverted" nature of cinema characterized by "robust bodies, lively actions, and emotional expression" constituted a generic definition of the cinematic medium: identified with the dynamic body in American male and female action films, cinema was considered to be expressive in nature.[43] Because the Chinese national character was diagnosed in terms of gender inadequacy (on the part of both men and women), the New Heroist embrace of action adventure and serial queen genre cinema implicitly linked gender and genre—and cinema with character—with the aim of revitalizing the national character.

The urge to remold the Chinese national character and Chinese cinema was, however, contemporary with derogatory Western cinematic representations of Chinese people in the films that were frequently screened in Shanghai and other urban theaters—ironically, in the very American action films the New Heroists favored. The serial queen thrillers (including Pearl White films), the male-starred action/adventures, the slapstick comedies, and the sentimental melodramas had no lack of racist depictions of Chinese people, which inevitably provoked local indignation. The reaction against such films was most famously documented in dramatist and screenplay writer Hong Shen's protest in front of the theater exhibiting Harold Lloyd's *Welcome Danger* (*Bu pa si*) in 1930 and in the banning of Von Sternberg's *Shanghai Express* in 1932. Audiences also complained about the derisive portrayal of the Chinese in D. W. Griffith's *Broken Blossoms* when it was exhibited at the Empire Theater in Shanghai in 1925.[44]

Criticizing Western films that "fabricated non-existent ugliness" in representations of Chinese characters, these reactions nevertheless distinguished between two kinds of unfavorable portrayals.[45] In an article comparing *Broken Blossoms* and *The Thief of Baghdad* (dir. Raoul Walsh [1924]) with regard to their racist treatment of the Chinese, the author felt that the racial profiles of the Chinese characters in the two films were different.[46] Although the Mongolian Khan (played by Kamiyama Sojin) and the female palace slave (played by Anna May Wong) were depicted as evil and conniving in the latter film, the author argued that they were nevertheless presented as strong and capable. Therefore, "even though the foreign audience might detest them, they will be feared and taken seriously." On the other hand, he considered the effeminate portrayal of the powerless Chinese man in *Broken Blossoms* to be "particularly embarrassing," although the story "meant well to our nation."[47]

These reactions amplified the contradiction between the internalized racial hierarchy in the discourse of "national character" and the anxiety of foreign "misrepresentation" that was acutely experienced in the global circulation of Hollywood cinema.[48] Yet the action adventure, in the eyes of the local beholder, also opened up a subaltern space of articulation precisely with the genre's peculiar portrayal of racial ugliness. This ugly image of the virulent but powerful Chinese Other bore an uncanny resemblance to the American icon of forceful mobility, to which Anna May Wong's shining dagger provided a brief glimpse. This unexpected proximity urges us to reevaluate the cultural politics underlying New Heroism in China after the mid-1920s. Apparently, New Heroists internalized a perception of China as effeminate weakling in their viewing of Hollywood action and serial queen thrillers, which provided them with the ideal symbolist and occidentalist model of robust, dynamic ugliness to pursue. Yet to dismiss New Heroists simply as passive, unreflective consumers victimized by the discourse of "Chinese characters" and enchanted by the hegemony of Americanism is to miss an important underside of the phenomenon. That is, what they embraced as the ugly sublime was actually an inverted image of the subordinate Chinese themselves that was projected by the same American film genres. At the back of the vigorous "White" figure of *The Thief of Baghdad*, therefore, stand the evil, yet no less powerful, Khan and Chinese slave woman, the abject by-product that Western dominance failed to exorcise. In a gesture of Occidentalism, the New Heroists unwittingly reappropriated the power of abjection assigned to the subordinate in Hollywood action and serial queen thrillers.

It is in this sense that we can understand the New Heroist enthusiasm for martial arts films and its connection with American serial and, later, feature-length adventures. Counteracting the national self-image of frailty and passivity, martial arts films portrayed a unique ugliness endowed with the proto-primitivist "life force" of the lower class competing against and emulating robust Western figures. The aesthetics and ethics of the ugly were furthermore endowed with the neo-romanticist scientific objectivism and symbolist sensibility, along with the nationalism and the New Heroist social activism that endorsed an alternative beauty and national image. Hollywood cinema, especially action films, provided both discourses with an object of anxiety and the language of critique/resistance. The early advocates of martial arts films contended that such films would boost the Chinese film industry not only through the great popularity they would generate but also by "mak[ing] the blue eyes see that we Chinese have our own Eastern culture and morality when the films are exported."[49] Still, as a source of inspiration, they turned to the "Martial Spirit" of Western action films—including *The Thief of Baghdad*—which, significantly, were translated as "martial arts films" (*wuxia pian*).

From Pearl White to White Rose Woo: The Dual Body of the Vernacular

While the discussion of New Heroism, with its modernist aesthetics, social critique, and nationalist agenda, was largely a male discourse, produced mainly by Western-educated, elite writers and critics, the female heroine was embraced by these writers in terms of modern subjectivity. For Lu Mengshu, the New Hero did not need to have "three heads and six arms" but could be anybody, including women and children, as long as they "have fiery emotion, a spirit of sacrifice, and lead the rest to oppose oppression and improve society."[50] The New Hero is not a privilege but a right. Women were particularly welcome in this cinema, as the effeminized national image needed an injection of the "life force" of the ugly. Defying the traditional image of beauty with power and prowess, the newly invented female body embodied the changes in national character and Chinese cinema.

The Huaju films starring Wu Suxin stood at the center of this modernist and nationalist configuration of Chinese cinema. Wu Suxin belonged to the second-generation movie stars of the mid- and late 1920s. She was contemporary with (but quickly obscured by) Hu Die and Xuan Jinglin.[51] Despite her frequent appearance in film journals and programs, very little is known about Wu Suxin's life. Born in 1905 of Cantonese origin, she graduated from Qixiu Girl's School in 1922 and started acting for small studios until she joined Tianyi Studio, where she gradually rose to stardom after acting in nine films (including one of the first martial arts films, *Nüxia Li Feifei* [Female heroine Li Feifei (1925)]) between 1925 and 1927. In 1927 Wu left Tianyi and joined the newly founded Huaju Studio (1926–1931). Between 1927 and 1931 she made about twenty-two films for Huaju, mostly co-starring with Zhang Huimin, the co-owner of the studio. Wu also undertook other roles in the production process, including associate director, costume designer, and makeup artist. After 1931, with the closing of Huaju Studio and the decline of martial arts films, Wu went to Dahua Studio, where her star status can be inferred from the fierce competition between Dahua and the major film studio Mingxin over the production rights for adapting the popular writer Zhang Henshui's *Tixiao yinyuan* (The fate in tears and laughter [1931]). Wu played dual leading roles in the Dahua production, while Hu Die did the same for the Mingxin version. Wu's rivalry with Hu Die, the soon-to-be "movie queen," can be traced back to 1926–1927, when the two stars acted in six films together at Tianyi studio. After the Japanese annexation of Manchuria in 1931, which provoked rising patriotic sentiment, Wu went on stage and toured in dozens of cities.[52] Little is known about her subsequent life.

Huaju was a relatively small-sized studio, founded by the brothers Zhang Qingpu and Zhang Huimin of the wealthy Zhang family of Cantonese origin. The studio made martial arts, adventure, and detective films exclusively and was particularly keen on parading its actors in Western attire while they wrestled with, competed against, and mastered modern technology. Despite its interest in ultra "low" genres, Huaju maintained close ties to various elitist writers and critics, including its screenplay writer, Gu Jianchen, one of the earliest spoken drama playwrights and the founder of the high modernist group Shanghai xiju xieshe (Shanghai Drama Society). Also, Huaju's studio journal, *Huaju tejuan*, published modernist poetry, essays advocating the May Fourth enlightenment project, discussions of screenwriting techniques, and philosophical arguments about cinema's affective impact and artistic status. Moreover, many of its messages had the exact wording and rhetorical style as the New Heroist discourse. The journal not only set a mission for martial arts films to serve the age of revolution and save China from its "subcolonial" condition, but also made explicit reference to Byron, Ibsen,

Huaju studio production stills, *Dianying yuebao*, no. 1, April 1928.

Wilde, and other romantic and neo-romantic idols in its appeal to the "life force" in a new kind of cinema.[53] These writings indicate how martial arts films were subject to heterogeneous interests and represent the New Heroist short circuit between the high and low.

At the center of popular and elitist interest in producing a Chinese martial arts cinema translated from American serial queen and male-starred adventure films, Wu Suxin presented an exemplary figure within this much mediated and elongated cultural encounter. While at first sight Wu looks nothing like Pearl White, the linguistic transplantation is obliquely registered. Pearl White's last name is partially maintained in Wu's English name, White Rose Woo, which became part of the film title *Nüxia Bai Meigui* (The female knight errant White Rose [1929]), a martial arts film that I will examine more closely below.

The word *rose* was loaded with rich intertextual references during this period. The flower, with the thorniness of exotic/occidental beauty, became an aesthetic currency in the May Fourth (1919–1925) and post–May Fourth period (1925–1931) across a variety of cultural planes. Du Shihuan's discussion of neo-romanticism used the rose as an example to illustrate the difference between romanticism, naturalism, and neo-romanticism, thus testifying to the circulatory power of the term within the realm of literature.[54]

The rose was also prominent in the Chinese cinematic and popular literary imagination of the 1920s.[55] One of the most popular Mandarin Duck and Butterfly fiction journals was edited by Zhou Shoujuan and called *Hong meigui* (The Red Rose), for which Yu Tianfen, a popular writer specializing in detective fiction, wrote an intriguing mini-photoplay titled *Meigui nülang* (1924), or "The lady of the roses."[56] In this story, several crimes are connected to a young female flower vendor selling roses at a recently opened entertainment park. It turns out that "the lady of the roses," who has already beguiled the patrolling policeman into a romantic liaison, is attached not only with a thorny link to the criminal underworld but also with a long black queue, or Chinese male pigtail, that turns out to be part of a wig and the gender disguise for the "lady's" male identity. The gender twist further builds its humor on the symbolic cutting by the Republican Revolution (1911) of the male queues. The queue, a Qing dynasty (1644–1911) definition of masculinity, had become a detachable sign of femininity, further confusing the "lady's" real gender.

Meigui nülang was produced just as the female film star began to replace the cross-dressed male of New Drama, making the latter increasingly denaturalized. Orchestrating the fiction with crude, scene-dissecting photos, the protocinematic mini-photoplay figured a kind of *nüxia*, although it was a negative portrayal containing a gender twist.[57] Despite his criminal identity, the "lady of the roses," like many female knights errant to follow, is homeless and nomadic, roaming in a landscape of *jianghu* (rivers and lakes), the unofficial version of a society in which chivalry and alternative justice reigned (although in this story, the alternative justice is still considered to be criminality). Accompanying its exotic beauty with aggression and gender ambiguity, the dual connotations of the rose were reproduced in many *nüxia* films of the period (1927–1931). Femininity and physical prowess tinted the flower symbolism with a touch of the ugly in the unusual color and image association in film titles such as *Heimudan* (Black peony [1931]), *Heiyi nüxia* (The black-cloaked female knight errant [1928]), and *Nü haidao* (The female pirate [1931]).

Nüxia Bai Meigui (1929) opens with a semi-actuality scene shot on location at a parade at the Women's Sports Academy. After an establishing long shot of the female students marching behind a male brass band, the camera pans slowly and cuts to a closer shot of a female sports group. A high angle presents all of the students wearing white tops and shorts, followed by a close-up of one student and the intertitle: "Bai Suying is an outstanding student at the academy. Because she likes wearing a white rose on her blouse and intervenes in any injustice, her classmates honor her with the nickname, 'the Female Knight Errant White Rose.'" The next sequence introduces a demonstration of the versatile training received by women that crosscuts among the female coach, the students' group demonstration, and Wu's individual performance. Performing gymnastics, club exercises, and rifle preparation, White Rose is shown together with the group yet is always singled out by the camera for each performance. She is the modern superindividual, a model for the group who at the end wins a martial arts costume, the award for best performance.

"One hour later," as marked by the intertitle, Wu seems to have regressed to an archaic time as she is seen wearing a *nüxia* costume and practicing archery in her Western-style garden. Swaggering and uncouth in gesture and language, Wu looks quite different from the disciplined body in the sports game. A male servant from her hometown arrives with a letter in which White Rose's father tells her that their farm is being robbed by the local bandits. Wu decides to disguise herself as her traveling brother so as to join the fight against the bandits. The scene orchestrates an intense exchange of gazes and reflections in this cross-dressing masquerade. A medium close-up shows Wu's back and her image reflected in the mirror. With the male servant peeking through the curtain from the side and her maid watching and applauding from behind, Wu puts on the various accessories of her attire step-by-step, recorded to the fullest detail by the camera. Wu first dons a moustache, followed by a headscarf, then a cowboy hat. Repeatedly shaping and adjusting her Douglas Fairbanks–type moustache, Wu highlights the flexibility of her gender display and poses in macho male gestures. Pulling her bow and posing for archery, she also adds a sword to her apparel. All of this hyperbolic gender construction is shown via the reflection in the mirror mediated by the camera and the reaction of the two onlookers: one a male voyeur intrigued by the scene and the other a female confidant celebrating Wu's gender transformation.

The immense pleasure generated in this scene is probably best captured by what Jane Gaines calls "vicarious transgression," "the kind of exhilara-

Wu Suxing cross-dressing in *The Female Knight Errant White Rose*.
Dianying yuebao, nos. 11–12, September 1929.

tion produced by the knowledge of how much 'trouble' gay/lesbian desire produces for heterosexuality."[58] According to Gaines, that pleasure can be metaphorically and performatively produced by dress, which allows a "complete fabrication" of gender. In several more films, including *Shandong xiangma* (The bandit of Shandong [1927]) and *Zhentan zhiqi* (The wife of the detective [1928]), Wu cross-dresses as male, performs martial arts stunts, and becomes involved in love triangles between a "male" peer and a female admirer. The acknowledgment of clothing—as well as gender—as detachable, constructed signs constitutes what Gaines calls the possibility of "good camp." Here the pleasure is doubled by another crossover, by Wu Suxing's re-assemblance of dominant cultural accessories. The "male" traits attached to the female body of Wu Suxin attested to the popularity of American male action stars in China between 1922 and 1925, among whom Douglas Fairbanks, John Barrymore, and Richard Barthelmess were the most popular. By trying out the Hollywood male star outfit and accessories, Wu staged the constructedness of existing cultural as well as gender assumptions.

In addition to trying out various gendered and cultural outfits, this vicarious transgression also extends to the décor. The excessive and chaotic stacking up of Wu's gender accessories is complemented by the symbiosis between costume and interior design. After Wu arrives home, we see the interior of the house draped in wallpaper with art deco geometrical patterns that blend in with the traditional decorative window frame. This design, in which orientalist modern art and traditional Chinese art are misidentified with each other, is echoed in the pattern on the headscarf of the male knight errant who comes to Wu's aid and in Wu's own decorative belt.

Wu pursues the bandits to their house, and upon her arrival the bandit leader and his gang rush out wearing cowboy shirts, jeans, and boots. The house is a familiar mechanized setting (*jiguan bujing*) of martial arts films as the site of evil, but in this film it strongly resembles a Buster Keaton slapstick setting.[59] Furnished with a Keaton staircase/slide flip-flop and indoor balconies, the house showcases Wu's extraordinary agility in overcoming the bandits, swinging on her rope with ease and performing acrobatic stunts. The house hosts the feverish encounter of mobile bodies dressed and moving in different genre codes and, like Wu's hybrid costume, stages an intensive and playful clash of Western, slapstick, and martial arts genres.

Wu's male personification complements the gender-bending of her peers in American serial queen adventures.[60] If cross-dressing is a familiar trope in serial queen adventures, Wu's hybrid body crosses not only gender, but also temporal and cultural alignments, displaying the attire and physique of the globe—be it Chinese or Western, traditional or modern, male or female—and questioning the rigid boundaries of these binary distinctions. Wu's body is illustrative of the translation process that links two realms in the gestures of boundary crossing. In the translating language, as Lydia Liu says, "The original and translation complement each other to produce meanings larger than mere copies or reproductions."[61] If the American serial queen film delivers a reflexive vernacular of the experience of modernity in its own local context,[62] the Chinese *nüxia*, never quite its equivalent and not always serial, engages similarly with technology and social mobility. But the female figure is further modified in *nüxia* by multiple cultural references to local and foreign genre inflections, including the male-starred action films. Together, the American serial queen and the Chinese *nüxia* pursue the composite experience of modernity on a continuous and expanding horizon of cultural encounter.

Nonetheless, our utopian celebration of this cultural translation epitomized in Wu's hybrid female body must be partial because of the military marching in the sports academy with which *Nüxia Bai Meigui* (The female knight errant White Rose) opens. Shot in semi-actuality style, this beginning registers the contemporary context from which Wu's trip home (her trip "out of time") departs. On the one hand, Wu's physical movements carve out an alternative body space, a wonderland where the multiple temporal and geopolitical forces are negotiated by way of the aesthetics of pastiche, montage, and ornamentation. On the other hand, the disciplined body shapes the very possibility of this fantastic departure and underscores the weight of the present tense in which a competing orchestration of the body is practiced. Within the narrative, Wu's hybrid and anarchic body is actually produced through discipline by the marching rituals through which she earns a martial arts costume.

A similar paradox also occurred in a Lianhua Studio production, *Yi jian mei* (A spray of plum blossoms [1931]), which appeared shortly after the studio's establishment in 1930, heralding a new decade of Chinese filmmaking.[63] Adapted from the Shakespeare play *Two Gentlemen of Verona*, the film is similar to "White Rose" in its stark contrast of military discipline and martial arts anarchy, and like that film, it resembles American adventure thrillers.[64] It brings the double presence of Western serial queen and male adventure films to the Chinese screen: while the female soldiers with long permed hair and military uniforms (jacket, skirt, and boots) look like sisters of Pearl White from *Pearl of the Army*, which was widely popular in China around 1922, the male lead (Jin Yan, China's soon-to-be "movie emperor" [*yingdi*]) plays a Robin Hood figure modeled on the American male adventure films that circulated between 1922 and 1925. Set in revolutionary Canton in the 1920s, the rivalry between the military and the martial arts—articulated through the male competition between a young officer (Wang Cilong) and an officer-turned-bandit in pursuit of the military general's daughter (Lin Chuchu)—is mediated by a utopian female space with a masculine exterior and hyperfeminine interior. Headed by the general's daughter, the women are seen on the exercise ground as wedged in and undifferentiated from the masculine squad, indicating the collective geometry of the nation. Inside Lin's boudoir, where female camaraderie and confidence are nurtured, the décor of a plum blossom motif is reproduced in an exaggerated fashion in an industrially designed glass door and window frame, in sofa pillows, and in Lin's chest pin. The military presence of the uniformed female soldiers in this exclusive, feminine space adds an element of empowerment to the romantic story of the male lead's sister (Ruan Lingyu), who travels to the south in pursuit of her womanizing lover (Wang Cilong) and is transformed into a woman soldier in this boudoir, aided by Lin's sisterhood.

The autonomy of this female interior, however, is undercut by the unchallenged class hierarchy, with the women soldiers serving Lin in her boudoir and also by the dual symbolism of the plum blossom as both the female bosom and the new Republic.[65] The gender connotations of the flower are further nuanced by Jin Yan's flying arrow, to which is attached a drawing of a signature plum blossom, reminiscent of another martial arts film, *Xiadao yizhimei* (The knightly bandit nicknamed "One Bough of Plum Blossom" [1929]), written by the advocate of New Heroism, Chen Zhiqin. This masculine, phallic association is inverted in turn when Mei Lanfang, the most prominent Beijing Opera male star of the time, who specialized in young female roles (*huadan*) and whose last name "Mei" means precisely plum blossom, is twice evoked in the film. He first appears when Jin Yan is seen standing beside him on a steamboat waving at people; a curious documentary-like shot places Mei at the focal point of the frame while Jin stands to the side. He is evoked again when Jin Yan's fellow bandit (Liu Jiqun) entertains the gang by performing the female role in "Tiannü sanhua" (Heavenly maiden scatters flowers), a Beijing Opera scene most famously played by Mei Lanfang. The association with Mei Lanfang adds another spin to the already dizzying swing of gender crossing in the film.

While the plum blossom motif of the feminine space is penetrated by nationalist, male, and cross-dressing symbolism, the frailty of the feminine utopia is also underlined by a serial queen "power and peril" narrative, although the structure is quickly turned on its head. During a cross-country horserace, Lin is endangered by two consecutive assault attempts by her pursuers. Rescued by her lover, Jin Yan, an officer-turned-bandit wronged by injustice, Lin and Ruan Lingyu join the bandits and stage a scene of female victimhood. Tied up and thrown in the middle of the road, they ensnare the military and serve as the vanguard of a successful ambush by the bandits led by Jin Yan. The film ends with justice restored; the bandits conscripted; and Jin Yan, Lin, Ruan, and Ruan's lover—dressed in military uniforms—marching toward the screen on horseback. This ending draws a full circle from the sports stadium parade that opens the film *Nüxia Bai Meigui* (The female knight errant White Rose) to the military march that ends *Yi jian mei* (A spray of plum blossoms). In both films, the female heroines gain entry into exhilarating knight errantry, yet they do so, paradoxically, through the militarized standardization of the body. This brings out the dual aspects of the vernacular as highlighted by the *nüxia* body: one associated with "dialect, promiscuity, the everyday" resulting in optimal hybridity via cultural translation, the other with a linguistic hegemony instituting the nationalistic and militarist ambitions in its own gesture of empowered expression and experience.

The interplay between these two discourses of the disciplined body and the fantasy body reappeared in subsequent Chinese films. The romantic pairing of a nationalist empowerment of the female body through discipline and the anarchic action of *nüxia* recurred in the most memorable female figures of Lianhua Studio productions in the 1930s. These include the barefoot embodiment of the neo-romanticist spirit by the agile Wang Renmei in *Ye meigui* (The wild rose [1932]) contrasted with her training of village children in simulated wars in the same film; Li Lili's athletic superwomanhood and the taming of it for the collective honor in *Tiyu huanghou* (Queen of sports [1934]); the secondary role of a female worker (A. Ying) in *Cai Chusheng* (The new woman [1934]) who is celebrated equally for her invigorating physical fight with the villain and for the Taylorist organization of her timetable; and lastly, Li Lili's free spirit and her heroic capture of a landlord for nationalistic purposes in *Dalu* (The big road [1935]).

These themes also recurred in yet another round of the *nüxia*: the female spies in wartime Resistance Films who replaced the gender masquerade with disguised social identities and whose painted faces of feminine frailty and glamour sheltered their physical and mental prowess in the service of the nation. However, the most striking reincarnations of the *nüxia* figure would appear in a cluster of heroic female figures in post-1949 "New Chinese Cinema," culminating in the militant and fantastic female soldiers in *Hongse niangzi jun* (The red detachment of women [1960]). Moving as a social and spatial nomad among gender stereotypes and modes of self-articulation, the modern girl measured the distance between freedom and discipline, mobility and constriction, sensation and sentimentality.

Situated at the local end of translation, my historical inquiry into the mediated cultural encounter between American serial queen films and Chinese *nüxia* films has centered on how the latter amalgamated, transfigured, and negotiated different cultural sources—domestic and foreign, high and low, aesthetic and political—to give birth to its own domestic vernacular. In this process, American serial queen films were integrated into a series of local agents of cultural translation. First, this translation involved an intermedial competition between the American films and a burgeoning local media culture that was dominated by Chinese popular drama. Second, American serial queen adventures and male action films were translated into Chinese martial arts films by way of the elite discourse of New Heroism. Martial arts films did not derive merely from popular interests entrenched in a folkloric imagination mobilized by modern commercial print culture and cinematic technology; rather, this popular and "low" film genre was also supported by the Chinese elite, which translated modernist aesthetics and American action films into the New Heroist agenda to address its own social and nationalist concerns.

The high modernist dimension in the formation of martial arts films complicates any limitation of the "vernacular" to the popular and the "low." It also leads us to interrogate the automatic equation of the vernacular with modernist alterity. It is evident that this modernist component of the vernacular is caught up in its own nationalistic agenda, which bears liberating as well as normative impulses. Nevertheless, this ambivalent agency of the national, as Pheng Cheah reminds us, is very much "inscribed within a global force field" and does open up venues for critical consciousness against the colonial global order.[66]

Third, the *nüxia* figure in martial arts films translated serial queen films by deploying the "power and peril" paradox and demonstrating physical agility and mobility while also combining features of other adjacent genres such as male action films and slapstick comedy to produce a hybrid female body. These levels of translation conditioned the extraordinary female body beyond self-empowerment and celebratory cultural hybridity. These plural forces generated a dual vernacular, turning the *nüxia* figure into a contentious and consensual site for the popular and the official, the low and the high, the modernist and the nationalist.

As I have explored it through the case of *nüxia*, the vernacular refers to global/local traffic, local heterogeneity, and the anarchic/hegemonic impulses within the generation of a domestic cinema. The mediated encounter between American serial queen films and the *nüxia* subgenre challenges the mythical "Chineseness" of the martial arts films and demonstrates this "local" genre as a product of international film exchange. It also illustrates the ideological implications of the vernacular in a particular historical context. In the end, this cinematic female heroism that fashions an anarchic *and* disciplinary body alerts us to the tensions between vernacular and authoritarian discourses, as well as to their proximity.

This proximity puts into question the geopolitical division within Chinese cinema between the commercial, "vernacular" Shanghai–Hong Kong axis and the socialist, propagandistic mainland axis. The figure of *nüxia* dating from 1920s Shanghai may have found her refuge in "liberal" and transnational Hong Kong cinema, but she has also remained, with various metamorphoses, central to mainland Chinese film history, as suggested above; hence the uncanny resemblance between the market-driven and the state-dictated cinemas. The alleged alterity of Shanghai cinema, here exemplified by its martial arts films, could only be understood through an emphatic notion of the "vernacular." Such a view reifies a geopolitical division between cosmopolitan Shanghai-Hong Kong and provincial/nationalistic China. In reality, though, the normative dimension of the "vernacular" was not fostered only in mainland socialist China but had already operated in Shanghai silent cinema as well as Hong Kong cinema.[67] Through this cross-cultural genealogy of *nüxia* films, I hope to have outlined an alternative account of Chinese martial arts films that might help resituate Shanghai cinema in a larger picture of Chinese cinema.

Remapping the various contours of the vernacular helps us traverse the geopolitical division and examine more closely the heterogeneity of the local. The geopolitics of alterity in Greater China has always been inscribed within a larger context of unequal cultural exchanges. This account also asks us to reassess the contemporary global cultural traffic in recent films such as Quentin Tarantino's *Kill Bill, Vol. II*, in which Uma Thurman's own cultural heritage has to be redeemed via her "yellow-haired" embodiment of *nüxia*. The return of the cultural and iconic "debt," now that we can recognize the reincarnated (and barely recognizable) Pearl White as the image of *nüxia*, may be among the most productive, perplexing, and economically profitable legacies of cultural translation.

NOTES

1. *Yingxi zazhi*, no.1 (1921). The film titles listed here are the Chinese distribution titles. Unless otherwise stated, all translations of the cited texts are made by this article's author.

2. Miriam Hansen, "The Mass Production of the Senses: Classical Hollywood Cinema as Vernacular Modernism," in *Reinventing Film Studies*, ed. Christine Gledhill and Linda Williams (London: Arnold, 2000), 332–50.

3. Lydia Liu, *Translingual Practice: Literature, National Culture, and Translated Modernity—China, 1900–1937* (Stanford, Calif.: Stanford University Press, 1995), 25–27.

4. Ibid., 26.

5. Miriam Hansen, "Fallen Women, Rising Stars, New Horizons: Shanghai Silent Film as Vernacular Modernism," *Film Quarterly* 54 (2000): 11; see also Hansen, "Mass Production of the Senses," 333.

6. See Zhang Zhen, "An Amorous History of the Silver Screen: The Actress as Vernacular Embodiment in Early Chinese Film Culture," *Camera Obscura*, no. 48 (2001): 229–63, esp. 251; see also Zhang Zhen, *An Amorous History of the Silver Screen: Shanghai Cinema, 1896–1937* (Chicago: University of Chicago Press, 2005).

7. Zhang Zhen, "An Amorous History," 253.

8. For a thorough study of the systematic invention of the modern vernacular as a national language, see Edward M. Gunn, *Rewriting Chinese: Style and Innovation in Twentieth-Century Chinese Prose* (Stanford, Calif.: Stanford University Press, 1991).

9. The scope of my research is limited to media practices in Shanghai, although other cities were reported to have screened the same serial films.

10. C. J. North, comp., "The Chinese Motion Picture Market," *Trade Information Bulletin*, no. 467, Bureau of Foreign and Domestic Commerce, U.S. Department of Commerce, 2. I am aware that North's data could be inflated, as demonstrated in David Newman's recent study, "U.S. Department of Commerce View of the China Film Market during the 1920s, with a Particular Focus on Hong Kong" (paper presented at the Centennial Celebration of Chinese Cinema Conference, Beijing, June 6–7, 2005).

11. North, comp., "Chinese Motion Picture Market," 3.

12. Ibid.

13. See film ads in *Shenbao* for *The Iron Claw* (June 6, 1917), 4, and for *The Clutching Hand* (June 26, 1917), 4.

14. See film ads in ibid., May 25, 1920, 2, and June 5–14, 1920, 2.

15. Ibid., May 2, 1921, 2.

16. *Shimpa geki*, or "New School Theater," was a form of Japanese theater originated in the 1880s from Japanese "political drama" and developed as a popular theater from the 1880s to the 1920s. The theater combined elements from Japanese *kabuki* and Western stage melodrama. It was often considered a "transitional form" before the introduction of Western realist theater, although recent scholars have given due attention to its own distinct character from which early Japanese cinema drew. See Scott Nygren, "Inscribing the Subject: The Melodramatization of Gender in *An Actor's Revenge*," in *Melodrama and Asian Cinema*, ed. Wimal Dissanayake (New York: Cambridge University Press, 1993), 127–42.

17. The distinction between Civilized Play (The New Drama) and the Reformed Beijing Opera remained rather blurry at this point. While the latter maintained singing sequences, more formulaic acting styles, and type character casting, the former contained no singing and often featured a notoriously improvisational style in speech and acting. See Xu Banmei, *Huaju chuchuangqi huiyilu* (Beijing: Zhonggu Xiju, 1957).

18. Ibid., 120–21; Gong Jianong, *Gong Jianong congying huiyilu* (Taibei, China: Zhuanji Wenxue She, 1967), 404.

19. Ben Singer, *Melodrama and Modernity: Early Sensational Cinema and Its Contexts* (New York: Columbia University Press, 2001), 176; Nicholas A. Vardac, *Stage to Screen: Theatrical Origins of Early Film, David Garrick to D. W. Griffith* (Cambridge, Mass.: Harvard University Press, 1949). Singer provides three connotations for "diegetic realism" concerning the spectator's relation to the image or stage: naturalism (the story unfolds in ordinary real life settings), apperceptive realism (the spectator is aware of realism as the aesthetic effect), and absorptive realism (the spectator suspends belief and takes representation as reality).

20. Singer, *Melodrama and Modernity*, 178–82.

21. Jennifer Bean, "Technologies of Early Stardom and the Extraordinary Body," in *A Feminist Reader in Early Cinema*, ed. Jennifer Bean and Diane Negra (Durham, N.C.: Duke University Press, 2002), 412.

22. On the cult of sentimentality in popular writers and May Fourth women writers, see Perry Link, *Mandarin Ducks and Butterflies: Popular Fiction in Early-Twentieth-Century Chinese Cities* (Berkeley: University of California Press, 1981), and Rey Chow, *Woman and Chinese Modernity: The Politics of Reading between West and East* (Minneapolis: University of Minnesota Press, 1991). On the debates about singlehood, cohabitation, and other aspects of the sexual revolution, see Lee Haiyan, *Revolution of the Heart: A Genealogy of Love in China, 1900–1950* (Stanford, Calif.: Stanford University Press, 2006). On the rationalization of prostitution from earlier courtesan culture and its role in Chinese urban modernity, see Gail Hershatter, *Dangerous Pleasures: Prostitution and Modernity in Twentieth-Century Shanghai* (Berkeley: University of California Press, 1997).

23. *Shenbao*, June 23, 1914, 7.

24. See, for example, Cheng Jihua, Xin Zuwen, and Li Shaobai, eds., *Zhongguo dianying fazhanshi* (Beijing: Zhongguo Dianying, 1963), 28.

25. See Zhang, "An Amorous History of the Silver Screen," and Michael G. Chang, "The Good, the Bad, and the Beautiful: Movie Actresses and Public Discourse in Shanghai, 1920s-1930s," in *Cinema and Urban Culture in Shanghai, 1922–1943*, ed. Zhang Yingjin (Stanford, Calif.: Stanford University Press, 1999), 128–59. Chang discusses how readers of a woman's magazine felt that the photographic realism of cinema almost demanded the "genuine" female presence and hence corroded a long convention of male cross-dressing as female leads.

26. On the generations of Chinese female stars in the 1920s and 1930s, see Chang, "The Good, the Bad, and the Beautiful."

27. Cheng Yan, "Tan yingpian zhong zhi wushu," *Huaju tejuan* (Huaju special publication), no. 2 (1927): 46.

28. Gu Kenfu, "Fa kan ci," *Yingxi zazhi* 1 (1921): 7–10, esp. 8.

29. Cheng, Xin, and Li, *Zhongguo dianying fazhanshi*.

30. Li Suyuan and Hu Jubin, *Zhongguo wusheng dianying shi* (Beijing: Zhongguo Dianying, 1996). In his most recent English-language history of Chinese cinema, Hu

Jubin has rearticulated the Northern Expedition as the predominant context for martial arts films. Hu Jubin, *Projecting a Nation: Chinese National Cinema before 1949* (Hong Kong: Hong Kong University Press, 2003).

31. Zhang Zhen, "Bodies in the Air: The Magic of Science and the Fate of the Early 'Martial Arts' Films in China," *Post Script* 20 (2001): 43–60.

32. Ibid., 55–57. The Shaw Brothers was a major Hong Kong film studio that dominated Hong Kong and Southeast Asian film exhibition and film production for decades. Tianyi (1925–1937), one of Shanghai's first film studios to make martial arts films, was owned by the same Shaw family. Relocated to Hong Kong, the Shaw Brothers studio contributed significantly to the wave of martial arts films in Hong Kong that peaked in the 1960s. On the history of the Shaw Brothers studio, see Huang Ailing, ed., *The Shaw Screen* (Hong Kong: Hong Kong Film Archive, 2003).

33. Du Shihuan, "Xin langmanzhuyi de dianying," in *Dianying yu wenyi*, ed. Lu Mengshu (Shanghai: Liangyou, 1928), 115.

34. Shih Shumei, *The Lure of the Modern: Writing Modernism in Semicolonial China, 1917–1937* (Berkeley: University of California Press, 2001), 55–58, 239. As Shih forcefully argues, May Fourth writers' and critics' pragmatic use of Western modernism as a natural extension of a Western literary teleology in the service of their own discourse of progress has contributed to interpretations of Western writers and thinkers in ways that sometimes run diametrically contrary to interpretations in Western modernism, for example, the May Fourth emphasis on the positivistic aspect of Bergson despite his suspicion of nineteenth-century scientific positivism. See ibid., 58–68.

35. Chen Zhiqing, "Zailun xin yingxiongzhuyi de yingju," *Yinxing*, no. 8 (1927): 11.

36. Ibid., 4.

37. Lu Mengshu, "Dianying yu geming," in his *Xinghuo: Yingju lunji* (Shanghai: Dianying Shudian, 1927), 30. The notion of national character at stake here was derived from the German romanticist discourse of Volksgeist and popularized and inflected in nineteenth-century missionary writings on the Chinese character, most infamously in Arthur Smith's book *Chinese Characteristics* (Shanghai: North China Herald Office, 1890). For a detailed discussion of European national character discourse and its Chinese appropriation in the service of May Fourth literary modernity, see Liu, *Translingual Practice*, 45–76.

38. The frequent use of "life force" in literary elitist discourse derives partly from the Japanese literary critic Kuriyagawa Hakuson's *Kumon no shōchō /Kumen de xiangzheng*, trans. Lu Xun (Shanghai: Beixin Bookstore, 1924), which was reprinted five times. Kuriyagawa used the notion of life force as a combination of Bergsonian "vitality" and Freudian "libido" and identified it as the source of literary and artistic creation. The New Heroist critics mixed Kuriyagawa's understanding with Schopenhauer's notion of "will" and the Nietzschean notion of "power," both of which were popular in China for over a decade.

39. In mid-1920s China, traditionalism was itself a counterdiscourse against the May Fourth enlightenment, significantly influenced by Western critiques of mo-

dernity and often comes close to a modernist self-Orientalism. For a cogent critical analysis of traditionalism, see Shih, *Lure of the Modern*, chap. 6. All quotations in this paragraph are from Chen Zhiqing, "Yipian jitu," *Yinxing*, no. 7 (1927): 16–17.

40. Lu, "Dianying yu geming," 49.

41. Du Shihuan, "Dong de minzuxing yu yangmeituqi," *Yinxing*, no. 7 (1927): 46–47. See also Zhang Weitao, "Yingxi zaji, 11," *Yinxing*, no. 7 (1927): 32–33.

42. Zhang Weitao, "Yingju zaji, 16," *Yinxing*, no. 10 (1927): 30.

43. Chen, "Yipian jitu," 16.

44. Tang Mengpu, "Guanyu *Canhua lei* de liangge wenti," *Yingxi chunqiu*, no. 7 (1925): 16–17. The film was first shown in 1923 in the Carlton Theater and was subsequently banned by the British for fear of its "harming the international relationship." Chen Dingyuan, "Kanle *Canhua lei* yihou," *Yingxi chunqiu*, no. 7 (1925): 8. Reexhibited in 1925, the film received massive criticism from Chinese viewers.

45. K. K. K., "Ping *Qingnian jing* yingpian," *Yingxi chunqiu*, no. 12 (1925): 4–5. "K. K. K." was the pen name for the renowned Chinese director Cheng Bugao.

46. Wu Qingmin, "*Yuegong baohe* jiqi zai hu zhi piping," *Yingxi chunqiu*, no. 7 (1925): 8–9.

47. Ibid., 9.

48. The modern Chinese literary icon Lu Xun was critical of Sternberg's negative portrayal of the Chinese in *Shanghai Express*, a portrayal evoking public outrage that resulted in its banning after only two days of screening in 1932. Sternberg's 1936 visit to China, much anticipated by Chinese intellectuals, was disappointing because of his defense of his orientalist representations in *Shanghai Express*. While remaining critical of Sternberg, Lu nonetheless asked the Chinese to reflect on Sternberg's and others' negative portrayals of them and even suggested a complete translation of Arthur Smith's notorious *Chinese Characters* for "self-reflection, analysis, and reform." Lu Xun, "Lici cunzhao, 3," in *Luxun quanji*, vol. 6, ed. Xuxun jinian weiyuanhui (Beijing: Renmin Wenxue, 1956), 505.

49. Yi Hanru, "Zenyang caineng shi Zhongguo dianying shiye fada," *Yingxi chunqiu*, no. 10 (1925): 11.

50. Lu Mengshu, "Xin Yingxiong zhuyi de yingju," in *Xinghuo*, 9. Lu Mengshu, "Dianying yu geming," in his *Xinghuo: Yingju lunji*.

51. Hu Die's, Xuan Jinglin's, and Ruan Lingyu's careers lasted well into the mid-1930s, and by then a much more established media had "enhanced" its coverage of stars with profuse gossip, biographical accounts, and photographs. This both heightened their visibility and sparked the memories of film industry veterans, contributing considerably to present scholarship on early stars.

52. Wu was most famous for playing the lead in a stage production that ridiculed the patriotic warlord Zhang Xueliang, who was taking the public blame for losing Manchuria. Arrested briefly for her participation in the play, she and her colleagues were released as a result of public pressure. Gongsun Lu, *Zhongguo dianyingshihua* (Hong Kong: Nantian shuye gongsi, 1977), vol. 2, 158–59.

53. *Huaju tejuan*, nos. 1–2 (1927).

54. Du Shihuan, "Neoromanticist Cinema," 113–15.

55. A few examples are *Fuhuo de meigui* (dir. Hou Yao [1927]); *La rose de Pu-chui*, the French export title the studio chose for *Xixiang Ji* (dir. Hou Yao [1927]); *Hong meigui* (dir. Xu Zhuodai and Wang Youyou [1926]), adapted from a widely popular New Drama of the same title; and the character name Meigui (Rose) in *Shanghai yi wunü* (dir. Wang Cilong [1927]).

56. Yu Tianfen, "Meigui nülang," *Hong Meigui* 1 (1924). Mandarin Duck and Butterfly fiction is a general term for republican period (1912–1949) popular fiction, including a wide range of genres—detective fiction, sentimental romance, and martial arts, among others—that had many parallels with early Chinese cinema. See Link, *Mandarin Ducks and Butterflies*.

57. The author Yu Tianfen arranged the scenes and shot eight photographs with actors on location, although the journal published only four of them because of the poor quality of the other pictures.

58. Jane Gaines, "Dorothy Arzner's Trousers," *Jump Cut*, no. 37 (1992): 88–98.

59. "Mechanized settings" characterize American and Chinese stage melodrama that used technical apparatus to create stage spectacles; this use was adapted in early Chinese action thrillers, including martial arts films.

60. Ben Singer discusses the cases of cross-dressing in American serial queen adventures as the female appropriation of the privileges and qualities associated with masculinity. See Singer, *Melodrama and Modernity*, 231–33.

61. Liu, *Translingual Practice*, 15.

62. Jennifer Bean and Ben Singer have described the American serial queens as exhibiting physical prowess and endangerment symptomatic of the catastrophic and redemptive promise of modernity; of a negotiation of social anxiety and public mobility; and of a kinesthetic impact upon audiences. See Bean, "Technologies of Early Stardom and the Extraordinary Body," and Singer, *Melodrama and Modernity.*

63. For the history of the rise of Lianhua, see Pang Laikwan, *Building a New China in Cinema: The Chinese Left-Wing Cinema Movement, 1932–1937* (Lanham, Md.: Rowman and Littlefield, 2002).

64. On the film's adaptation from the Shakespeare play and the practice of other Chinese film adaptations of Western canonical literature, see Zhang Zhen, "Cosmopolitan Projections: World Literature on Chinese Screens," in *A Companion to Literature and Film*, ed. Robert Stam and Alessandra Raengo (Malden, Mass.: Blackwell Publications, 2004), 144–63.

65. The national symbol for the Republic (1911–1949) was the plum blossom, as expressed in the choice of both the national flower and the title of the national anthem, "Meihua zhi ge" (Song of plum blossom), with the five petals of the flower symbolizing the five ethnic groups of China (expanded to fifty-six ethnic groups in the People's Republic).

66. Pheng Cheah, "Given Culture: Rethinking Cosmopolitan Freedom in Transnationalism," in *Cosmopolitics: Thinking and Feeling Beyond the Nation*, ed. Pheng Cheah and Bruce Robbins (Minneapolis: University of Minnesota Press, 1998), 303.

67. To wit, for example, the various kinds of subjection of *nüxia* in the service of a patriarchal order in the 1960s and 1970s in Shaw Brothers films such as *Jin yanzi* (dir. Zhang Che, Hong Kong [1968]). Another example is *Kongzhong xiaojie* (dir. Yi Wen, Hong Kong [1955]), in which the famous singer/dancer Ge Lan plays an airline stewardess balancing her singing and dancing energy while embracing the body discipline of the flight attendant. Significantly, she is nicknamed Shisanmei (Thirteenth Sister), a famous *nüxia* character in a widely popular nineteenth-century Chinese martial arts novel, Wen Kang's *Ernü yingxiong zhuan* (1878).

Contributors

WEIHONG BAO is an Assistant Professor at the Department of Film and Media and the Department of East Asian Languages and Cultures at the University of California, Berkeley. Her book on early Chinese cinema, *Dances of Fire: Aesthetic Affect and the Intermediation of Chinese Cinema*, is forthcoming from the University of Minnesota Press. She has published in such journals as *Camera Obscura*, *Nineteenth Century Theater and Film*, *Opera Quarterly*, the *Journal of Chinese Cinemas*, and the *Journal of Modern Chinese Literature*. She is currently working on her second book project, this on the historical interaction between cinema, theater, and architecture in China.

RUDMER CANJELS is a scholar and lecturer working at the Netherlands Institute for Sound and Vision and VU University Amsterdam/Erasmus University Rotterdam, with an interest in filmic paratexts, crossmedia storytelling, industrial films, fan culture, and silent cinema. He has published various articles on industry-sponsored films (in *A History of Royal Dutch Shell* [Oxford: Oxford University Press, 2007] and *Films that Work* [Amsterdam: Amsterdam University Press, 2009]) as well as written a study on the international distribution and cultural transformations of silent film serials (*Distributing Silent Serials* [New York: Routledge, 2011]). Currently he is part of an international HERA (Humanities in the European Research Area) project, researching the construction of a collective imaginary of innovation, science, and technology within the industrial films of the 1950s and 1960s.

MARINA DAHLQUIST is an Associate Professor in Cinema Studies at the Department of Media Studies at Stockholm University. She has published articles on cinema and civic education, health discourses, and colonial structures. She is a recipient of a research grant from the Swedish Research Council (2011–2013) within the project "Cinema and Uplift: Health Discourses and Social Activism in the U.S., 1910–1930." Her primary research interests are historical reception, educational films, and issues of globalization.

MONICA DALL'ASTA is an Associate Professor of Film and Media Studies at the University of Bologna, Italy. She is the author of *Trame spezzate: Archeologia del film seriale* (Broken plots: An archeology of serial cinema [2009]) (Limina Award as Best Italian Book in Film Studies in 2009). She is co-editor, with Jane Gaines and Radha Vatsal, of *Women Film Pioneers Project* (New York: Center for Digital Research and Scholarship, Columbia University Libraries, forthcoming). In 2008 she edited a new Italian translation of Alice Guy's *Memoires* (*Memorie di una pioniera del cinema*) and the first collection on women involved in filmmaking in Italian silent cinema (*Non solo dive: Pioniere del cinema italiano* [Not just divas: Women Pioneers of Italian cinema]). Her latest work is a collection on Guy Debord's films (with Marco Grosoli), *Consumato dal fuoco: Il cinema di Guy Debord* (Burn by fire: The cinema of Guy Debord [2012]).

KEVIN B. JOHNSON is currently Visiting Assistant Professor of German and Film Studies at Lawrence University in Wisconsin. He is the author of several articles on Czech and German cinema of the 1930s and 1940s. In addition, he was primary translator (from Czech and German) for the volume *Cinema All the Time: An Anthology of Czech Film Theory and Criticism, 1908–1939* (2008). Together with Petra Hanáková, he edited *Visegrad Cinema: Points of Contact from the New Waves to the Present* (2010), for which he also contributed an essay.

CHRISTINA PETERSEN is Christian Nielsen Assistant Professor of Film Studies at Eckerd College. She is the author of several articles on film in the 1920s and is currently at work on a monograph concerning the historical and theoretical phenomenon of the American youth spectator and its influence on the genre of the American youth film. Her other research interests include race, ethnicity, and gender in American cinema; genre studies; space in melodrama and the Gothic; theories of embodiment; and the moving picture experience of youth as a historical category.

ROSIE THOMAS is Director of the Centre for Research and Education in Art and Media (CREAM) and Co-director of the India Media Centre at the University of Westminster. She is a pioneer of the academic study of the Bombay film industry and since 1985 has published widely on Indian cinema. Throughout the 1990s she worked as a television producer making documentaries, arts, and current affairs programs for Channel Four, many on South Asia–related topics. Rosie's current research interests include pre-independence popular Indian cinema and South Asian arts and documentary. She is co-founder and co-editor of the international Sage journal *BioScope: South Asian Screen Studies*, a forum for new research on the history and theory of South Asian film, screen-based arts, and new media screen cultures.

Index

Note: page numbers in *italics* refer to illustrations.

WOMEN AND FILM HISTORY INTERNATIONAL

A Great Big Girl Like Me: The Films of Marie Dressler *Victoria Sturtevant*
The Uncanny Gaze: The Drama of Early German Cinema *Heide Schlüpmann*
Universal Women: Filmmaking and Institutional Change in Early Hollywood
Mark Garrett Cooper
Exporting Perilous Pauline: Pearl White and the Serial Film Craze
Edited by Marina Dahlquist

The University of Illinois Press
is a founding member of the
Association of American University Presses.

Designed by Jim Proefrock
Composed in 10.75/13.5 Marat Pro
with Nickelodeon display
at the University of Illinois Press
Manufactured by Thomson-Shore, Inc.

University of Illinois Press
1325 South Oak Street
Champaign, IL 61820-6903
www.press.uillinois.edu